POLITICAL PHILOSOPHY NOW

Chief Editor of the Series:
Howard Williams, Aberystwyth University, Wales

Associate Editors:
Wolfgang Kersting, University of Kiel, Germany
Steven B. Smith, Yale University, USA
Peter Nicholson, University of York, England
Renato Cristi, Wilfrid Laurier University, Waterloo, Canada

Political Philosophy Now is a series which deals with authors, topics and periods in political philosophy from the perspective of their relevance to current debates. The series presents a spread of subjects and points of view from various traditions which include European and New World debates in political philosophy.

For other titles in this series, please see the University of Wales Press website: *www.uwp.co.uk*

POLITICAL PHILOSOPHY NOW

Imperfect Cosmopolis
Studies in the History of International Legal Theory and Cosmopolitan Ideas

Georg Cavallar

UNIVERSITY OF WALES PRESS • CARDIFF • 2011

© Georg Cavallar, 2011

All rights reserved. No part of this book may be reproduced in any material form (including photocopying or storing it in any medium by electronic means and whether or not transiently or incidentally to some other use of this publication) without the written permission of the copyright owner except in accordance with the provisions of the Copyright, Designs and Patents Act 1988. Applications for the copyright owner's written permission to reproduce any part of this publication should be addressed to The University of Wales Press, 10 Columbus Walk, Brigantine Place, Cardiff, CF10 4UP.

www.uwp.co.uk

British Library Cataloguing-in-Publication Data
A catalogue record for this book is available from the British Library.

ISBN 978-0-7083-2367-0 (hardback)
      978-0-7083-2382-3 (paperback)
e-ISBN 978-0-7083-2368-7

The right of Georg Cavallar to be identified as author of this work has been asserted by him in accordance with sections 77 and 79 of the Copyright, Designs and Patents Act 1988.

Printed by CPI Antony Rowe, Chippenham, Wiltshire

Contents

Acknowledgements		vii
1	Introduction	1
2	Vitoria, Grotius, Pufendorf, Wolff and Vattel: Accomplices of European Colonialism and Exploitation, or True Cosmopolitans?	17
3	British Enlightenment: the Triumph of Commercial Cosmopolitanism	39
4	Kant and the 'Miserable Comforters': Contractual Cosmopolitanism	64
5	Late Eighteenth-century International Legal Theory: from *Cosmopolis* to the Idea of Europe	85
6	Immigration, Rights and the Global Community: Pufendorf, Vattel, Bluntschli and Verdross	109
7	Conclusion	128
Notes		141
Select Bibliography		193
Index		205

Acknowledgements

This book grew out of several papers I delivered at various conferences over the last three years, and articles I published in different journals. Above all, I want to thank my wife Angelika for her almost stoic indifference when I was continuously absent-minded, especially during shared meals, conversations, and whenever she had something important to tell me. With kind amusement, she allowed me to work on this book which, in her opinion, has one major disadvantage: it is not going to make me rich. I am grateful to our children Clemens, Antonia and Valentina for tons of hugs, kisses, and laughter. The Stoics conceived humans as surrounded by a series of concentric circles, one of them being one's immediate family. I realized the truth hidden in Edmund Burke's famous statement that affections begin at home, and that we should not forget to 'love the little platoon we belong to in society', as it is 'the first link in the series by which we proceed toward a love . . . to mankind.'

I am indebted to many people for their help and continuous support, sometimes for years, especially to Sharon Anderson-Gold, Gideon Baker, Moritz Csáky, Lisa Ellis, Bardo Fassbender, Jörg Fisch, Pauline Kleingeld, Chris Laursen, Rebecka Lettevall, Herta Nagl-Docekal, August Reinisch, Karl-Heinz Ribisch, Garrett W. Sheldon and, above all, Howard Williams. I am grateful to University of Wales Press and their staff for their helpful and patient supervising of this book project.

Several chapters are based on previous papers and articles: Chapter 2 was published in the *Journal of the History of International Law*, 10 (2008), 181–209. Chapter 3 is a modified version of a paper delivered at a conference in Frankfurt am Main, and subsequently published in German. 'Late eighteenth-century international legal theory' grew out of a conference at Tours, October 2007. Chapter 6 is based on 'Immigration and sovereignty. Normative approaches in the history of international legal theory (Pufendorf – Vattel – Bluntschli – Verdross)', published in *Austrian*

Review of International and European Law, 11 (2006), 3–22, and presented at a conference in Tilburg, The Netherlands, May 2007.

I am fully aware of the fact that a book like this has its limitations. The range of publications I have consulted is limited, including only relevant ones in English and German. As English is not my native tongue, I should like to ask my readers' forgiveness, still hoping that I have succeeded in presenting my ideas clearly and intelligibly in spite of this fact. In any case, I trust that this book is a convincing example of what in the first chapter I will call intellectual cosmopolitanism, and that my readers will be able to feel my fascination with the intellectually vibrant and fascinating eighteenth century.

1 • Introduction

It seems that 'cosmopolitanism' is the new buzzword of a new century. Several factors are usually mentioned which might have contributed to the reactivating of the concept: the end of the Cold War, a growing awareness of global risks such as climate change which cannot be dealt with at a national level, economic and cultural globalization, the new global terrorism, and the US 'war on terror' during the presidency of George W. Bush Jr. (2001–9). Others have stressed cultural or intellectual factors such as the rise of ethnocentric nationalism and liberal and/or leftist attempts to counter it, or a broad disappointment with theories of multiculturalism, universalism, economic globalization or pluralism.[1]

In particular, cosmopolitanism has been linked with the expansion and deepening of the European Union and Europeanization. Authors have expressed hopes of a 'post-national, cosmopolitan form of loyalty', or see the European Union as a transnational institution which might realize the principles of cosmopolitan democracy.[2]

The new buzzword has begun to mean or denote almost anything: the frequent traveller who is 'critical' towards her own country, the white Western male who considers nation-states outdated and nationalists retarded, the intellectual who has come to disdain the former buzzword 'globalization'.[3] John Cameron has found nine possible interpretations, from the global citizen to the cultural explorer.[4] Others have added a range of adjectives to give an apparently flaky concept more substance or to refine it. We can read, among others, about 'exclusionary cosmopolitanism', 'oppositional cosmopolitanism', 'eccentric cosmopolitanism', 'consumer cosmopolitanism', 'banal cosmopolitanism' or 'emancipatory cosmopolitanism'.[5] Sometimes cosmopolitanism is just a perspective or a point of view, sometimes it is an activity. Cosmopolitanism may coincide with universalism, or might just be a negative concept, 'the critique of a nationalist *Weltanschauung*'.[6] If we consider all this confusion, and if we keep in mind that cosmopolitanism might turn into an ideology, it is not surprising that several authors have recently opted to keep the concept open and indeterminate, 'precisely because specifying cosmopolitanism positively and definitely is an uncosmopolitan thing to do'.[7] Alas, this reasoning is a bit unfortunate, because the adjective 'uncosmopolitan' already implies – or begs for – a definition.

Contemporary debates

Conceptual confusion could not stop a boom of publications on cosmopolitanism in recent years. In particular philosophers, political scientists and sociologists have joined a fascinating debate.[8] David Held made a start and developed the theory of a cosmopolitan democratic law in 1995, acknowledging the origin of the concept in Kant's political philosophy (see Chapter 4 below). Noting the 'democratic deficit' of international organizations, Held claimed that democratic practices have to cross territorial boundaries if a commitment to democracy, representation, and accountability should be retained. Held's normative ideal is a cosmopolitan system where people 'would come . . . to enjoy multiple citizenships – political membership in the diverse political communities which significantly affected them'.[9]

In a hotly debated essay entitled 'Patriotism and Cosmopolitanism' (1996), Martha Nussbaum argued for our primary allegiance 'to the worldwide community of human beings', and for cosmopolitan education.[10] Her provocative theses led to a string of essays which discussed her use of the concept of 'world citizenship', the problem of normative universalism, and the relationship between nationalism, patriotism and cosmopolitanism(s). In a more recent publication, *Frontiers of Justice* (2006), Nussbaum criticizes the limitation of the social contract tradition, arguing that Rawlsian liberalism excludes those who cannot take part in such a contract.

Two other US scholars also deserve to be mentioned. Taking neo-Kantian and Rawlsian theories of international justice as a starting point, Seyla Benhabib develops a post-metaphysical 'vision of *just membership*' on a global scale, tackling issues of migration, immigration, hospitality and democratic iteration, which mediates 'between universal norms and the will of democratic majorities'. She argues for a weak juridical cosmopolitanism and a 'dialogic universalism' which avoids the pitfalls of natural law-universalism and normative relativism.[11] Ghanaian philosopher Kwame Anthony Appiah has developed what he calls 'rooted cosmopolitanism', with people identifying with the local and the embedded, while also conceiving themselves in terms of universal norms and global identities. Cosmopolitanism is, in a nutshell, 'universality plus difference', and therefore combines two aspects: universal obligations towards others and a deeply felt respect for 'legitimate difference'. The task of philosophy is to spell out the details of the relationship between these two aspects, especially when they (seem to) clash. Like Nussbaum and Benhabib, Appiah disdains the idea of a world government.[12]

Jürgen Habermas is one of the few contemporary philosophers who argue for a world federation, where nation states have voluntarily ceded substantial portions of their sovereignty. He claims that we live in a post-Westphalian world and that a global civil society has become reality, while lacking adequate theorization. He believes in the universal nature of human rights and rationality, while urging governments to put neoliberal market economy under political control, exercised by a reformed and strengthened United Nations.[13] German sociologist Ulrich Beck proposes a new methodology in the social sciences and calls it the 'cosmopolitan perspective', which overcomes the allegedly monologic national perspective and manages to include 'the otherness of the other'.[14] Critics have complained that Beck constructs a vision of sociology that is a caricature of the actual state of the art, and that existing sociology is actually much more cosmopolitan than Beck wants to admit.[15]

This short overview cannot do justice to all contributions. French philosophers Jacques Derrida and Emmanuel Levinas deserve to be mentioned. Some authors have contributed one article or book, some are not noticed because they do not publish in English or in one of the major journals. Kok-Chor Tan, Massimo La Torre, Robert Fine, Toni Erskine have recently joined in, but lists of this sort can only be selective.[16] At any rate, they show a clear predominance of Anglo-American and English-speaking scholars: the current cosmopolitan discourse has, in spite of its noble aspirations, not yet become truly global.

The blind spot: the current cosmopolitan discourse and history

Many attempts to revitalize the concept of cosmopolitanism are historically uninformed. We may come across unwarranted assumptions, myths, clichés, glaring mistakes or the occasional inaccuracy. The envisioned recollection is often very selective or reductive.[17] Here are some examples.

Political scientists and philosophers like to refer to the 'Westphalian order', and sometimes claim that our world has entered a post-Westphalian, cosmopolitan order beyond the nation state and based on a global civil society. Robert Frith, for instance, picks up the term 'Westphalian cartography' from Richard Devetak and Richard Higgott.[18] Historians have countered that the notion of a 'Westphalian order' is rather misleading and should be used sparingly, if at all, and with the knowledge that it is nothing but a convenient shorthand. None of the key concepts of modern international law – which are associated with this notion – namely state sovereignty, the balance of power or legal equality, can be found in the Westphalian Peace Treaties, 'at least not as principles of international law'.[19] In Heiner Steiger's division of the epochs of international law, the magic year of 1648 is completely dropped. He suggests separating the international law of Christianity (from the thirteenth to the eighteenth century) from the international law of the civilized states in the nineteenth century. In the thirteenth century, Steiger claims, the law of nations as law among sovereign princes (rather than states) of equal standing was fully developed, in practice as well as theoretically.[20] The concept of a 'Westphalian order' also tends to obscure the differences between eighteenth and nineteenth-century international law and legal theories – and differences abound (see Chapters 5 and 6 below).

Another convenient, but misleading concept is the so-called 'Enlightenment project', sometimes identified with the 'project of modernity'. Research of the last decades has shown that the plurality and diversity of eighteenth-century Enlightenments render the notion of a 'project' virtually meaningless. As Robert Wokler put it: 'Genuine scholars of the period characteristically disaggregate such global terms, so as to situate the ideas and discourses they study only in specific and local contexts, with reference to all their rich particularity and texture.'[21] According to another widespread assumption, the Enlightenment was cosmopolitan, so we get the phrase 'cosmopolitan Enlightenment'.[22] Upon close scrutiny we have every reason to challenge this entrenched belief, as I will try to show in some chapters (see especially Chapters 3 and 5). Here, let me just briefly mention three outstanding examples.

At first sight, Welsh philosopher Richard Price (1723–91) seems to be a typical representative of 'Enlightenment cosmopolitanism'. In a key passage, he asserts:

> Foreign trade has, in some respects, the most useful tendency. By creating an intercourse between distant kingdoms it extends benevolence, removes local prejudices, leads every man to consider himself more as a citizen of the world than of any particular state, and, consequently, checks the excesses of that love of country which has been applauded as one of the noblest, but which, really, is one of the most destructive principles in human nature.[23]

The passage summarizes stock themes and arguments of the cosmopolitan discourses in the eighteenth century: the possibly beneficial moral effects of international trade and commerce, the reference to a metaphorical world citizenship, and the tension between patriotism and moral cosmopolitanism. We could argue that Price defends a weak form of moral cosmopolitanism, that he even alludes to political cosmopolitanism (in a passage on the US articles of confederation), and that he presents a unique version of cosmopolitanism that combines Christian and liberal elements.[24] However, upon closer analysis, there is this nagging doubt about Price's cosmopolitan disposition. While he criticizes excessive patriotic feelings and our tendency to partial reasoning, Price is clearly prejudiced against Native Americans and Arabs (who are inclined to 'plunder and massacre'), Jews (who are full of 'proud contempt' towards other nations), and Spaniards, Turks and Russians (who love the slavery they are subject to). While most parts of the world are in a 'state of humiliation' and exposed to 'darkness' or 'barbarity', Price praises the British constitution as a unique guarantee of political and religious freedom.[25] In short, we have every reason to doubt whether Price deserves the label 'cosmopolitan'. The passages which support the claim are counterbalanced by 'uncosmopolitan' statements.

Another interesting example is Fougeret de Monbron, who published his travel memories under the title *Le Cosmopolite ou le*

Citoyen du Monde (London, 1753). Again, appearances are deceptive. His cosmopolitan attitude is aesthetic and individualistic rather than reflective. He does not offer a theory, but resembles the contemporary frequent traveller or tourist who is prejudiced and uncritical of himself. 'Some would perhaps not call him a cosmopolitan at all, because he permanently uses his own subject as the norm, and notes what is different from his habits without reflecting on himself.'[26]

Finally, there is the confusing example of Kant. He is usually considered to be a cosmopolitan, because of his moral universalism, his scathing criticism of European colonialism and his advocacy of a world government. On the other hand, there are openly racist statements, which simply do not go together with Kant's cosmopolitan 'disposition' or *Gesinnung* elsewhere.[27] These examples suggest that a pluralistic model of cosmopolitanisms is more appropriate. There is no 'typical form' of cosmopolitanism, the 'cosmopolitan Enlightenment' is most likely a myth, and the diverse forms of cosmopolitanisms have different functions in the discourses as well.[28]

I want to continue with two glaring examples of historical distortion. Arguing that the United States is on the way to become a worldwide empire, Massimo La Torre ends his essay on 'Global citizenship' (2005) with a suggestion how it could preserve its republican tradition. The solution is to 'take the Ancient Romans' great example and grant American nationality to all members of the globalized world community'. This way the US could buy the world's 'everlasting gratitude'.[29] If we leave aside the political aspect of the demand and focus on its historical dimension, we quickly find that the reference to the *Constitutio Antoniania* of 212 is completely mistaken. It is true that the Antonine Constitution of Emperor Caracalla granted all free inhabitants of the Roman Empire full citizenship. However, it is hard to see what was 'great' about this law, and it is even more difficult to detect any cosmopolitan dimension. In the first place, the law conveniently widened the circle of subjects who had to pay inheritance tax (applicable only to full citizens). By the beginning of the third century, the status of Roman citizenship had already been devalued by constantly extending the number of recipients. On top of that, the distinction between Roman citizens and free non-citizens had been eroded, while new class distinctions had been set up.[30] It is hard to see how the Antonine Constitution should serve as an example or point of reference for contemporary conceptions of world citizenship espoused by David Held and others.

I am highly critical of cleansing operations which seem to be at work in several contemporary cosmopolitan discourses. There is a certain tendency to distinguish 'true' cosmopolitanism from allegedly 'degenerated' forms, or inconvenient evidence is simply ignored. This brings me to my second example. For a long time, Hugo Grotius has been revered as the founding father of modern international law and, implicitly, as a cosmopolitan pacifist. This might be the main reason why Martha Nussbaum has offered a surprisingly rose-tinted view on Grotius. Her reference to Grotian 'international society' is reminiscent of Hersch Lauterpacht. Grotius is the knight in shining armour. As a moral philosopher, he developed a progressive theory of 'humanitarian intervention', influenced Kant, and even turned into a forerunner of Nussbaum's own capabilities approach. As a cosmopolitan, he believed 'that all human beings form part of a single moral community'.[31] The context of the article was Bush's invasion of Iraq in 2003. While I am sympathetic to the view that the invasion violated the UN Charter and international law, I believe that Nussbaum simply picked the wrong author. Recent scholarship has convincingly shown that Grotius is an emperor who has no clothes. Nussbaum ignores the pragmatic, bellicose and imperialist dimension of Grotius' legal thinking (see the following chapter). It is mistaken to refer to 'the Grotian/Kantian vision', since Grotian and Kantian international legal theories have little in common (Chapter 4).

I believe that Nussbaum's distortions point to a deeper problem. She has also offered an interpretation of Cynic and Stoic cosmopolitanism which is highly dubious as well. For instance, Nussbaum repeatedly refers to the Stoic idea of a moral community of equal human beings all over the globe, or describes Cicero as a pacifist.[32] This is at variance with textual evidence. Some scholars claim that there might be no positive content at all to the Cynic Diogenes' famous and often-quoted claim: 'I am a citizen of the cosmos.' Sellars asserts that Diogenes aimed at an independent, personal ethic directed towards happiness or *eudaimonia* rather than endorsing the idea of human fellowship. Zeno's *Republic* probably proposed an isolated and elitist community of intellectuals or sages, where the non-wise were considered sub-human. Finally, Roman Stoicism was definitely rather lenient towards Roman patriotism (to say the least), and formed an uneasy alliance with (not always benevolent) Roman imperialism.[33] All this suggests that it is very problematical to subscribe to Nussbaum's approach, which she describes in one essay as follows: 'to begin writing a different chapter in the history of our classical heritage, one from which I think we can derive lessons of direct political worth.'[34] Can we really 'derive lessons' from ancient authors whose scant texts are open to divergent interpretations? Are not the lessons we have to derive from Grotius' work completely different from Nussbaum's? I think we must keep this problem in mind when we start digging in the past 'with a cosmopolitan purpose', to use Kant's phrase.

The concept and forms of cosmopolitanisms

I have already pointed out that the term 'cosmopolitanism' often remains quite vague in current debates and leads to sweeping generalizations. We can define cosmopolitanism as the belief or the theory that all humans, regardless of race, gender, religion or political affiliation, belong to, or should belong to, one single community. Cosmopolitanism's two basic tenets are: its reach is global in scope, all humans belong to this community. Second, this commonwealth should be cultivated, for instance, by trying to understand cultures different from one's own or – see Richard Price – by mutual trade and commerce.[35]

We can flesh out the concept if we compare cosmopolitanism with related webs of belief, theories or its 'enemies'. Cosmopolitanism has to be distinguished from forms of regionalism such as patriotism, nationalism or Europeanism. A pro-European attitude, for instance, is sometimes mistaken for a cosmopolitan attitude. The Abbé de Saint-Pierre and his focus on the idea of European unity is a case in point (see the beginning of Chapter 3). Cosmopolitanism is at odds with political realism and statism, and might conflict with liberalism or civic republicanism. It does not easily go together with communitarianism.[36]

We can distinguish between different types or forms of cosmopolitanisms.[37] The core idea of human rights (or moral) cosmopolitanism is that there are universal rights and obligations, and these should not be limited in scope, that is, they should be applied to all human beings. For instance, moral cosmopolitans argue that we have a duty to help strangers who are in need or suffering, or that we should promote basic human rights everywhere. Moral cosmopolitanism usually includes an element of normative universalism: all humans enjoy equal moral status, and they share certain essential features. Thomas Pogge refers to the main features of normative individualism (humans are the key units of concern), universality and equality (all humans without exception are equally considered), and generality (humans should count for everyone).[38] Moral cosmopolitanism is an offspring of natural law cosmopolitanism (see Chapter 2), goes back to Greek and Roman Antiquity, and was reactivated, for instance, by Christoph Martin Wieland (1733–1813) in the Age of Enlightenment. Martha Nussbaum's concept of world citizenship is meant metaphorically and denotes membership in a worldwide moral community. As moral cosmopolitanism implies normative individualism, it clashes with multicultural or postmodern normative relativism.

Political cosmopolitanism usually argues for some sort of global legal world order. Habermas advocates a thin version of world government with layered sovereignty, David Held has developed a theory revolving around cosmopolitan democracy and cosmopolitan democratic law, others favour a strengthening of existing international political institutions, or the evolution of a global civil society.[39] Habermas is close to Kant, whereas Anacharsis Cloots (1755–94) envisioned a world government where states have been absorbed (see Chapters 4 and 5).

Cultural cosmopolitanism acknowledges the diversity of cultures across the globe, and claims that 'we should recognize different cultures in their particularity'.[40] This implies the appreciation of cultural diversity and multicultural hybridization while rejecting (strong) nationalism, but also strong moral relativism. Cultural cosmopolitans work on the scope and limits of the 'rights to culture', cultural self-determination, and the rights of minority cultures. Georg Forster (1754–94) is a good example of an eighteenth-century cultural cosmopolitan, and in contrast to the superficial Fougeret de Monbron, he realized that it is difficult to free oneself from prejudice completely and admitted that he himself did not always succeed, while he was in fact rather successful in the enterprise (by challenging Eurocentric racist assumptions, for instance).[41]

In the eighteenth century, economic or commercial cosmopolitanism held 'that the economic market should become a single global sphere of free trade'.[42] Major representatives were Adam Smith and other intellectuals of the Scottish Enlightenment (see Chapter 3), but also the German Dietrich Hermann Hegewisch (1746–1812). In recent years, economic exchange unrestricted by state intervention has been attacked as neoliberalism, and economic cosmopolitanism has been reformulated by some philosophers in a way that includes elements of moral and political cosmopolitanism.[43] Epistemological cosmopolitanism is a way of thinking ('global thinking', according to Ulrich Beck), a cognitive orientation with the key feature of impartiality. It is a disposition which entails openness towards others, and an appreciation of diversity.[44]

This taxonomy of cosmopolitanisms can be further refined. I will briefly mention romantic cosmopolitanism, patriotic cosmopolitanism and the *cosmopolitisme littéraire* towards the end of the eighteenth century in a later chapter. Cloots could be described as a representative of revolutionary or republican cosmopolitanism (see the end of Chapter 5). Francisco de Vitoria or John Locke (Chapter 2), William Penn and John Bellers (Chapter 3) are Christian cosmopolitans (just like today's German theologian Hans Küng). We even find a 'Christianized Ciceronian tradition of cosmopolis' in sixteenth-century neo-Stoicism.[45] Thomas Paine or Kant might deserve the label early liberal cosmopolitans (or cosmopolitan liberals). Some equate legal or judicial cosmopolitanism with political cosmopolitanism, whereas others distinguish between them.[46] The various forms of cosmopolitanisms are quite different from each other, might clash, but could also overlap. At any rate, they can still be subsumed under the heading of 'cosmopolitanisms'. As Charles Jones puts it: 'Cosmopolitanism is actually a range of views – moral, political, and cultural – affirming the importance and value of the community of all human beings.'[47]

We should not only distinguish among forms of cosmopolitanism. There is another dimension: all forms can come in thin (moderate, weak) or thick (strong, extreme) versions. Strong moral cosmopolitanism, for instance, claims that loyalties, affiliations and preferences at the local level can *only* be justified 'by reference to the interests of all human beings considered as equals'. Thin moral cosmopolitanism, on the other hand, claims that the moral ideal of world citizenship is not the ultimate source of legitimization.

This type of cosmopolitanism simply insists 'that one's local attachments and affiliations must always be balanced and constrained by considerations of the interests of other people'.[48] Here, local duties are not derived from duties to humanity as a whole. In the 1990s, Nussbaum started off as a strong moral cosmopolitan, now she seems to have moved towards a moderate version, endorsing open-minded patriotism.[49] Appiah's rooted cosmopolitanism is another form of weak moral cosmopolitanism. We will see that most authors in the following chapters favoured this thin or moderate version.

Cosmopolitans, especially adherents of moral cosmopolitanism, usually defend a form of moral or normative universalism. This leads us to the familiar debates with moral relativists, and attempts to mediate between these positions, or develop an alternative approach. I do not want to go into this any further. Suffice it to say that this problem will be with us in all the following chapters.[50]

The state of the art and the aims of the book

The current interest in cosmopolitanism has led to publications which usually follow conventional academic disciplinary boundaries. The writers mentioned in a previous section are mostly philosophers, such as Martha Nussbaum, Kwame Anthony Appiah, Seyla Benhabib, Jacques Derrida, Emmanuel Levinas or Jürgen Habermas.[51] Cultural histories, which are often highly specialized and cover the eighteenth century or later periods, are widespread. A fine example is the volume edited by Peter Uwe Hohendahl on patriotism and cosmopolitanism in Hamburg between 1700 and 1933.[52]

Historical or cultural studies with a broader perspective are surprisingly rare. However, recently two excellent studies have been published. Margaret C. Jacob looks into early science and alchemy, into Masonic lodges, stock markets, international commerce and the radicalization of the late eighteenth century to show how everyday cosmopolitan practices led to new forms of engagement with strangers or unbelievers. Michael Scrivener illustrates how intellectuals in the eighteenth century tried to expand the public sphere, wrote against slavery, race and empire, or advocated Jewish emancipation.[53]

Literary studies usually define cosmopolitanism in a broad sense, pick several authors and put them in context. Amanda Anderson, for instance, focuses on Charles Dickens and Oscar Wilde, among others, and defines cosmopolitanism as a practice which encompasses above all 'the capacious inclusion of multiple forms of affiliation' and the capacity of detachment, which in turn involves 'an attempt to transcend partiality, interests, and context: it is an aspiration toward universality and objectivity' (interestingly, this definition takes her close to epistemological cosmopolitanism).[54]

Especially important for the present study are works in the fields of conceptual history and philosophical or intellectual history. An outstanding example is Andrea Albrecht's dissertation on the cosmopolitan discourses in German-speaking countries around 1800. Derek Heater has offered a string of books on cosmopolitan themes, revolving around the theme of world citizenship.[55] Simone Zurbuchen's focus is on the Swiss Enlightenment and the familiar tension between patriotisms and cosmopolitanisms, whereas Francis Cheneval's seminal study discusses the political philosophy of cosmopolitanism in early European thought up to Kant.[56]

This book tries to show how contemporary debates on cosmopolitanism could benefit from a deeper historical understanding. In an essay entitled 'Emancipatory cosmopolitanism', Jan Nederveen Pieterse states: 'The relationship between cosmopolitanism and history is less often discussed. But cosmopolitanism that does not acknowledge its lineages and does not examine its positionality is unreflexive, unexamined cosmopolitanism.' He claims that normative abstraction could be problematic and wants us to 'bring history back in'.[57] By giving depth and texture to the concept of cosmopolitanism, this study attempts to practise the very self-reflexivity which is so central to philosophical discourse. It investigates cosmopolitan theories, their ramifications and developments in modern European history. It does not offer a comprehensive history of cosmopolitanisms or a conceptual history, but focuses on a neglected aspect, namely on the cosmopolitan dimension of international legal theory, from the sixteenth to the twentieth century, with an emphasis on the eighteenth.[58]

According to traditional interpretation, the so-called 'classical' writers of international law like Vitoria, Grotius, Wolff or Vattel were cosmopolitans. The second chapter examines whether more recent interpretations should be preferred, where these writers are seen (and condemned) as accomplices of European colonialism and exploitation. Unlike some commentators such as Robert Williams or Brett Bowden, I argue for a nuanced assessment. The charge is rather justified in the case of Grotius, who was a lobbyist and ideologue of Dutch colonialism, and Vattel, who followed Locke's agricultural argument, saw savage peoples as inferior and moved towards legal positivism, which in turn favoured Europeans. However, the indictment does not make sense in terms of Vitoria, Pufendorf or Wolff. Vitoria develops a form of moral cosmopolitanism and hints at legal cosmopolitanism. Pufendorf holds that there are no special rights for Europeans. Wolff presents the first culturally sensitive international legal theory, rejects the civilization or agricultural argument, and foreshadows Kant's elaborate philosophy with elements of epistemological, moral, political and cultural cosmopolitanisms. As texts are often ambiguous or open to divergent interpretations, even Vattel is a difficult case. If some from Europe and the US used his writings to justify colonialism and imperialism, other passages were quoted by Chinese politicians to criticize imminent British military measures in the 1840s (though to no avail). I propose a rather lenient overall assessment of these authors, and point to the fallacy of another great narrative if a 'totalizing Western legal discourse' is constructed.

The third chapter looks at several eighteenth-century British authors. It seems that members of minorities like the Quakers (Penn and Bellers) or members of disadvantaged communities (like Fletcher) were especially liable to develop progressive, pan-European or cosmopolitan schemes. They endorsed various types of moral and political cosmopolitanisms. If they focused on Europe, their Europeanism was pacifist rather than imperialist. Penn in particular did not abandon or dilute his Christian, cosmopolitan attitude when dealing with the Native Americans. If we take a look at other British Enlightenment thinkers, we usually find a clear focus on the modern state, or a state-centred perspective: issues like the defence of religious and political liberties, the revolution of 1688 or the idea of patriotism were the centre of interest, as in Algernon Sidney or Joseph Priestley. If international relations issues were touched upon, the most frequent debates concerned standing armies and militias, the idea of a balance of power, or the fear of military or political hegemony. Hume, Smith, Paine and Bentham offered rather conventional international legal theories, and usually favoured economic cosmopolitanism over more supposedly flaky versions of moral or legal cosmopolitanism.

It is surprising how many contemporary authors seem to believe that Kant almost single-handedly invented or conceptualized modern cosmopolitanism. Daniel Chernilo, for instance, refers to 'Kant's pioneering translation of cosmopolitan principles into legal and institutional arrangements',[59] ignoring the work of Wolff, Fletcher and others who simply did not just 'prepare the ground' for Kant. According to Walter D. Mignolo, Kant articulated the 'civilizing global design' of the 'cosmopolitan project'.[60] I have already expressed my doubts about the so-called cosmopolitan project; I also doubt that Kant deserves a special place in its civilizing global design.

This undue emphasis on Kant is even more surprising as soon as we realize that many contemporary authors reject what Kant probably saw as his main contribution to the discourses on political cosmopolitanism: his qualified endorsement of a world state. Most present-day cosmopolitans vehemently deny that they favour a world state. Many also assert that Kant 'was against it'. If interpreters read Kant as endorsing a world government, they offer a caricature rather than an apt description. Hedley Bull is an almost classic case in point (see Chapter 5). His misreading has recently been repeated by Michael Walzer:

> there is a unified global state, something like Immanuel Kant's 'world republic', with a single set of citizens, identical with the set of adult human beings, all of them possessed of the same rights and obligations. This is the form that maximum centralization would take: each individual, every person in the world, would be connected directly to the center.[61]

This is a parody of Kant's ideal (see Chapter 4), and probably also of the plan which would come closest to Walzer's exaggeration, that of Cloots (see end of Chapter 5).

My starting point in the fourth chapter is a paragraph of the Second Definitive Article of *Perpetual Peace*, where Kant characterizes the natural lawyers Grotius, Pufendorf and Vattel as *leidige Tröster* or 'miserable comforters'. If we look at his arguments that are the basis of his restrained criticism we are led to his cosmopolitan contractualism: Kant takes social contract theory and normative individualism to their logical, cosmopolitan conclusion. The true Kantian legacy is striving for the partial realization of the idea of international right, a world federation with coercive powers. In practical politics, this also includes support and reform of the second best option, a free federation as the surrogate of this idea.

The fifth chapter offers a sketch of late eighteenth-century international legal theory, which seems to have abandoned all cosmopolitan elements. The chapter takes a closer look at certain authors (Vattel, Martini, Moser and Martens), analysing their methodologies and their underlying assumptions. I was particularly interested in what they wrote about the relationship between natural, voluntary and positive law, about the balance of power, about Europe, about peace projects, and about the right to wage war (their just-war theories). These lawyers believed in a common European, Christian culture, in a European society of states that were politically independent but culturally, historically and economically related to each other. They followed a general trend of the late eighteenth and early nineteenth century, when the last traces of *cosmopolis* and the *societas humanis generis* were gradually and partly replaced by the ideas of 'Europe' and 'civilization'. They illustrate the transformation of the cosmopolitan discourses to Europeanism. In final sections, I present the fascinating theories of Robert Ward and Anacharsis Cloots. Ward, a qualified normative universalist, holds that Christianity is the true foundation of the law of nations, which has become a historical phenomenon. Cloots's cosmopolitan republicanism envisions a world republic with departments, but without states.

According to a widespread assumption, cosmopolitans are in favour of open or porous borders, whereas communitarians or proponents of the so-called 'Westphalian system' of sovereign states opt for the right of communities to decide who may immigrate and who not. The sixth chapter analyses what the international lawyers Pufendorf, Vattel, Bluntschli and Verdross wrote about the right of immigration. All the authors argue for a qualified right of free movement. They differ in their respective background theories. Some are natural lawyers, some move towards legal positivism, some offer an eclectic, all-inclusive theory. But all reject the theory of absolute state sovereignty, a theory that was widespread in European legal theory roughly between 1870 and the First World War. Instead, they endorse a peculiar type of legal cosmopolitanism, something Hans Kelsen calls the primacy of international law over state law. They deal with a real problem concerning the right of immigration and the right of communities to determine who may come in and who not: Where do we draw the line, and how can we justify drawing it? They turn out to be halfway cosmopolitans: on the one hand, they argue for a qualified right of free movement. On the other hand, they accept that there is a fundamental asymmetry between those inside and those outside, and they see no reason to overcome this asymmetry. They wind up with some sort of middle position, which tries to balance out divergent claims.

2 • Vitoria, Grotius, Pufendorf, Wolff and Vattel: Accomplices of European Colonialism and Exploitation, or True Cosmopolitans?

Traditionally, authors like Vitoria, Grotius, Pufendorf, Wolff or Vattel have casually been assigned to the camp of the cosmopolitans. Quoting Patrick Henry and Sir James Mackintosh, Henry Wheaton, for instance, called them 'illustrious authors', 'friends of human nature', 'kind instructors of human errors and frailties', 'impartial witnesses' who developed the principles of international morality, writers 'with enlarged views of the welfare of nations'.[1]

Many recent interpreters have seen, and usually condemned, these writers as accomplices of European colonialism and exploitation. In one way or another, the theory runs, they provided the ideological basis of conquest, and were thus implicated in one of the most appalling crimes of modern history. Robert Williams is a rather outspoken representative of this approach. He endorses three related claims: the West has tried to impose its vision of truth on other cultures since the Middle Ages, mistakenly believing in its own superiority and the corresponding inferiority of others. Secondly, the West has used (international) law as an effective instrument of empire, genocide and exploitation. Finally, Williams claims that Francisco de Vitoria was a kind of founding father of this discourse: 'Vitoria's Law of Nations provided Western legal discourse with its first secularly oriented, systematized elaboration of the superior rights of civilized Europeans to invade and conquer normatively divergent peoples.'[2] According to Williams, Vitoria offered an apology of and ideology for Spanish colonial practice, endorsing Eurocentric norms. 'While the normative foundation of Vitoria's Law of Nations was constructed according to a secularized, as opposed to an ecclesiastically dictated, vision of reason, it was a vision no less totalizing and hierarchical in its outlook than the medieval response to radical difference.'[3] Vitoria is modern in the sense that his thinking is more secularized, but the frame of thought has remained unchanged: it is still (or even more) totalizing, hierarchical, Western, repressive and exclusive.

In an influential essay originally published in 1996, Antony Anghie expounds four theses. First, he asserts that international law was created because of the Spanish–Indian encounter rather than preceding it. Secondly, pretended universalism is a mere fake: Vitoria is said to have been biased in favour of the Christians, thus creating a Catch-22 for the Amerindians (whatever they did, their wars were unjust). According to the third thesis, the international lawyers since Vitoria were accomplices of colonial exploitation and created an imperialist international legal theory whose allegedly universal language 'was devised specifically to ensure [the natives'] disempowerment and disenfranchisement'.[4] Finally, Vitoria paved the way for later legal constructions of the allegedly uncivilized other.

Once the initial determination had been made and accepted that the colonial world was not sovereign, the discipline could then create for itself, and present as inevitable and natural, the grand redeeming project of bringing the marginalized into the realm of sovereignty, civilizing the uncivilized and developing the juridical techniques and institutions necessary for this great mission. Within this framework, the history of the colonial world would comprise simply the history of the civilizing mission.[5]

Anghie's thesis of a Western civilizing 'project' or 'mission' looks like a retrospective construction. The connections between Vitoria and nineteenth-century international law are suggested rather than demonstrated.

Brett Bowden draws on Williams and Anghie's article. His claims are similar: international law was an accomplice of imperialism and implicated in the 'Western imperial project'. The 'standard of civilization' was the 'legal mechanism' which admitted communities, peoples or states into the international society – in fact, usually excluded them. Part of this mechanism has been the construction of a non-European, exotic, uncivilized and barbaric 'other' – from the Middle Ages to the wars on terrorism of George W. Bush.[6]

In a 1995 article, Paul Keal partly follows a similar approach, referring to Western 'universalising discourse' and 'cultural imperialism',[7] but is more considerate with the international lawyers. He is rather dependent on what Lindley, Todorov and others write about them instead of listening to what these lawyers themselves had to say. Keal's criticism of nineteenth-century international legal theory is justified, but tends to project their thinking back to earlier periods. In his recent book (2003), Keal is even more nuanced, though he still refers to 'cultural imperialism'. Following Lindley's seminal 1926 study and its distinctions as a heuristic device, Keal differentiates among three groups of writers. The first group includes international lawyers 'who recognised sovereignty in non-European peoples', among others Vitoria, Gentili and Pufendorf. Authors like Grotius, Vattel or Philimore only granted 'limited or conditional sovereignty' to non-Europeans (the second group). Finally, the major representatives of nineteenth- and early twentieth-century international legal theory such as John Westlake or William Edward Hall simply denied that non-Europeans enjoyed sovereign rights.[8] Keal concludes that 'the earlier writers were more willing to concede rights to non-Europeans'. Things got worse in the nineteenth century, when rights were systematically denied. In particular, this was the case whenever peoples were regarded as 'uncivilised'. Keal's overall assessment is not only more nuanced, but also more lenient towards some writers. 'Not all international law was either a universalising discourse or a form of cultural imperialism. Parts of it applied only to particular non-European entities and did not involve the imposition of European cultural values.'[9]

Unlike commentators such as Robert Williams, Antony Anghie or Brett Bowden, and like Paul Keal, I argue for a nuanced assessment. I emphasize the complexity of the history of international legal theory, which suggests that we cannot conveniently pigeonhole divergent authors under a heading such as 'Western totalizing discourse'. Very often, false continuities are constructed, for instance, between the eighteenth and the nineteenth centuries. Against Keal, I argue that there is no linear development from a more cosmopolitan to a narrow Eurocentric international legal theory. Sometimes it seems that the influence of this theory on politics and international legal practice is overestimated. Some contemporary critics seem to have chosen the wrong authors and ignored the ambiguity of texts. I claim that several international lawyers endorsed, or tried hard to arrive at, some form of moral/ ethical, legal and/or intellectual cosmopolitanism.[10]

Francisco de Vitoria: Christian mission and thin justice

Francisco de Vitoria (1486–1546) is the author who has probably attracted the most divergent assessments. Williams claimed that Vitoria's law of nations 'justified the extension of Western power over the American Indians as an imperative of the European's vision of truth'.[11] Others, especially Catholic, Spanish and Latin American authors, have been more lenient, sometimes even enthusiastic. They see Vitoria's idea of an international community at the heart of his innovative theory. Antonio Gómez Robledo appreciates Vitoria as the prophet of contemporary *ius cogens* norms and legal cosmopolitanism. Roberto Irigoyen claims that popular sovereignty, equality, the liberty of the peoples or communities, and international solidarity are the cornerstones of Vitoria's theory.[12]

Not all Spanish authors are enthusiastic (and often uncritical) fans of Vitoria. Seeing parallels between Sepúlveda and Vitoria, José Antonio Maravall seems to have been one of the first who argued that Vitoria provided an ideology of colonialism and early capitalist interests.[13] At the same time, Vitoria has been appreciated outside Spain (and the Catholic world). James Brown Scott, for instance, praised Vitoria as the founding father of international law: 'The corner-stone of Vitoria's system was equality of states, applicable not merely to the states of Christendom and of Europe but also to the barbarian principalities in the Western World of Columbus.' According to Scott, there are no traces of Eurocentric bias, just an all-embracing cosmopolitan attitude. 'The international community is not a superimposed state; it is coextensive with humanity – no longer merely with Christianity.'[14] And finally, there are those who offer mild criticism, aiming at some middle ground between enthusiasm and condemnation. Fernández-Santamaria appreciates Vitoria's postulate of an international order, but holds that his universe is still Christian, denying the Amerindian communities true equality.[15]

Who is right? Is Vitoria the cosmopolitan founder of modern international law, or just a biased Eurocentric accomplice of Western colonialism? Or is this the wrong question? Should we embark on the famous search for the 'third way'? The main problem with Vitoria is that his key lecture 'On the American Indians' falls into two sections which seem to be incompatible with each other. In the first part, he claims that the Spaniards had no right to invade and conquer the territories of the 'barbarians'.¹⁶ In the second part, Vitoria argues that the Spaniards had several 'just titles' to do so. A favourable interpretation of Vitoria shows that he succeeded at least in part to develop a concept of thin justice as impartiality, forming an uneasy relationship with his Christian, thick conception of the good.

In the second part of his lecture, Vitoria developed four substantial arguments in favour of Spanish invasion: 1) the right of humanitarian intervention, 2) the right of hospitality, 3) the right to missionize, and 4) the argument based on the mental incapacity of the natives. The first two titles were conditional. Intervention was justified if acts of human rights violations such as cannibalism had actually occurred and if Spanish intervention was limited to the goal of helping the victims. Hospitality rights implied that Spaniards were not violent or unjust when visiting the natives. As Vitoria puts it, the Spaniards were allowed to visit the natives, so long as it was done without trickery or fraud and without inventing excuses to make war on them. But on these grounds, if the barbarians allowed the Spaniards to carry on their business in peace among them, the Spaniards could make out no more just a case for seizing their goods than they could for seizing those of other Christians.¹⁷

Vitoria's title based on the mental incapacity of the natives has received most attention in recent years. Here we have to keep in mind that Vitoria's reasoning is merely hypothetical. He asserts that he mentions this title merely 'for the sake of the argument'. In addition, he reminds us that even if we should wish to endorse the title, it is (again) a conditional one, as everything would have to be done *'for the benefit and good of the barbarians, and not merely for the profit of the Spaniards.* But it is in this latter restriction that the whole pitfall to souls and salvation is found to lie.'¹⁸ Vitoria admits that some natives 'seem to us insensate and slow-witted', even 'foolish'. However, he quickly adds that this can be attributed to their 'evil and barbarous education'. Vitoria engages in a balancing act, arguing that they are 'like us', that is, human beings, but also different at the same time. The differences are seen as a matter of degree rather than kind, and explained by reference to contingent historical factors such as education. 'Even amongst ourselves we see many peasants (*rustici*) who are little different from brute animals.'¹⁹

Vitoria's main aim is to evangelize the natives and bring salvation to the unbelievers, and this implied that gross injustices were avoided in the first place. His framework is theological, based on a thick, Christian definition of the good life. In this respect it is wrong to assume – with Robert Williams – that Vitoria's thinking is secularized. Vitoria writes about the Native Americans that 'belief in Christ and baptism is necessary for their own salvation'.[20] The Spanish obligation to missionize is central. The right of ambassadors is closely connected with the right to preach Christianity. But Vitoria sees that a thin conception of justice is the necessary condition of a successful mission. The natives should get a real chance to 'listen to peaceful persuasion about religion', which in turn requires that 'the Christian faith is set before the barbarians in a probable fashion, that is with provable and rational arguments and accompanied by manners both decent and observant of the law of nature, such as are themselves a great argument for the truth of the faith', and this should be done 'not once or in a perfunctory way, but diligently and observantly'.[21] Spanish injustices make any genuine Christian mission impossible. Vitoria claims that Spanish behaviour or manners must conform to the standards of the law of nature. A thick conception of the good is part and parcel of a more fundamental thin concept of justice.

There is a tension in Vitoria's third section on the 'just titles' of the Spaniards. It revolves around two conflicting propositions: if the Spaniards had injured the Amerindians, the latter were entitled to expel them. The Amerindians had waged a just war. On the other hand, if the Spaniards had not injured them, they were entitled to defend themselves and their natural right of hospitality. They could wage a just war.

Vitoria writes: 'Since these travels of the Spaniards are (as we may for the moment assume) neither harmful nor detrimental to the barbarians, they are lawful.'[22] The decisive part of the sentence is the one in brackets. May we really assume this? The resolution of the above dilemma rests on our judgment of the situation; moral principles do not help here. Throughout the third section, Vitoria points out that some of the just titles enumerated are only 'possible', that they 'might' or 'could' be legitimate. It is important to bear in mind that Vitoria is very careful in his assessment. He does not state bluntly that the titles are inapplicable, but comes close to it: it 'appears' that this is the case and, if so, then 'the barbarians gave no just cause for war', with the consequence that *'the whole Indian expedition and trade would cease*, to the great loss of the Spaniards'. Vitoria's conclusion is that the Spaniards should do what cannot be wrong, that is, using the right of hospitality as specified and trading with the natives as equal partners, who 'have a surplus of many things which the Spaniards might exchange for things which they lack'.²³ Vitoria does not feel sure about all of his arguments, and concludes that trade and hospitality, based on reciprocity and fair exchange, are the best remedies in the given situation.

Why was Vitoria not more outspoken? Perhaps Vitoria found it imprudent to condemn the policy of the emperor in a public lecture. On 10 November 1539, after Vitoria had delivered his second lecture on the Native Americans, de Soto, the prior of his convent, received a letter from Emperor Charles V, demanding that the theologians hand in all material on the Indian question and stop writing or lecturing on it.²⁴ However, Vitoria was very outspoken in a letter to Miguel de Arcos, and revealed his personal attitude. Commenting on the conquest of Peru by Pizarro (1533), Vitora writes in a very emotional way that he is shocked by the events, and that the news of the massacre at Cajamarca and the execution of the Inca Atahuallpa 'freezes the blood in [his] veins'. He points at the difficulties he encounters when speaking his mind: the *conquistadores* or *peruleros*, if criticized, 'lose their temper' and accuse Vitoria of heresy or of condemning the emperor and his policy. Vitoria's arguments are rather straightforward. As the Peruvians had apparently never injured the Spaniards, they did not 'give them the least grounds for making war on them'. The conquest was 'butchery', the natives were *'most certainly innocents in this war'*, and Spanish conduct, apparently motivated by greed, amounted to 'sheer robbery'. Twice Vitoria compares the plundering of Peruvian towns with the pillaging of Spanish cities.²⁵ Vitoria's arguments are based on traditional just-war doctrine and basic features of thin justice such as reciprocity and impartiality.

With his postulate or ideal of an international society, Vitoria hints at legal cosmopolitanism, and his concept of human rights suggests a form of moral cosmopolitanism that is not fully developed.²⁶ However, his theory has its limitations. In his lectures, Vitoria never explicitly denies the right of the Spanish crown to conquer Mexico or Peru. Perhaps he wants to show that the emperor's 'sovereignty' could and should go together with the Amerindians' right to keep ownership of the land or *dominium*.[27] Secondly, as Sankar Muthu argues, Vitoria's egalitarian understanding of humans was too insubstantial to bear much moral weight. What is missing is an understanding of humans as cultural agents who have developed, in the course of history, diverse and incommensurable ways of life, none of which is in any way inferior. Vitoria never questions the European standard of civilized life. The cultural values and practices of Christian societies are taken for granted and are the infallible yardstick.[28]

Hugo Grotius: profit and power politics rather than principles

As in the case of Vitoria, we have a wide spectrum of possible interpretations. At the one extreme, authors imply or claim that Grotius was a cosmopolitan who refused to use the law of nations as an ideological instrument to justify European conquest. At the other end of the spectrum, Grotius is condemned as biased and inadequate, because his theory 'did not in any way restrict the endeavour of subjugating the non-European nations to European authority. Grotius' system could afford a pretext for every desired act of violence.'[29] One group of more recent publications (which are usually in German) stresses the systematic quality of Grotius' writings, and is rather lenient. The other group, including members of the Cambridge School of Political Thought, is more contextual, critical, and debunks Grotius. Martine Julia van Ittersum's book is a splendid example.[30]

Several aspects of Grotian international legal theory suggest that he is cosmopolitan. He appeals to the Stoic and Ciceronian concept of a moral community of humankind (*humani generis societas*).[31] Grotius' claim that war is just if waged against those who actively persecute Christians because of their faith can hardly be called biased. As a norm, it is of course in need of interpretation and application, and here abuse and prejudice may creep in. But it can be accommodated with the principle of self-defence, and the norm is counterbalanced by the prohibition of waging war against those who are unwilling to accept Christianity.[32] Vitoria had presented the outlines of an international moral community, and Grotius repeatedly referred to him, stressing that the Spaniard was right. The natives of the East Indies 'enjoyed public and private ownership' like the natives of the Americas. Taking their property or natural rights away was 'an act of thievery and rapine no less than it would be if perpetrated against Christians'.[33] Grotius explicitly rejects special rights of the Europeans: the argument of papal donation, that of Christianizing the unbelievers, and the duty to civilize the barbarians. The first title was rejected by Vitoria and other Spanish authors who followed him, with exceptions such as Solórzano. The right to missionize and convert was usually endorsed. It was debated when and to what extent coercion was acceptable. Grotius weakens the scholastic emphasis on religious issues. Along these lines, and in contrast to Gentili and other Protestant authors of the time, he asserts that 'alliances and treaties with infidels' or non-Christians are binding. We have to keep in mind that there are not two spheres of law in Grotius' system, one for Christian, European communities and another one for non-Christians.[34]

At the same time, Grotius does not simply replace privileges based on Christianity with those based on civilization, as many other more secularized authors after him would do. He is quick to reject another argument in favour of European conquest, the 'excuse of introducing civilization into barbaric regions'.[35] Grotius' argument can be divided into three propositions. The first one is of course the rhetoric of human rights pertaining to all. The second one, again echoing Vitoria, points to the fact that the natives are 'neither insane nor irrational'. The third is psychological: Europeans use civilization as a pretext, their real motivation is greed. He buttresses the first proposition with a rejection of consequentialist thinking. The civilization argument implies that one group of persons imposes on another their own thick conception of the good, pretending or really believing that it is for their welfare and happiness. Consequentialist thinking of this sort, however – popularized in the phrase that 'the end justifies the means' – is potentially incompatible with natural rights theory. '[T]hose who have the use of their reason ought to have the free choice of what is advantageous or not advantageous, unless another has acquired a certain right over them.'[36] The qualification in the relative clause seems to leave a loophole for European conquest, but Grotius sees only children (and in another passage the mentally handicapped) as an exception.

The evidence that Grotius was not impartial and cosmopolitan revolves around three issues: the political purpose of his writings; his theory of punishment; and his doctrine of property. In a meticulous study, Martine van Ittersum has shown that Grotius was a lobbyist and ideologue of Dutch colonialism, writing *De Jure Praede* (1604–6) on behalf of the United Dutch East India Company (VOC or *Vereenighde Oostindische Compagnie*). The book aimed at vindicating the VOC's privateering campaign in the East Indies. Grotius used the language of natural law and rights to achieve this pragmatic, political goal.[37] Politics and profit triumphed over principles. When Grotius argued that treaties with non-Christians were binding, and the latter enjoyed true dominion, he had the Sultan of Johore as a strategic partner of the Dutch in mind. When he famously pleaded for the freedom of the seas, he followed an explicit request of the VOC directors, and so on.[38] Grotius did not refrain from bending facts, applying principles selectively, and condoning unfair contracts. In the words of Richard Tuck, *De Jure Praede* is 'a major apology for the whole Dutch commercial expansion into the Indies'.[39]

What about his major feat, *De Jure Belli ac Pacis* (1625), a work written when Grotius was no longer a lobbyist for the VOC? Did he turn from politics and profit to principles then? There can be no doubt that *De Jure Belli* is more systematic and more scholarly, and less of a piece of propaganda. However, even here we find traces of a clear European bias, and arguments that justify European expansion. It is just that the relevant passages are buried under masses of learned, sophisticated, ornate and seemingly innocuous expositions. *De Jure Belli ac Pacis* shares with *De Jure Praede* the same starting point, namely the domestic analogy: 'That power is called sovereign (*summa*) whose actions are not subject to the legal control of another, so that they cannot be rendered void by the operation of another human will.'[40] This power can be the state (*civitas*), but an individual enjoys the same power and rights, provided it has not transferred them to a civil society. Both natural individuals and states have the right to use force, the right to punish, and thus the right to make war. In a second move, Grotius assigns the same status to private trading companies – such as the VOC. War itself is seen as a kind of lawsuit, the administering of justice by force.

In contrast to Vitoria and other Second Scholastics, Grotius holds that natural individuals may punish persons over whom they do not possess rights if they (allegedly) grievously violate 'the law of nature or nations'. In particular, this applies to cannibals, inhospitable communities, those who 'are inhuman to their parents', and pirates. In a key passage, Grotius sides with Pope Innocent IV (1243–54), who had argued that as the 'vicar of Jesus Christ', the Pope had power 'not only over Christians but also over infidels'.[41]

> Thus far we follow the opinion of Innocent, and others who say that war may be waged upon those who sin against nature. The contrary view is held by Vitoria, Vázquez, Azor, Molina and others, who in justification of war seem to demand that he who undertakes it should have suffered injury either in his person or his state, or that he should have jurisdiction over him who is attacked. For they claim that the power of punishing is the proper effect of civil jurisdiction, while we hold that it is also derived from the law of nature.[42]

It goes without saying that this imprecise and sweeping provision generously legitimated a large variety of European colonial practices. In addition, there seems to be an inconsistency in Grotius' work: in other passages, he advocates free choice and a qualified form of pluralism, a result of taking scepticism into account.[43]

Finally, Grotius' theory of property clearly favours European agricultural societies. Grotius himself notes the colonial context, and the colonial debates in the wake of the Spanish *conquista*, with participants such as Vitoria, de Soto, Cano, Covarruvias, Molina and Gentili.[44] Grotius presents an embryonic form of the agricultural argument, popularized by Locke and Vattel later on: '[I]f within the territory of a people there is any deserted and unproductive soil, this also ought to be granted to foreigners if they ask for it.' Grotius distinguishes between *dominium* and *occupatio*. Dominion and jurisdiction still reside with the native population. However, settlers have a perfect natural right to occupy (as long as occupation is effective), which means that the consent of the natives is immaterial.[45]

Grotius' key aim in *De Jure Belli ac Pacis*, it seems, was to show a way to establish peace among the Christians in Europe. His sphere of natural law is global in scope, but there is an inner, Christian circle, with Grotius hoping that Christian states would form a federation or league (*foedus*) 'against the enemies of Christianity'.[46] Given the naive and often anachronistic hagiography of past centuries – Grotius as the founder of the modern law of nations, as the champion of native rights, as the theorist of the modern states system, as the founding father of the 'Grotian tradition' in international relations, as 'the tutelary deity of the Peace Palace at The Hague' (Richard Tuck) – the current debunking is just and proper.[47] Nevertheless, we should keep in mind that Grotius undoubtedly made important contributions in other disciplines and areas: for instance, in theology, contract theory, moral theory or the theory of natural rights.

Samuel Pufendorf: criticizing the rights of conquest

Samuel Pufendorf (1632–94) has also been included among those European authors who justified colonialism.[48] If we take a closer look at his major work, *The Law of Nature and Nations* (1672), however, we get a very different picture. It is true that his theory is more state-centered, moving away from the idea of a moral community of humankind, and favouring states (rather than individuals) and their interests instead. But Pufendorf is fair enough to include non-European communities, even if they should not meet modern European standards of statehood. Like Gentili before him, Pufendorf mentions the Chinese as a people that avoids contacts with foreigners, and is justified in doing so.[49] In another passage, he explicitly rejects Vitoria's reasoning in favour of Spanish perfect hospitality rights. Pufendorf dismisses Vitoria's first just title of 'natural partnership and communication'. The perfect right of ownership trumps the imperfect right to visit and live in foreign countries. The property-holder simply has 'the final decision on the question, whether he wishes to share with others the use of his property'.[50] Pufendorf adds the pragmatic consideration that any unrestricted influx of immigrants who might stay for an unlimited period of time may have detrimental effects on the native community. In the language of natural law, this inflow could conflict with the community's duty of self-preservation. Secondly, there is no natural, enforceable right to trade. Again, the natives have to grant permission and may renounce it 'if the well-being of the state demands it'. Thirdly, Pufendorf rejects Vitoria's claim that a unilateral grant of rights is unjust. Pufendorf asserts that rights do not have to be symmetrical in this respect. In matters of imperfect obligations, a property-holder can be 'more liberal to one than to another'. This gave the Japanese, for instance, the right to admit Dutch traders, but refuse admission of other Europeans. Here and in other instances, Pufendorf applies the domestic analogy. In this case, he argues that the relationship between communities can be compared with the owner of a garden who grants exclusive privileges to one of her/his neighbours.

Pufendorf also refuses to accept Grotius' incipient agricultural argument (the claim that native nomads do not really own their land because they failed to enclose and farm it permanently). He stresses the factor of agreement rather than natural rights. Rejecting Grotius' subtle distinction between (European) effective occupation and (native) dominion, Pufendorf asserts that if no individual owner can be detected, the land 'should not at once be regarded as unoccupied, and free to be taken by any man as his own, but it will be understood to belong to the whole people'.[51]

Pufendorf explicitly refers to the Amerindians when he criticizes Francis Bacon's claim that Europeans have a right of humanitarian intervention to stop acts of cannibalism and human sacrifice. Like Bacon, most authors before Pufendorf took this right for granted. In Pufendorf's account, state or community rights trump those of the global moral community. (He might argue that they serve the latter, albeit indirectly). There is clear indication of a paradigm shift. State sovereignty entails a strict duty of non-intervention. Foreign states may only intervene if their own citizens are victimized, provided that they have come as 'innocent guests, or driven by storms'. Pufendorf distinguishes between foreign visitors who come to visit 'as enemies and robbers', and those who behave peaceably or are in need of help. An explicit reference to European colonialism is missing, but perhaps implied: 'For *only in the last case* does a right of war lie with those whose citizens are treated with such cruelty, not in the others.'[52] In sum, there are no special rights for Europeans. Pufendorf rejects the Aristotelian doctrine of natural slavery as implausible and conflicting with natural equality, and any titles of conquest based on civilization.[53]

Christian Wolff: the first culturally sensitive international legal theory

The innovative international legal theory of Christian Wolff (1679–1754) has rarely been appreciated. Brett Bowden is a case in point. He asserts that Wolff's belief in European civilization is biased: the first step is the familiar distinction between civilized and barbarous nations. Next there is the assertion that 'nations ought to be civilized'.[54]

From this assessment, it was just a short leap to the assumption that it was the task of the civilized to assist with the training of the uncivilized in their aspiring to the realms of the 'civilized world', should their minds be so pliable and adept at accepting such conditioning.[55]

This phrasing creates the impression that Wolff was one of the accomplices of colonialism. The opposite is true. Like Gentili or Pufendorf before him, Wolff defends Chinese isolationist policy. The Chinese have a perfect right to restrict or altogether refrain from international trade and commerce 'for the purpose of preserving their own interests'. Wolff interprets Chinese intentions, claiming that the government was interested in perfecting the state, which is of course compatible with the duty of self-perfection. Wolff does not stress the right of self-preservation or self-defence, but points out instead that the Chinese are entitled to keep their morals 'pure and uncorrupted'.[56] If Chinese policy is perfectly lawful, Wolff nevertheless hints at the possibility that it may be imprudent, an argument elaborated on by political economists like David Hume and Adam Smith (see Chapter 3 below). Foreign commerce 'makes a nation rich, consequently powerful'.[57] Nations which refrain from it, Wolff suggests, might gradually lose their power, actually China's fate in the nineteenth century.

Like Pufendorf, Wolff rejects any exclusive rights for Europeans. The right of each nation to decide on foreign commerce effectively abandons Vitoria's first title. Nations may persuade, but must never force or compel others to embrace their religion. Unlike Vitoria and Francisco de Suárez, Wolff makes sure that no back doors are left open. If other nations reject 'the true worship of God ... that must be endured'. Probably again referring to Chinese practice, Wolff holds that states may expel missionaries, prohibit their entrance and ban their books.[58] Wolff's system of natural law allows for a clear distinction between rights and religion. He holds that, given religious pluralism in the world, the true religion is notoriously difficult to define. In cases of doubt, the rights of nations as specified in *ius gentium* are of primary importance, as religions are juridically equal.[59] Wolff does not edorse relativism; his juridical framework implies religious neutrality or impartiality. Finally and in agreement with some previous authors like Vitoria, Wolff accepts the true ownership of natives, employing hypothetical thinking to arrive at the golden rule and the idea of impartiality. Thus,

> no nation ought to do to another what it does not wish to be done to itself. Indeed, if it is allowable for one nation to occupy lands inhabited by another nation, because they have been hitherto unknown to it, by the same reasoning it will be allowable also for the second nation to occupy the lands of the first, or for any other foreign nation to do so.[60]

European policy of conquest, though not explicitly mentioned, is rejected with the simple, but convincing argument that it cannot be universalized.

This kind of impartial thinking has been employed by authors before Wolff. It usually boiled down to the tricky question of whether there was a loophole left for European prerogatives to sneak in (such as the right to preach Christianity). Here, Wolff does not allow for compromises. He is culturally sensitive, not imposing European standards of statehood and sovereignty on native communities. Admittedly, 'groups of men dwelling together in certain limits but without civil sovereignty' are not nations but, like nomads, they have 'jointly acquired ownership' and must not be subject to civil sovereignty without their consent, 'even if at the time those who inhabit the territory are not using those lands'.[61] The basic units of *ius gentium* are families, not states.

Finally and most importantly, there are no special rights for civilized peoples (*gentes*) against barbarians, who may not be expelled at will.[62] In a footnote based on natural-law thinking that combines the notions of natural liberty, consent, culture, and injury, and contrasts them with advantage and usefulness, Wolff, while accepting the distinction between civilized and uncivilized nations, refuses to establish rights for the former to 'subject to the civil sovereignty separate families dwelling in a certain territory or staying there'.[63] States do have duties towards others, but they are imperfect, so that

> no right arises to deprive another of his natural liberty without his consent or to restrict it for his benefit as much as the purpose of the state demands; for where you desire to promote the perfection of another, you have no right to compel him to allow that to be done by you.

There is a clear criticism of Locke's agricultural argument: 'no right is created for you in regard to that which belongs to another, because he does not use and enjoy his own property as much as he could.' Wolff blends three different types of arguments in the passage. First, there is the familiar language of natural law and natural rights: 'liberty' must not be taken from legal persons who are 'unwilling'; free consent is required by those who are affected; nobody injures anyone just by his/her mere existence. And 'as long as your neighbours do not injure you, no definite right arises in your favour against them'. Secondly, Wolff uses the domestic analogy to show that dispossessing 'barbarous and uncultivated nations' contradicts our common sense. Thirdly, Wolff rejects the (European) concept of usefulness as a basis of rights: 'And how, I ask, can you show that for the sake of your advantage or that of another nation families may be made subject to sovereignty without their consent, when from that which is useful to you no right arises?'[64] Finally, and most importantly, Wolff hints at a new social and cultural theory which denies that agricultural or commercial societies are morally superior to nomadic forms of life.

Wolff's international legal theory has usually either been ignored, rejected or ridiculed. He was misunderstood even by his followers in the eighteenth century, by Michael Hanov (1695–1773) and by Hermann Friedrich Kahrel (1719–87). Some recent authors, especially Francis Cheneval, see him as a brilliant and innovative international lawyer and as one of the founding figures of modern political cosmopolitanism (see also Chapters 4 and 5).[65] In contrast to authors like Grotius and Vattel, Wolff has a systematic legal theory. For instance, he criticizes Grotius who simply juxtaposed the natural and the positive law of nations, asserting that the latter is based on the will of nations (in case of doubt, on the will of European nations). Wolff, by contrast, wants to bridge the hiatus between natural and positive law with the concept of voluntary law (*ius gentium voluntarium*), which is positive, but has to meet basic normative standards (and thus cannot simply be a matter of state will).⁶⁶

Wolff's theory is not flawless. He does not distinguish (as Kant would later do) between deontology and teleology. The norms of the *civitas maxima*, the democratic global commonwealth, are derived from 'what has been approved by the more civilized nations'.⁶⁷ But on the whole, his achievement is impressive. As far as European relations to non-Europeans are concerned, Wolff's system of *ius gentium*, together with Kant's, marks the triumph of epistemological cosmopolitanism. His moral cosmopolitanism is based on universalist ethics where every human being counts. He combines this approach with a cultural theory that is sensitive to cultural difference, non-European practices and beliefs. Thus he anticipates Denis Diderot's concept of natives as cultural beings (and not as 'noble savages') with a different, albeit not inferior, way of life, and contemporary forms of cultural cosmopolitanism.⁶⁸

Emer de Vattel: the agricultural argument

Traditionally, Emer de Vattel (1714–67) has been seen as Wolff's pupil, who famously rejected his postulate of a *civitas maxima*. Wolff and Vattel do not have much in common, also – and particularly – in terms of the rights of non-Europeans. Here, it makes more sense to emphasize similarities and parallels between John Locke and Vattel.

Probably elaborating on Grotius, Locke developed the agricultural argument fully in his *Two Treatises of Government* (1689). His labour theory of property was fully compatible with, and explicitly justified, European expansion at the expense of native nomadic populations. Historically, the argument applied only to a small portion of the land acquired by Europeans. However, Locke was highly selective in his use of available literature. The overall result was, as Barbara Arneil convincingly argues, the 'defence of England's colonial policy in the New World' and the 'dispossession of the aboriginal peoples of their land'.⁶⁹

Like most natural lawyers before him, Vattel endorses the idea of an original community of ownership, for instance, when he claims that 'the earth belongs to mankind in general'. He states that discovery establishes merely *ius ad occupationem*, a rudimentary and inceptive title contingent upon follow-up effective occupation. 'Hence the Law of Nations will only recognize the *ownership* and *sovereignty* of a Nation over unoccupied lands when the Nation is in actual occupation of them, when it forms a settlement upon them, or makes some actual use of them.'[70] Vattel supplements this theory of effective occupation with the argument of better use. '[N]ature . . . destines the earth for the needs of all mankind, and only confers upon individual nations the right to appropriate territory so far as they can make use of it.'[71] Humans may only legitimately claim as much territory as they actually need and use. These humans belong to agricultural and commerical societies. Vattel distinguishes among three types of nomads. First, there are the 'ancient Germans' and 'modern Tartars', who plunder, pillage and injure others and should therefore be 'exterminated like wild beasts of prey'. The second group of nomads, including the Native Americans, is more peaceful. However, their territory can be settled without injustice, provided sufficient land is left to them. Finally, there are the Arabs who do not use the soil efficiently, but may do it their way as long as cases of 'urgent necessity' of territory do not arise.[72]

The argument of better use is closely following Locke's agricultural argument. Vattel's reasoning includes the following steps. The cultivation of the soil is an obligation of natural law. There is an additional utilitarian calculation involved. Population increases make an intensive use of the soil necessary. Pastoral and hunting ways of living are no longer deemed feasible, and have to give way to an agricultural form of existence, which is economically superior. This utilitarian calculus is supported by the emphasis on effective occupation mentioned above: nomads do not occupy their hunting grounds in a strict sense, as they roam over rather than inhabit them. Vattel calls this 'uncertain occupancy'. Actual occupation, that is settlement and use, are decisive.[73] Vattel concludes: '[W]hile the conquest of the civilized Empires of Peru and Mexico was a notorious usurpation, the establishment of various colonies upon the continent of North America might, if done within just limits, have been entirely lawful.'[74] The emphasis on the status of the Peruvian and Mexican empires as civilized supports the familiar distinction between civilized and savage peoples. The group of civilized nations is no longer exclusively European. Vattel can be defended with his insistence on the idea of impartial justice, specified in the phrase 'if done within just limits'. In addition, sufficient land has to be left to the natives. As we have seen, however, it is up to the sovereign state to decide where to draw this line, and given the human propensity to abuse power, an assumption Vattel himself subscribes to, there was little reason to assume that the Dutch, English or French in North America would meet even this minimal requirement.

Was all this the result of Vattel's Eurocentric bias? It is more plausible to explain the outcome with the flaws in Vattel's overall legal theory. His work can be seen as the perfect synthesis of a refined natural law theory and actual state practice. In other words, his theory is both descending and ascending, combines a top-down with a bottom-up procedure, 'giving to the more acceptable principles of contemporary practice the respectable and fashionable cloak of a universally binding rational rule'.[75] Vattel's theory moves towards legal positivism, with state practice becoming more important. Nations are identified with states; individuals or families do not play any significant role in his system. In these respects, he laid the foundation of classical nineteenth-century international legal theory.

Conclusion

In this chapter, I have tried to show how many interpreters lump very different authors together, assuming that they are bound together by a common 'colonial project'. This approach is unwarranted. My own interpretation emphasizes each author's individuality and (limited) originality, and their profound differences in terms of arguments, legal theories and judgements on non-European peoples. The main errors of the authors mentioned in the introduction can be summarized in the following way.

1. *The fallacy of another great narrative*

Some authors explicitly or implicitly assume a totalizing 'Western legal discourse', especially Williams and Anghie. This theory, however, is an illusion, committing the fallacy of constructing a meta-narrative of modern history. What we really get is a complex picture: the small story that is being told here about Vitoria or Wolff is not necessarily part of a bigger one. The fallacy lies in assuming a false continuity and connectedness that is in fact the work of the interpreter's mind. There are often several types of over-schematization involved: the cliché of a coherent 'Europe' or 'Western civilization' and a corresponding discourse, the sweeping reference to the category of 'the other' and misleading labels like 'Western imperial project' or 'Enlightenment project' (see also Chapter 1). The narrative itself is totalizing, essentialist and thus epistemologically unconvincing.

2. The construction of false continuities

For instance, Anghie makes fanciful connections between the sixteenth-century theologian Vitoria and the secularized discipline of nineteenth-century international law – when key concepts and approaches were civilization, race, sovereignty, state will and legal positivism, all of them rather alien to Vitoria's natural-law thinking. There is a sweeping reference to 'classical international law' without an attempt to define this term. Bowden offers us some daring jumps: for example, from Allen (1939) to Wolff (1749), then to Hall (1890), with quotations from Ward (1795) in between.[76] The complexity and pluralism of the discourses from various, and often very divergent, centuries get lost.

3. The influence of international legal theory is overestimated:

This is suggested by recent studies. McHugh and MacMillan stress the importance of the common law tradition for the English colonies, rather than the impact of international lawyers such as Vitoria, Suaréz, Gentili or Grotius. International legal theory and international legal practice did not always overlap, especially when theories had a philosophical bent. Fisch points out that law in general was indeed an instrument of colonialism, but adds several qualifications. Law 'also set some limits to European intervention and manipulation'. He warns us not to overestimate the importance of legal mechanisms, let alone of legal writings. 'One might suppose that, after all, legal policy was not of a decisive political importance: the end of European rule came in all areas within a short period regardless of the particular legal policy of the respective colonial power.'⁷⁷ Often, indigenous law was used as a means of controlling the natives. It remains to be shown that European legal traditions by their very nature or essence lend themselves to be used as an instrument of oppression. The emancipatory, subversive potential of these traditions, for instance in terms of the concept of equality, should not be underestimated. Sometimes they turned against Europeans. There were unintentional effects, especially in the areas of legal equality and human rights.[78]

4. The ambiguity of texts

Vitoria's lecture in particular is deeply ambiguous. It is definitely one-sided to present him as an unequivocal accomplice of European colonialism or imperialism. Even Vattel is a difficult case: texts are often multidimensional and open to divergent interpretations, and if Europeans and US-Americans used Vattel to justify colonialism (with the help of the agricultural argument), we should not forget that Commissioner Lin Tse-hsu quoted Vattel to criticize British pressure and impending intervention in the 1840s. When he took rigid measures to protect the health of China's population and destroyed British chests of opium, he could have found support for that policy in the doctrines of several European natural lawyers. His scant knowledge of Vattel based on deficient translations apparently convinced him that his course of action was in agreement with norms of the European law of nations.[79]

At the end of the day, it is obvious that debunking Grotius and Vattel as accomplices of European expansion and colonialism is justified. However, we can also discover strong cosmopolitan traditions in some of the international lawyers. Vitoria's moral cosmopolitanism is incomplete, but still an impressive feat, whereas Pufendorf's and Wolff's moral and legal cosmopolitanisms belong to the impressive intellectual achievements of modern European legal theory.

In his excellent book *From Apology to Utopia*, published some twenty years ago, Martti Koskenniemi simply did not mention the 'colonial dimension' when discussing international lawyers such as Grotius. In his more recent study *The Gentle Civilizer of Nations*, he devotes a whole chapter to late nineteenth-century European international legal theory and how it constructed the standard of civilization, ways of excluding non-Europeans and methods of justifiying imperialism.[80] This indicates a significant shift of emphasis in contemporary scholarship, and one that should be welcomed.

3 • British Enlightenment: the Triumph of Commercial Cosmopolitanism

Introduction: a cosmopolitan Enlightenment?

The eighteenth century has usually been seen as a cosmopolitan age before the advent of nationalism in the wake of the French Revolution. In a recent publication, for instance, we find the claim that 'the Enlightenment ... was cosmopolitan in style and content', and the Abbé de Saint-Pierre and Rousseau are cited as examples.[1] This standard interpretation has to be qualified. I illustrate this claim with a few examples: Hume is often regarded as a cosmopolitan thinker, an assessment which is primarily based on his famous statement that 'not only as a man, but as a BRITISH subject, I pray for the flourishing commerce of GERMANY, SPAIN, ITALY, and even FRANCE itself'.[2] The context of the passage is decisive: Hume argues that jealousy of trade is largely unfounded. The 'enlarged and benevolent sentiments' of the cosmopolitan coincide with the self-interest of a particular state's citizen. Presumably not all communities qualify as potential trading partners, although Hume takes for granted that poorer countries can undersell richer ones, as long as they are industrious and ambitious. At any rate, Hume mentions only European countries. In another famous passage, Hume is blatantly racist. He considers 'negroes, and in general all the other species of men ... to be naturally inferior to the whites' and praises white civilization as the pinnacle of human evolution.[3] Hume is apparently Eurocentric rather than cosmopolitan. If he endorsed cosmopolitanism, then it was its economic rather than its moral version. He was not a narrow-minded Scot (or Briton), but perhaps a narrow-minded European.

The Abbé de Saint-Pierre is another case in point. Often praised as one of the founding fathers of the United Nations, the Abbé in fact focused on European affairs, stating that the aim of his proposed league was to establish 'everlasting peace amongst all the Christian states'. The designed European Union was supposed to fight the Turks and throw them out of Europe, Asia and Africa. Global peace was not intended.[4]

Voltaire does indeed refer to 'the citizen of the world', but he is in fact a moderate patriot who tolerates other nations and despises inter-state envy, rivalry and aggression. 'The man who would want his homeland never to be larger, or smaller, or richer or poorer would be a citizen of the world.' This is an extremely thin notion of moral cosmopolitanism. The main thrust of his article *'La Patrie'* in the *Dictionnaire Philosophique* is that most people do not have anything they could legitimately call their 'homeland'. Either they are suppressed by their leaders and priests, or they are greedy merchants who 'have no country apart from their stock exchange and their ledgers', or they are, for instance, 'pleasure-loving', narrow-minded, arrogant and monolingual Parisians.[5] Voltaire's main focus is on a genuine form of patriotism, and cosmopolitan attitudes apparently serve to counterbalance national pride.

I hasten to add that some thinkers of the Enlightenment were cosmopolitan, but we should stay clear of sweeping generalizations.[6] In particular, we should not overlook the category of Europeanism 'in between' patriotism and cosmopolitanisms. Another cliché is the assumption of harmless, unpolitical and cosmopolitan theories of patriotism in the eighteenth century, until 'the fall' into xenophobic and extreme nationalism triggered by the French Revolution. This assessment is apparently in need of qualification. Some authors, even in the territories of the Holy Roman Empire (which are usually seen as rather backward and provincial, compared with France or England), endorsed a militant, aggressive and brutal form of nationalism long before 1789.[7]

How can we characterize the cosmopolitanisms of the eighteenth century? I think that we can distinguish several common trends or aspects. First of all, there is a widespread openness towards and fascination with other cultures, especially in art and literature. Typical examples are Johann Wolfgang von Goethe and Johann Gottfried Herder, but there are lesser-known attempts such as Sir William Jones's translations of Sanskrit poems or the contributions in the journal *Der Patriot* (1724–6, published in Hamburg).[8] It goes without saying that many intellectuals were not free from prejudice (examples abound), but a considerable number at least aimed at open-mindedness, tolerance, and impartiality. For instance, Montesquieu's theory of oriental despotism, developed in his extremely influential work, *The Spirit of the Laws* (1748), became widely accepted by the end of the eighteenth century. However, even then European intellectuals repeatedly challenged Montesquieu's claim (which was based on a misreading of Sir John Chardin). An outstanding example is Abraham-Hyacinthe Anquetil-Duperron, who argued in *Législation orientale* (1778) that the category of 'oriental despotism' was biased and unfounded. John Crawfurd visited Vietnam and neither found tyranny nor terror, but a happy population – 'as if they had nothing to complain of'. Edmund Burke was among those who challenged Montesquieu (see below). Hume's racism also did not go unchallenged.[9]

These lively debates took place among intellectuals who saw themselves as members of a transnational 'republic of letters' which they deemed as important as, or even more important than, membership of their particular communities. The *philosophe* could be at home 'anywhere in the world', provided that he (sometimes, even, she) could communicate with like-minded intellectuals and exchange ideas in journals such as the *Journal encyclopédie*. This intellectual cosmopolitanism was not truly global: in fact, the enlightened *cosmopolite* was at home in western Europe and North America. In principle, the *res publica litteraria* or *Gelehrtenrepublik* disregarded social hierarchies and denominational or national differences. It continued a tradition going back to fifteenth-century humanists like Erasmus.[10]

Lively debates across borders also led to an impressive diversity of attitudes, opinions and theories, and especially with respect to cosmopolitanisms. German-speaking authors are a case in point. I can only hint at this diversity, mentioning two authors. Friedrich Schiller's cosmopolitanism is moral at its core. He focuses on the emotional development of the individual who aims at the cosmopolitan transformation of her society. While Kant's political writings serve as Schiller's starting point, he later moves towards a theory of aesthetic education, believing that beauty paves the way towards (political) freedom.[11] Partly following Adam Smith (see below), Dietrich Hermann Hegewisch (1746–1812) espouses market or economic cosmopolitanism, arguing for porous borders, the right to emigrate, the free movement of labour and perpetual mobility. He combines this with a thin form of moral cosmopolitanism, postulating that there are natural human rights and that all humans should be seen (and tolerated) as equal trading partners.[12]

Finally, Enlightenment cosmopolitans usually tried hard to strike a meaningful balance between patriotism and cosmopolitan obligations. Rousseau opened the debate with his intricate – and often misleading – theory. Rousseau emphatically rejected various forms of cosmopolitanism as deformed, immoral or degenerate, such as cultural or economic cosmopolitanism. He tried to balance defensive republican patriotism with genuine moral cosmopolitanism.[13] A string of authors took part in this debate on the proper relationship between patriotism and cosmopolitanism, among them Thomas Paine, Christoph Wieland, Kant, Richard Price, Voltaire and Edmund Burke.[14]

Types of cosmopolitanism in Locke, Hume, Smith, Paine, Bentham and Burke

I start with an assessment of so-called 'classical' or more or less mainstream British authors. John Locke's vision of international relations (to use a modern term alien to Locke himself) is reminiscent of Hugo Grotius (see the previous chapter): he starts off with the traditional idea that, originally, humankind was one community.[15] Later on, people formed separate, smaller and distinct communities. When citizens united to establish 'one body politick', these independent communities were still in a state of nature with each other.[16] 'So that under this Consideration, the whole community is one Body in the State of Nature, in respect of all other States or Persons out of its Community.'[17]

Locke holds that, in general, the state of nature is unbearable and has to be left. Though this condition is characterized by equality and freedom, it is 'full of fears and continual dangers' and the enjoyment of property is 'very unsafe, very insecure'.[18] The key argument against Hobbes and Filmer is that the right of individual self-preservation must not be replaced by reasons of state, or the self-preservation of the state itself. For instance, Locke criticizes absolute monarchy as arbitrary because from an individual perspective, it does not overcome the state of nature. As far as individual self-preservation is concerned, absolute monarchy, tyranny, oppression and the state of nature coincide. It would be foolish, Locke asserts in a famous passage, that citizens agreed 'to avoid what Mischiefs may be done them by Pole-Cats, or Foxes, but are content, nay think it Safety, to be devoured by Lions'.[19]

Now the logical step would have been to overcome the equally 'unsafe' and 'insecure' international state of nature and form a social contract among states. Locke notes that there is a difference between mere promises and compacts or treaties where states or individuals are still in a state of nature and a social contract or compact where parties agree 'together mutually to enter into one Community, and make one Body Politick'.[20] Locke seems to hold that this community of states is theoretically possible. We do not get the standard argument that international anarchy 'is not that bad' (as in Hobbes and others). Locke does assert that being judge in one's own case – a key feature of the state of nature – is unreasonable. But Locke does not draw the logical conclusion that the international state of nature has to be left. Instead, we get a rather conventional theory of the law of nations: for instance, defensive wars are acceptable and politics should be based on the people's consent.[21] As in Hume, foreign policy is a matter of 'prudence' and 'wisdom' of politicians, and cannot be regulated by 'antecedent, standing, positive laws' as in domestic affairs. In short, Locke gives foreign ministers a free hand as long as 'the advantages of the Commonwealth' are not lost sight of.[22]

Locke's famous labour theory of property has important consequences on an international level. His labour theory is fully compatible with colonial expansion at the expense of native nomadic populations who, according to Locke, do not really own the land because they do not permanently enclose and farm it (see Chapter 2). Locke's international relations theory is incomplete and contradictory. His contractual theory and his normative individualism hint at an inherent cosmopolitan dimension but do not spell it out.[23]

David Hume's vision of international society is clear, but also rather conventional. Enlightened political economy teaches us that transborder interaction is usually both mutually advantageous and 'even sometimes necessary', because resources and commodities are unevenly distributed over the globe. However, all states can exist without international society, albeit perhaps not luxuriously. Individuals, by contrast, depend on civil society for their very survival.[24] With this distinction between domestic and international society in mind, Hume rehearses arguments of the natural law tradition, for example Pufendorf. Compared with his attempt to revolutionize moral philosophy, Hume's account of the law of nations and international society is highly conventional. The same principles of natural justice, namely 'the stability of possession, its transference by consent, and the performance of promises', should be operative both in the domestic and the international sphere.

However, the domestic analogy is soon qualified. The principles of natural justice have lesser 'force' based on the just-mentioned utilitarian calculus: the comparatively smaller usefulness or utility of international society translates into reduced *moral* necessity.[25] As the philosopher is in no position to assess with accuracy the precise degree of the moral 'force' of the right of nations, it is left to the politicians and their experience and judgement to do so. Again, this is reminiscent of Pufendorf: state sovereignty is emphasized, international lawlessness accepted as inevitable and political decisions are most likely a matter of reasons of state. Like some other representatives of the Enlightenment, Hume goes out of his way to argue for the European system of a balance of power. For him, it is a safeguard against the threat of a universal monarchy, checks the ambition of rulers such as Charles V and Louis XIV, maintains the independence of states and guarantees common security and relative stability.[26]

Hume endorses what could be labelled qualified, indirect or long-term economic cosmopolitanism. The upshot of his economic analysis is that trading partners naturally profit from commercial interaction, without directly intending this result. In other words,

> while every man consults the good of his own community, we are sensible, that the general interest of mankind is better promoted, than by loose indeterminate views to the good of a species, whence no beneficial action could ever result, for want of a duly limited object, on which they could exert themselves.[27]

It is better to focus on specific objects or projects than on lofty ones, Hume asserts. Because of the law of unintended consequences, the more limited perspective inevitably promotes the broader 'general interest of mankind'. It does not make sense to characterize Hume as either cosmopolitan or anti-cosmopolitan. To some extent, he is both: there is no doubt that the interests of one's own state or community come first. However, assuming that interests converge if unintended consequences are operative, Hume can also claim that his version of economic cosmopolitanism is more efficient and thus better than direct, traditional natural law cosmopolitanism. He implies that only if societies or regions become trading partners and thus part of the economic market, do they qualify as members of this – either European or truly global – community.

Of the classical British authors, Adam Smith is the most original thinker. To some extent, Smith can be interpreted as a representative of political realism who follows a Hobbesian approach: he does not assume a natural harmony of interests across borders, his focus is on the state or commonwealth, he views international relations as anarchic, endorses the balance-of-power doctrine, and emphasizes the importance of defence.[28] Smith combines a weak form of political realism with a state-centred and patriotic perspective and cosmopolitan ideas. On the one hand, he asserts that the love of humanity is too vague, that patriotism is more feasible and that Britain should be loved 'for its own sake'. However, as in Hume, the great society is indirectly supported by efforts consciously focusing on the domestic sphere. Worldwide economic gains are an unintended by-product. Free trade would turn states into a sort of 'provinces' of one great empire: the idea of a *monarchia universalis* is transformed into the vision of a truly global free exchange of commodities, with overall beneficial results such as the end of local famines, and a situation where respect for rights is guaranteed by a roughly equal distribution of economic and military power. In addition, people with 'enlarged and enlightened' minds would overcome the passions of 'savage patriotism'.[29]

Distinguishing between European politics and global international relations, Smith holds that the balance of power in Europe is efficient, with the overall result being 'peace and tranquillity' and the protection of the freedom and independence of the sovereign European states. The situation is different on a global scale. Since 1492, Europeans have enjoyed military superiority, which enabled them 'to commit with impunity every sort of injustice' wherever they wanted to.[30] Smith speaks as an impartial spectator; he is not interested in defending or trivializing European atrocities, or constructing a teleological theory of possible benefits arising from these injustices. However, as in European politics, the global remedy is a system of power balance (the standard remedy of political realism). Smith speculates that perhaps in the future, European power will decline and that of non-European communities will increase, so that in the long run 'the inhabitants of all the different quarters of the world may arrive at that equality of courage and force which, by inspiring mutual fear, can alone overawe the injustice of independent nations into some sort of respect for the rights of one another'. This equality of force can be established by worldwide commerce and the transfer of technology.[31] In short, commerce reduces material inequalities among nations and parts of the globe, and contributes to peace and 'respect for rights' in the long run. A natural superiority of Europeans, or a right to civilize backward barbarians, is not implied.

Smith became famous for his elaborated version of the so-called four-stage theory. While his account is developmental and culminates in the commercial society, Smith avoids, and warns against, what he sees as civilizational self-deception: the belief that one's own society or culture is superior to others. Smith's moral balance-sheet of commercial society is much more nuanced than Hume's, emphasizing the paradoxes, ambivalences and negative side-effects of commercial progress.[32] In addition, Smith explains societal change in Europe, at least partially, with the help of material or physical factors, thus enabling him 'to avoid the self-congratulatory note common in discussions attributing such developments to European's special understanding of the values of freedom or political equality'.[33]

While Smith's assessment of European achievements was mildly sceptical (and never enthusiastic), his treatment of non-European societies was quite tolerant and non-judgmental. The often arrogant and condescending tone of numerous nineteenth-century historians is missing. Practices and institutions of earlier forms of society are usually depicted as reasonable. Smith implicitly denies that Europeans are qualified to export their type of society to other continents; he warns that the 'man of system' is bound to neglect contexts, 'interests' and 'prejudices' when attempting to realize his ideal plan.[34] Smith's culturally sensitive judgements are rooted in his moral theory, which aims at what Kant would later call 'enlarged thinking' or *erweiterte Denkungsart*: we should see ourselves from the perspective of others, should reflect upon the cultural and social contexts of our judgements, should step beyond the narrow confines of our own group, should try to broaden the circle of comparison. Smith arrives at a delicate balance between a thin version of moral universalism (the traditional, but modified natural law element) and a contextual theory of moral judgements (the new element of history). Smith does not upset this balance in favour of fully fledged moral relativism, similar to Pufendorf, Wolff or Kant (see Chapters 2 and 4). The outcome is a 'posture of humility in the evaluation of unfamiliar practices' of non-Europeans, even if Smith sometimes does not refrain from criticism.[35] These practices are usually understood as possibly reasonable responses to different contexts and circumstances.

Smith's cosmopolitanism combines patriotism with indirect, long-term economic as well as natural law (or human rights) cosmopolitanism. Smith's criticism of colonialism corresponds with these three elements: colonies are detrimental for the metropolitan state (they may lead to war, for instance); they contradict economic prudence because they are simply too expensive; they lead to destruction, oppression, abuse and arbitrary rule, as the case of the East India Company illustrates.[36] As in Bentham (see below), there is a delicate balance between economic (or utilitarian) and moral arguments.

Born in England, Thomas Paine (1737–1809) pursued several occupations and finally emigrated to the American colonies in 1774, with a letter of introduction and recommendation by Benjamin Franklin in his pocket. His first major work and an immediate best-seller, *Common Sense* (1776), helped inspire the Declaration of Independence. It has been said that his work leaves us

> with all the features of cosmopolitan thinking in international relations: Faith in reason and progress, the evils of authoritarian regimes, the democratic peace, the peaceful effect of trade, nonprovocative defense policies, open diplomacy, obsolescence of conquest, the universal respect for human rights, and the democratic propensity to engage in messianic interventionism.[37]

This generous use of the label 'cosmopolitan thinking' must be rejected: 'cosmopolitan' should not be mixed with 'liberal' or 'liberal internationalist'. In the first place, Paine is a liberal thinker who criticizes monarchies, argues for republican and democratic principles of government, and defends the American and French revolutions. He also develops an early version of the democratic peace proposition. However, these are liberal, not cosmopolitan convictions or theories.

As a cosmopolitan, Paine endorses commercial as well as moral or human rights cosmopolitanism. His most succinct statement on commerce is in the second part of *The Rights of Man* (1792): 'I have been an advocate for commerce, because I am a friend of its effects. It is a pacific system, operating to unite mankind by rendering nations, as well as individuals, useful to each other.' This belief is backed up by the ancient 'doctrine of universal economy' (Jacob Viner), endorsed in the fourth century by Libanius. The elements of this doctrine are the moral cosmopolitan belief in a universal commonwealth, the conviction that the exchange of goods is beneficial in a world where resources are distributed unequally, and finally the religious and teleological faith that God or Nature arranged all this to promote peaceful cooperation and social relationships. This doctrine had been a standard argument of cosmopolitan thinkers before Paine such as Montesquieu and representatives of the Scottish Enlightenment.[38]

Paine's moral or human rights cosmopolitanism is based on the optimistic belief that 'man, were he not corrupted by governments, is naturally the friend of man, and that human nature is not of itself vicious'.[39] Human rights are universal, and the 'morning of reason' will make sure that in the long run the people all over the world will overcome 'corrupted' and 'wretched' governments, and establish a 'universal civilization'.[40] This ultimate goal, this natural and peaceful harmony, is achieved with the help of two key factors, by commerce and by the spread of democratic governments. Free trade and commerce have two beneficial consequences: first, trade makes conquest inefficient and obsolete. An open world-market helps nations to obtain what they tried to get through conquest in previous centuries. Secondly, trade fosters cosmopolitan understanding between nations, a claim that is reminiscent of Hume and others.[41]

The second factor that helps to establish a 'universal civilization' is the spread of democratic governments. According to Paine's democratic peace proposition, monarchical government is the main source of war and if it was abolished 'throughout Europe, the cause of wars would be taken away'. Monarchies are always in a 'state of nature' with each other as they 'put themselves beyond the law as well of God as of man'. For Paine, war is a special form of exploitation, where the productive classes at home and abroad become an easy prey for the 'plundering classes' such as government officials, aristocrats or the established clergy. Paine's 'idealistic internationalism' (David Fitzsimons) aims at liberating societies from oppressive governments or states.[42]

Paine's optimism concerning the spread of democracy and the triumph of a universal civilization is partly rooted in his millennial thinking, partly the result of his American experience. Eighteenth-century America was a very unlikely but confirming case for a naturally emerging harmony.

> If there is a country in the world, where concord, according to common calculation, would be least expected, it is America. Made up, as it is, of people from different nations, accustomed to different forms and habits of government, speaking different languages, and more different in their modes of worship, it would appear that the union of such a people was impracticable.[43]

Paine dismissed the emigration from England as an irrelevant factor, and stressed the national and religious diversity of the immigrants. Why is the American experiment so successful? Because the government, Paine replies, is based on the only true principles and the rights of man. Paine apparently holds that this 'cordial unison' can be instilled all over the world.

Paine's 'model of a new democratic world founded on international brotherhood' (Thomas Walker) is rather vague. He mentions the plan of Henry IV and proposes a 'European congress' and 'one great republic' for all of Europe along these lines.[44] The institutions and principles of this republic are not spelled out. Paine seems to believe that the harmony of interests and economic cooperation would suffice to keep this loose federation together. Paine is very suspicious of government; along these lines, he might have detested the idea of a transnational government. Paine is not a profound thinker, but he has the gift to express popular ideas in a very persuasive way. His brand of cosmopolitanism – a mixture of economic and human rights cosmopolitanism – corresponds with standard interpretations of the Enlightenment.

Jeremy Bentham is the most outspoken advocate of economic cosmopolitanism, but keeps the moral perspective. Bentham has traditionally been seen as a utilitarian imperialist, just like his successors James and John Stuart Mill, who misunderstood or misrepresented his views. In fact, Bentham is closer to authors like Smith, who argued *against* empire with the help of utilitarian (and moral) arguments. A juxtaposition of two statements illustrates the point. John Stuart Mill asserted that '[d]espotism is a legitimate mode of government in dealing with barbarians, provided the end be their improvement, and the means justified by actually effecting that end', thus anticipating standard nineteenth-century arguments of imperial liberalism based on Europe's civilizing mission, race and economic as well as technological development (see ending of Chapter 5). Bentham belongs to the late eighteenth-century critics of empire, refuting Mill's claim in advance. 'Reform the world by example, you act generously and wisely: reform the world by force, you might as well reform the moon, and the design is fit only for lunatics.'[45] Bentham shows that English liberalism was not necessarily imperialist. The quotations also document that within a few decades, attitudes changed profoundly.

In 'Principles of international law' (1786/9) and 'Rid yourselves of ultramaria' (1793), Bentham asserts that the emancipation of the colonies or 'foreign dependencies' is above all in the interest of the home countries. His arguments against the Spanish, British and French empires are predominantly utilitarian, stressing economic aspects. Long tables and calculations are supposed to show that colonial expenses by far overbalance profits. In addition, the colonies have a detrimental domestic impact, and increase national insecurity by diverting manpower.[46] Like domestic law, international law is based on the principle of utility, or 'the most extensive welfare of all the nations on the earth'. Utility overrides national interests with the exception of self-preservation. As in Benjamin Constant, commerce should replace conquest and colonial exploitation. Britain can trade better with independent states or communities than with rebellious and expensive colonies.[47]

Bentham supplements his economic arguments. Like Edmund Burke, he believes that administrators and colonial rulers cannot be trusted, and that great distances make good government impossible. We do not find a downright support of Europe's civilizing mission; Bentham's statements are rather ambiguous and contradictory on this point.[48] However, Bentham is quite outspoken on the issue of justice:

> Suppose ... that hitherto ... a colony has been a source of net profit to the ruling country. Still, it is not in the nature of the case that it should long continue so to be. Over the inhabitants of the dependency in question, power cannot be exercised, – from them such profit cannot be extracted, without manifest injury done to them, without manifest oppression exercised upon them.[49]

Colonies *may* be profitable; in the long run, however, the indigenous population or the settlers will be suppressed to maintain order, and this is not only unjust but may lead to a destructive civil war, as in the case of the American colonies. Bentham combines in a creative way two standard arguments against colonies. From a moral perspective, they are unjust; from an economic perspective, they are counter-productive, and only an elite will benefit. Bentham's moral cosmopolitanism is emphasized by the fact that unlike his utilitarian successors, he does not distinguish between settler colonies and those populated mainly by indigenous peoples. The same moral standards apply to them and the moral verdict is identical, namely colonialism is a waste of money, leads to an abuse of power, oppression, corruption, corruptive influence on the constitution, despotism, profits for the ruling few and prejudice.[50]

While Edmund Burke became (in)famous for his attack on the French Revolution and his conservatism, he is rarely appreciated for his criticism of British colonialism, especially in connection with Warren Hastings, the systematic oppression in India and the exclusion of the Irish.[51] As in Hume and Smith, we find elements of political realism: the emphasis on prudence, on the balance of power, on a qualified duty to intervene, and on war. Burke also refers – in a manner reminiscent of, but going beyond, Vattel and other eighteenth-century international lawyers (see Chapter 5) – to 'the community of Europe', 'the brotherhood of Christendom' and 'the system of Europe'.[52] Like many other eighteenth-century authors, Burke does not think that patriotism, Europeanism and cosmopolitan sentiments are incompatible with each other. This is expressed in his famous statement: 'To be attached to the subdivision, to love the little platoon we belong to in society, is the first principle (the germ as it were) of public affections. It is the first link in the series by which we proceed toward a love to our country and to mankind.'[53] This is the familiar image of concentric circles.

Burke's cosmopolitanism revolves around three elements. First, there is Burke's 'peculiar universalism' (Jennifer Pitts) which combines universal principles with historically evolved values of a particular society and the 'law of nations'. The latter encompasses the collective reason of ages and cultures, distilled from an observation of various customs and traditions.[54] The novel element here is that Burke forcefully continues the path taken by the Scottish Enlightenment from 'universal moral order' to 'historical reason' (see ending of Chapter 5). Secondly, Burke attacks what he denounces as the 'geographical morality' of Warren Hastings: the claim that, depending on the region, different sets of rules and norms apply. Against Hastings, Burke asserts that the British are not entitled to suspend their moral and legal standards when dealing with non-Europeans. Instead, 'the British had an obligation to extend universally the fundamental standards of respect, lawfulness, and humanity that applied at home'.[55] A way to overcome geographical morality was to boost the moral imagination and increase sympathy for strangers. In a manner reminiscent of Francisco de Vitoria (see Chapter 2), Burke compared India with Germany: 'not for an exact resemblance, but as a sort of middle term, by which India might be approximated to our understandings, and if possible to our feelings; in order to awaken something of sympathy for the unfortunate natives'.[56] This comparison only worked – and this is the third element – if Indians and their culture and institutions were not seen as inferior. So Burke is at pains to show that Indian alleged inferiority and so-called oriental despotism are psychological or cognitive problems of *Europeans* in the first place: a convenient myth of Hastings and other British administrators to justify their own oppression, injustices and arbitrary rule. And Burke, with considerable historical accuracy, identified Montesquieu as the main culprit of this distorted picture of India (see above).[57]

It is time for a brief summary: most authors tend to favour long-term, predominantly economic and indirect cosmopolitanism. The natural law tradition is strongest in Smith, and there are traces of natural law cosmopolitanism in Locke, Paine and Bentham. Political and contractual cosmopolitanism is not an issue in these authors. Locke and Paine are the ones who get close to it.

Thinkers with a European or cosmopolitan perspective: Penn, Bellers and Fletcher

I will now turn to authors who develop a clear European or cosmopolitan perspective. Their political or contractual cosmopolitanism may not be fully developed. However, in contrast to the thinkers in the previous section, economic or commercial considerations are subordinate to political issues, and the goal is to establish some sort of European or international federation.

William Penn (1644–1718) was an English Quaker and founded the colony of Pennsylvania. In 1682, he held a famous interview with Native American tribes and made a treaty of friendship with them. His religious convictions brought him in conflict with the authorities, he practised an early form of civil disobedience, supported toleration and was imprisoned several times. In the 1690s, when he withdrew from public life in exchange for not being harassed by the crown any more, he wrote several tracts and titles, among them *An Essay Towards the Present and Future Peace of Europe* (1693).[58]

Penn proposes a European 'league, or Confederacy' where the representatives of states meet on a regular basis 'in a general diet, estates, or parliament' to establish norms of European international law.[59] Depending on size, states send up to twelve delegates. In his plan, Penn does not favour England: it gets only six votes, compared with ten for France and twelve for the German Empire. The parliament would include ninety seats and the room should be round to 'avoid quarrel for precedency'. Laws are passed or decisions become binding if they have a three-quarters majority. States that do not submit to these decisions will be compelled to accept them. Penn does not specify what form the ultimate sanction would take. Perhaps he has economic sanctions or financial penalties in mind; it is also possible that he envisions military force against the recalcitrant.[60] The scheme 'leads to the benefit of an universal monarchy, without the inconveniencies that attend it'. The benefit is overcoming the international state of war, or the advantages of 'peace and security'; the inconveniencies that are avoided are high taxes, exploitation, suppression and dependence on the imperial authority.[61]

How does Penn argue for this European confederacy, how does he justify it? Apart from moral outrage at the tragedies of war, we can detect two distinct lines of argument. First, Penn follows a utilitarian approach, as in Hume or Bentham. The first section talks of the advantages of peace. A typical statement runs: 'Peace preserves our possessions; we are in no danger of invasions: our trade is free and safe, and we rise and lie down without anxiety.' Peace in Europe would of course save money and 'beget and increase personal friendship between princes and states', which would in turn make war more unlikely.[62]

The second line of argument builds on the domestic analogy. Without mentioning the concept of a state of nature, Penn implicitly refers to this condition as one where each person is judge in one's own cause. Government by contrast is characterized by the rule of law, impartial judges and a civil authority based on consent. Penn writes:

> justice is the means of peace, betwixt the government and the people, and one man and company and another. It prevents strife, and at last ends it: for besides shame or fear, to contend longer, he or they being under government, are constrained to bound their desires and resentment with the satisfaction the law gives. Thus peace is maintained by justice, which is a fruit of government, as government, is from society, and society from consent.

By analogy, the European confederacy amounts to a government constraining the freedom or sovereignty of states. Penn is quick to add that only external, not internal, sovereignty would be limited.[63]

Do we get a cosmopolitan perspective in Penn? Well, we do not, but it would be exaggerated to call Penn's perspective Eurocentric. There is a clear focus on Europe, Penn is convinced of European cultural and religious superiority, he hopes that a European peace would improve the reputation of Christianity and make more attacks of the Ottoman Turks impossible (Penn wrote his essay ten years after the siege of Vienna in 1683).[64] On the other hand, Penn's federation is clearly defensive (in contrast to Saint-Pierre and many others). He finds it 'fit and just' to include the Ottoman empire in the league and implies that it would keep its European possessions on the Balkans. European colonies and colonial atrocities are not mentioned, but Penn the pacifist points out that

European Christians have fought 'many bloody and unjust wars' with native populations (the so-called 'infidels').[65] This evidence supports the thesis that Penn endorsed a thin version of natural law cosmopolitanism.

What about Penn's colonial policy? Was he cosmopolitan in practice? His record in terms of dealing with the Native Americans is a complex matter. It was in Penn's interest to cooperate with the natives – and the other way round. But he also wanted to show that with a just treatment of neighbours, the Quakers would not need a militia. Penn was an English patriot and he was often willing to compromise to save his 'holy experiment'. In fact, as in his writings, he combined pacifist idealism with pragmatism. Like Vitoria and several other natural lawyers (see Chapter 2), Penn was convinced that the Native Americans enjoyed full ownership over their lands, as 'tis the natives by the *jus gentium*, by the law of nations'. All things considered, we may conclude that 'Penn and his fellow Quakers were an exception' to European practices in North America.[66]

Like his friend Penn, John Bellers (1656–1725) was a Quaker and therefore a pacifist. He has sometimes been called a Quaker socialist because he was engaged in fighting poverty, and helping prisoners as well as the sick and old. Eduard Bernstein, leading thinker of modern social democracy, praised the essay as 'far ahead of his age', and a successful combination of idealism and realism.[67]

Written in 1710, during the Spanish War of Succession, Bellers's *Some Reasons for an European State* is similar to, and apparently influenced by, Penn's essay. Bellers proposes a league that would include a supreme court, and an annual congress or parliament to set up European international law. As in Penn, governments would remain sovereign 'at home'. Bellers offers two new ideas: he suggests that Europe is divided into one hundred equal provinces; and he hopes that the league will evolve out of the present Grand Alliance against France.[68]

How does Bellers argue for his federation? One argument is economic, the other is religious. He is especially interested in ecumenical progress, citing the Grand Alliance as an example of Protestants and Catholics cooperating peacefully with each other. As in Penn, Bellers hopes that a European peace would improve the reputation of Christianity among the Turks and 'infidels', and spread the faith.[69] Like Penn, Bellers focuses exclusively on 'the Universal

Peace of Europe'. He refers to America as 'those Dark Corners of the World' and to the Native Americans as 'barbarous' people.[70] On the other hand, Bellers rejects the plan of the French king Henry IV (actually written by the Duc de Sully), which excluded the Muscovites or Russians as well as the Turks from the federation. His reasoning should be quoted in full:

> The Muscovites are Christians, and the Mahometans Men, and have the same faculties, and reason as other Men, they only want the same Opportunities, and Applications of their Understandings, to be the same Men: but to beat their Brains out, to put sense into them, is a great Mistake, and would leave Europe, too much in a state of War; whereas, the farther this civil Union is Possible to be Extended, the greater will be the Peace on Earth, and good will among Men.[71]

The last sentence highlights once more the religious background of the essay. Bellers's league is not exclusively Christian; it is European, but with a cosmopolitan touch. We can call his approach cosmopolitan and pacifist (as opposed to imperialist) Europeanism (see Chapter 6; an example of imperialist Europeanism would be Saint-Pierre). Bellers is careful not to create inside–outside distinctions. Emphasizing the sameness of Muslims again points at some sort of moral cosmopolitanism.

Andrew Fletcher of Saltoun (1653–1716) is the most complex of the three authors, and the most interesting as well. It is not at all clear whether he should be assigned to the 'camp' of cosmopolitans. However, he deserves to be mentioned here, as he could be interpreted as outlining an early version of republican cosmopolitanism. Fletcher was a member of the Scottish Parliament in the years before 1707, when the Act of Union united Scotland with England to form the Kingdom of Great Britain. Fletcher was a Scottish patriot who vigorously fought against an incorporating union and for a federal union. He resented centralized power and sought to limit the power of the Crown and of English ministers in Scottish affairs, proposing an Act of Security with 'Limitations' in 1703. In vain he argued for an independent Scottish parliament and against standing mercenary armies. After the Act of Union, a desperate Fletcher turned from politics. His last words, according to his nephew, were: 'Lord, have mercy on my poor country that is so barbarously oppressed.'[72]

An Account of a Conversation Concerning a Right Regulation of Governments for the Common Good of Mankind was published in 1704, at the climax of his career, intended to support his opposition to an incorporating union. The dialogue is most likely fictitious, and takes place between Fletcher, the Earl of Cromarty (a Scots peer advocating an incorporating union), Sir Christopher Musgrave (a Tory MP) and Sir Edward Seymour (an ultra-royalist and Tory who resented the Scots).[73] Fletcher proposes to divide Europe into ten roughly equal confederations. He was probably influenced by Pufendorf's theory of a 'system of states' (*systema civitatum*). These ten parts should form 'mutual alliances'.[74]

Fletcher's intended league is unique, but equally interesting is the way he argues for it. We can detect three distinct themes in his account: the European international system; the fate of small states; and the threat of big cities. According to Fletcher, the European states-system is threatened by states aspiring to the universal monarchy or, more recently, attempting to establish political as well as commercial hegemony. This is the main topic of his *Discorso delle cose di Spagna* (1698). In this essay, Fletcher asserts wryly: 'I am speaking of what princes have and will always do, which is, by any means, wherever they can, to enlarge their kingdoms by occupying neighbouring provinces.'[75] In the 'Account', Fletcher laments that in the last decades, European conflicts have developed into devastating worldwide wars and that states are in constant danger of being 'enslaved by a foreign invasion' (the second danger is the 'corruption of manners').[76]

As a patriotic Scot, Fletcher is particularly interested in the way this states-system affects small countries like Scotland. Fletcher reasons that they should not only support larger states in their fight against hegemonic powers; they should also be careful to obtain guarantees to protect their territorial integrity, freedom and trade. Along these lines, Fletcher contrasts the ideal 'alliance' between England and Scotland based on equality and independence with a disastrous 'incorporating union' that would ruin the Scottish economy. In addition, in the long run Scotland might face the fate of Ireland and become a conquered nation:

> Now if after a union with us the least commotion should happen in Scotland, suppose on account of church government; might we not

expect that the suppression of this would likewise be called a conquest, and we or our posterity be treated as a conquered people?

(Scotland indeed became a conquered nation after the Battle of Culloden in April 1746 between an English army and the forces of the Jacobites (mainly Highland Scots), who supported the claim to the throne of Charles Edward Stuart.) There is one remedy, namely a third party that guarantees 'that all the conditions of union shall be duly observed'. Other European states would have to be this third party.[77] This implies that a league with a system of mutual alliances has to be established.

Fletcher's other main argument in favour of a league of confederations is based on his analysis of big cities. Fletcher himself loved cities like London, Paris or Amsterdam where he visited chocolate houses and engaged in conversation. His 'Account' starts with a praise of London and its advantages: the beauty of its location, the variety of life it offers and the amount of 'liberty and rights' that citizens enjoy 'in matters civil and religious'. However, the conversation soon turns to the 'corruption of manners' that great cities inevitably generate. They are hotbeds of luxury, prostitution and corrupt government. Corruption spreads like cancer, infecting the masses as well as newcomers who try to reform others. 'In a word,' Sir Christopher Musgrave summarizes, 'this city abounds with all manners of temptations to evil; extreme poverty, excessive riches, great pleasures, infinite bad examples, especially of unpunished and successful crimes.'[78]

Fletcher is a neo-Machiavellian and representative of the civic humanist tradition which emphasizes *virtus*, *vertu politique* or civic virtue and the political participation of citizens, also and especially in matters of military defence. To qualify for citizenship, the (always male) citizen must be master of his own household, and possess property in order to be economically independent. Civic humanists, who are sometimes called civic republicans, are extremely worried about the threat of corruption, caused by citizens who put private interests above the common good, or material concerns above civic virtue. The classic opposition between virtue and corruption is complemented by that between virtue and commerce.[79]

As a civic humanist, Fletcher is apparently more worried about the dangers of corrupt cities than about the dangers of international anarchy. This makes his proposal unique, and distinguishes him from Penn, Bellers and others who are rooted in the natural law tradition influenced by Christianity. Authors like Adam Smith established a third tradition that revolved around the notion of a 'commercial society' where the division of labour has been established and members exchange goods for their mutual benefit, and everybody thus 'becomes in some measure a merchant'.[80]

So Fletcher's major threats are the big cities, and this is reflected in his proposal. According to this, 'unnatural' cities like London would be reduced to capitals of the neighbouring counties, and complemented by ten or twelve cities 'of equal advantages'. Smaller governments would be 'duly executed', because control is tight and the citizens' participation is facilitated. Even virtue would be encouraged. 'So many different seats of government will highly tend to the improvement of all arts and sciences; and afford great variety of entertainment to all foreigners and others of a curious and inquisitive genius, as the ancient cities of Greece did.'[81] Fletcher's European union is a league of confederations, each in turn consisting of ten city states and their territories. Fortifications would make them 'unfit for conquests', militias unfit for aggressive wars. The confederations would unite 'for their common defence'.[82]

As a civic humanist, Fletcher furnishes his league with republican elements. He expresses doubts about 'absolute monarchy', argues for a limited monarchy, and formulates an early version of the democratic peace proposition. In the dialogue, Fletcher himself points out

> that the true interest and good of any nation is the same with that of any other. I do not say that one society ought not to repel the injuries of another; but that no people ever did any injustice to a neighbouring nation, except by mistaking their own interest.[83]

The democratic peace consists of two elements: peoples are usually peaceful and just, and their interests converge across borders. Secondly, militias, by their very nature, are unfit for aggressive wars. All in all, we get a clandestine if not outspoken statement for a league of small republics – long before Rousseau.[84]

Civic humanists like Machiavelli focused on the state and its survival in a condition of international anarchy – with the help of fortifications, efficient military leadership, strong armies, alliances and, possibly, aggressive wars. Fletcher goes beyond this state-centred perspective. In addition, and again in contrast to Machiavelli and the like, he attempts to change the modern, anarchical states-system towards a more peaceful condition. These two elements turn Fletcher into a neo-Machiavellian of a very peculiar mould. A key passage runs as follows:

> It is indeed . . . a most surprising thing to me, that not only all those who have written on that subject, and contrived schemes of constitutions, have, as I think, always framed them with respect only to particular nations, for whom they were designed, and without any regard to the rest of mankind.

Humans have a natural inclination to ignore 'the general good and interest of mankind, on which that of every distinct society does in a great measure depend'.[85] In other words, societies are mutually dependent on each other, and because of that interdependence, the whole (humankind) affects its parts (distinct societies). In another passage, Fletcher, in reply to Sir Edward Seymour, explains how his patriotism has led him to a cosmopolitan outlook:

> To tell you the truth, the insuperable difficulty I found of making my country happy by any other way, led me insensibly to the discovery of these things, which, if I mistake not, have no other tendency than to render, not only my own country, but all mankind as happy as the imperfections of human nature will admit.[86]

This implies that there is a harmony of interests across borders. Patriotic and cosmopolitan attitudes do not contradict each other, but may converge.

There is a passage where those two attitudes seem to be in conflict with each other, and there is a gap between the 'good citizen of a particular commonwealth' and 'a citizen of the world'.[87] However, Fletcher argues against Sir Christopher Musgrave that there is only a conflict or contradiction if we distinguish between morality in private affairs and morality in politics, between ordinary morality and the reason of state. If we do not accept this distinction, and if we look at real interests, patriotic and cosmopolitan attitudes do in fact converge. Put in Kantian terms, the political moralist 'who frames morals to suit the statesman's advantage' is responsible for the gap between particular state interests and the good of humankind.[88]

Several succinct passages highlight Fletcher's cosmopolitan attitude. Fletcher is worried about Scotland's future, but he is also very outspoken about the English conquest of Ireland and the oppression in the North American colonies. The European league of confederations should be complemented by similar arrangements 'through the other three parts of the world'.[89]

Francis Cheneval has praised Fletcher as an author who anticipated the republican projects of Rousseau and Kant, surpassing the Abbé de Saint-Pierre (who later proposed an exclusive European union of despotic monarchies; on Kant see Chapter 4).[90] This assessment is correct but, as in Rousseau, there are ambiguities that cannot be ignored. First of all, Fletcher's proposal seems to be self-defeating: the envisioned division of Europe would mean the end of Scotland as an independent political community, Fletcher's starting point.[91] Secondly, Fletcher is worried about the corruption of manners in big cities. However, one might say that if his proposal was realized, even more cities would be created, and they also might turn into hotbeds of vice, rather than creating more virtue. So Fletcher is between the devil and the deep blue sea. Finally, as a civic humanist, Fletcher is very sceptical about the new force of commerce or trade, 'the constant stumbling block, and ball of contention' of their discussion. Fletcher believes that the union with England has ruined Scottish trade – a belief that is historically not accurate.[92] At any rate, his proposal would have encouraged the economy and trade of the new city-states (at the expense of unnatural mega-cities like London). This in turn would again have fostered vice rather than virtue and have abandoned the civic humanist ideal of autarky.

I now come to my tentative conclusion: It has been argued that many cosmopolitan cynics and stoics in antiquity were in fact social outsiders, and that their ideas could therefore never become mainstream.[93] It seems that the same holds true for the authors of the last section. Especially members of (persecuted) minorities like the Quakers or members of disadvantaged communities like Fletcher were apt to develop progressive, cosmopolitan schemes. If we take a brief look at other British Enlightenment thinkers, we usually find a clear focus on the modern state, or a state-centered perspective: issues like the defence of religious and political liberties, the revolution of 1688 or the idea of patriotism were the centres of interest, as in Algernon Sidney or Joseph Priestley. If international relations issues were touched upon, most debates concerned standing armies and militias, the idea of a balance of power, or the fear of military or political hegemony. In the second half of the eighteenth century, solutions for problems within the British empire, especially with the North American colonies, were urgently needed and discussed. Priestley, Adam Smith and Edmund Burke were cases in point. The late eighteenth century produced a row of 'enlightened critics of empire' (Anthony Pagden) and colonialism, among them Charles Davenant and Edward Gibbon. Authors like Penn, Bellers or Fletcher do not fit into this pattern.[94]

My second observation harks back to what I said in the opening paragraphs of this chapter about Enlightenment cosmopolitanism: authors like Smith, Penn or Fletcher try to keep a balance among, or form a synthesis of patriotism, Europeanism and cosmopolitanism. Their ideas are very diverse and often creative. They frequently show a considerable degree of openness towards other cultures, Penn being the most impressive example. Finally, economic and indirect cosmopolitanism seems to have carried the day: the influence of Adam Smith and the new science of political economy on the following two centuries were considerable, to say the least. The authors of the last section, by contrast, have remained rather unknown until today. Penn's essay, for instance, was only rediscovered in 1849, and republished in 1896, for the first time since 1726.[95]

The French Revolution was a turning point for European attitudes and political theories, and this also applies to cosmopolitanisms. In the early phase of the revolution, French patriotism and moral as well as political cosmopolitanism complemented each other. This synthesis was personified by Count Volney, Condorcet and, above all, by Anarcharsis Cloots, who addressed the national assembly as '*l'ambassadeur du genre humain*' in June 1790. After 1793, revolutionaries became increasingly xenophobic and nationalistic, criticizing the *cosmopolites* as enemies of the revolution (see the ending of Chapter 5). Effects on European mentalities were considerable. Cosmopolitan theories were increasingly identified with the goals and practices of the French revolutionaries, and rejected together with them. Many, among them even moderate thinkers, challenged the precarious balance between patriotism and cosmopolitanisms, and became increasingly nationalistic. In this tense atmosphere Kant wrote his famous essay *Zum ewigen Frieden* (1795).

4 • Kant and the 'Miserable Comforters': Contractual Cosmopolitanism

Comparisons of authors with their predecessors are always fraught with a problem: we tend to exaggerate the differences at the expense of similarities. If we realize this tendency in our thinking, we might fall into the opposite extreme: we see parallels and similarities and ignore the differences. So we often settle for a middle course, a third way (and critics see this as a feeble compromise). Walter Mignolo follows the 'similar rather than different' approach. He compares Vitoria with Kant and concludes:

> I have the impression that if one stripped Vitoria of his religious principles, replaced theology with philosophy, and the concern to deal with difference in humanity with a straightforward classification of people by nations, color, and continents, what one would obtain indeed would be Kant. Is that much of a difference? In my view it is not.[1]

There is some truth in this statement: if we look at cosmopolitan right, there is, in terms of content, little new in Kant. Many natural lawyers criticized European colonialism before him, and defended aboriginal rights, Diderot anticipated Kant's distinction between the right to visit and the right to be a guest, and Wolff's universal commonwealth can be interpreted as foreshadowing Kant's rational idea of an original contract and original community (see Chapter 2). On the other hand, the concept of hospitality rights changed considerably after Vitoria. His critics, some of them members of the Second Scholastic themselves, stressed that the freedom of travel was conditional, not unconditional. Adam Smith in particular subsumed hospitality rights under personal rights, and his account was embedded in his four-stage theory and encompassed a historical dimension. They were (not only) part of a hierarchy of natural laws, but subject to state legislation and change. Wolff emphasized that the freedom of communication had to be mutual, not unilateral. Finally, Kant distinguishes between juridical duties and duties of virtue, and (like the natural lawyers), between perfect and imperfect duties. Revising the traditional argument from original ownership, Kant offers a new justification of hospitality rights.[2]

In some respects, Kant is close to Saint-Pierre, who analysed the European great power system in a Hobbesian fashion and concluded that it was little more than a system of mitigated anarchy: 'First, the present constitution of Europe can never produce anything else but almost continual wars, because it can never procure any sufficient security for the execution of treaties. Secondly, the equilibrium of power ... cannot procure any security either.'[3] In this respect, Kant sided with Saint-Pierre and his commentator Rousseau, and did not follow Vattel's analysis (see below). However, Kant also rejected Saint-Pierre's and Rousseau's design of an exclusive alliance for European (that is, Christian) states (see beginning of Chapter 3). Kant's ultimate aim is to establish a juridical condition on a global scale. In this respect, he is close to Eméric Crucé and his *Nouveau Cyneas* (1623), which ridiculed writers preaching a holy war against the Turks. He proposed a federation that deliberately included non-Europeans.[4]

Is Kant a cosmopolitan at all? Recent interpreters have been shocked and vexed by Kant's racist statements on non-Europeans and his obvious Eurocentric bias. For instance, Kant, citing Hume's racist comments (see the beginning of Chapter 3), claims that there are 'essential' differences between whites and blacks and that they seem to be 'as large with regard to mental powers as they are in colour'.[5] These assertions do not go together with Kant's professed moral universalism, his defence of the rights of the Khoikhoin or Hottentots and the Evenki or Tungusi, and his explicit rejection of the agricultural argument of Locke and others (see Chapter 2). Most interpreters conclude that Kant's moral universalism is inconsistent and that his racism violates his own theory. There is a widespread consensus that if Kant was a racist, then he could not have been a moral cosmopolitan, and his legal cosmopolitanism would be compromised. Kant seems to be just another White western male whose universalism masks naked Eurocentrism. As two commentators put it: 'Kant's views on race would not discomfort the average Nazi.'[6]

There are various ways to deal with Kant's inconsistencies. The most convincing interpretation argues that Kant dropped his 1780s race theory in the 1790s, restricted the role of race, and arrived at a coherent version of moral cosmopolitanism by the time he wrote *Zum ewigen Frieden* (1795).[7] There is evidence that the late Kant had second thoughts on race. He granted full juridical status to non-Europeans like the Hottentots, rejected slavery and criticized European colonialism. Secondly, he also revised his views concerning migration, asserting that it was Nature's will that all humans, regardless of race, will eventually live everywhere in the world. Third, the issue of race disappeared almost completely from his writings. In his *Anthropology* (1798), we get next to nothing on the 'character of races'.[8]

Kant's change of thought is a fascinating example of (the process of) autonomy in thinking, and perhaps of epistemological cosmopolitanism, while also showing that the road to Enlightenment is long and arduous. Finally, we should not forget that several contemporaries of Kant developed non-racist theories, among them Georg Forster (who criticized Kant in the *Teutsche Merkur*), Johann Gottfried Herder (who also rejected Kant's racist theory in his *Ideas for a Philosophy of the History of Mankind*) and Johann Heinrich Gottlob von Justi, who published *Vergleichungen der europäischen mit den asiatischen und andern vermeintlich barbarischen Regierungen* in 1762. Justi probably motivated Kant to include the favourable remark on the Hottentots or Khoikhoi. Referring to travel reports, Justi claimed that their legal system was superior to European versions. He concluded that European arrogance was unfounded.[9]

The 1790s saw the climax of cosmopolitan discourses in German-speaking countries. Apparently influenced by Rousseau and his psychology (see Chapter 3), Kant criticizes the indifferent *Weltliebhaber*, 'because of too much generality, he scatters his affection and entirely loses any particular personal devotion'.[10] The rich cosmopolitan discourses of the Enlightenment leave their mark on Kant's philosophy. We can discern different types of cosmopolitanisms: epistemological, economic or commercial, moral, political and cultural.

Epistemological cosmopolitanism revolves around the world citizen who tries to transcend the 'egoism of reason', the unwillingness to test one's judgements with the help of the reason of others. The ideal is one of the principles of common understanding: the 'extended way of thinking' (*erweiterte Denkungsart*; the other two principles are thinking for oneself and thinking consistently).[11] We try to adopt 'the standpoint of others', accept a possible plurality of interpretations. A comparison with Adam Smith is helpful. No matter what their differences are, Kant agrees with Smith that justice has to do with the impartial judgment of a neutral spectator. In the words of Smith, one and the same person can be both agent and judge or spectator. As a spectator, I abstract myself from my own position or perspective by placing myself in another's situation 'and by considering how it would appear to me, when seen from that particular point of view'.[12] The impartial spectator is a recurrent theme in Kantian philosophy, as the *Contest of Faculties* testifies, among other writings. More than anyone else, the impartial spectators are in a position to enlarge their own thinking and aim in their judgments at the universality and consistency that is the hallmark of the moral law.[13]

Kant defends moral cosmopolitanism in the 1790s with the claim that all rational beings, irrespective of their race, nationality, religion and so on, should be regarded as 'citizens of a supersensible world' and should thus belong to a cosmopolitan moral community.[14] Kant's clear-cut distinction between legal and moral spheres, one focusing on mutual restrictions of domains of external freedom, the other on the free adoption of ends, enables him to draw a clear line between legal and moral cosmopolitanism. Kant expresses the latter in the idea of a 'kingdom of ends' or 'kingdom of God,' where humans unite freely into a commonwealth based on equality and self-legislation, rational beings are respected as ends in themselves, and a moral whole of all ends is achieved. This ethical commonwealth is founded by God, the author of its constitution (but not the organizer), who also guarantees the harmony of nature and morality.[15]

We can find a second line of reasoning arguing in favour of moral cosmopolitanism, which is not based on the concept of practical reason, but follows a more conventional, biological approach. Moral cosmopolitanism is justified because all humans descend from common ancestors. The love of others is based on 'the general global ancestry' (*allgemeine Weltabstammung*). Kant assumes that there are properties 'common to all human beings as such', presumably rationality and moral capacities.[16]

Kant became famous and well known for his political or legal version of cosmopolitanism. That is also the main focus of this chapter. The starting point of contractual cosmopolitanism is a theory Kant takes over (but also transforms) from natural lawyers like Grotius, Locke or Wolff: 'All human beings are originally in *common possession* of the land of the entire earth.'[17] The 'original community' is, analogous to the original contract, not a historical fact but a rational idea. 'Original' refers to principles of reason, in contrast to a 'primitive' community, which has a historical or temporal dimension. Kant thus states explicitly that the original community of land is *not* a community of possession but a community of possible interaction.[18] Kant agrees with Locke that unilateral external acquisition in the state of nature is possible. He departs from him by claiming that this acquisition is only provisional and has to be sanctioned by the general will after the establishment of a civil condition. Physical possession 'holds *comparatively* as rightful possession' only in anticipation of this public lawgiving, where it is acquired conclusively. In Kant's terminology, external original acquisition or *occupatio* entails three principles: apprehension, declaration (not necessarily labour) and finally the appropriation by the general will.[19] Kant rejects Locke's labour theory of property and the agricultural argument (see Chapter 2). There are many 'forms' or 'external signs' of taking possession or first acquisition: developing land is just one of them. First acquisition does not exempt us from the duty to sign a contract for conclusive or peremptory acquisition. In view of the common possession of the earth, a regionally limited social contract on the state level, though indispensable, is not sufficient. Any acquisition will remain provisional unless the social contract 'extends to the entire human race'.[20] The idea of an original community requires a global implementation.

Kant's main idea is the moral necessity and practical possibility of a universal juridical commonwealth. The ultimate goal in the distant future (we can approach it asymptotically) is an original contract that encompasses all humans. Then, and only then, the juridical relations among people and their property rights have become peremptory. From a cosmopolitan perspective, the sovereign state, even if it has turned into a republic, is a necessary but incomplete step in the evolution of right.[21] This would also mean that the third definitive article becomes obsolete as soon as a full juridical condition (the world republic, if this is Kant's ultimate ideal) has been established. Domestic, international and cosmopolitan right would finally merge.

Economic or commercial cosmopolitanism in Kant is closely connected with his reading of Rousseau, Smith and the Scottish Enlightenment philosophers. Kant seems to hold that modern history moves towards a global economy, where the South American gold and silver mines, for instance, are inextricably linked with European manufacture of goods. Both productive industries stimulate each other, causing a mutually reinforcing process: 'In this way industry [*Fleiss*] always keeps pace with industry.'[22] The effects of commercial interdependence were assessed in different ways during the eighteenth century. On the one extreme, Rousseau asserted that interdependence breeds wars. On the other end of the spectrum, it was claimed to have the opposite effect. Smith offered the compromise that interdependence *may* create wars, depending on the economic theory embraced: if free trade policies rather than balance-of-trade mercantilism were adopted, peaceful interaction was more likely (see Chapter 3). Kant accepts Smith's contention that transborder interactions have become progressively more global in the modern age, with important moral repercussions: 'Since the ... community of the nations of the earth has now gone so far that a violation of right on *one* place of the earth is felt in *all* ...'[23] Kant's point seems to be that more intense interaction on a global scale propels people to look for solutions to the moral problems connected with this increased interaction. In other words, Kant is looking for forces that might promote his cosmopolitan ideal of a legal world community. The key factor he mentions in this respect is the spirit of commerce [*Handelsgeist*], supposedly incompatible with war, 'which sooner or later takes hold of every nation.'[24] The last remark is another endorsement of Smith's analysis. All communities move naturally through various stages, until they become commercial societies. This historical development has a moral potential, or at least Kant hopes that it does. Commercialization leads to increased interaction, which in turn urges peoples to look for institutional solutions to international problems – a federation, ultimately a world republic – which again might transform a mere aggregate into a moral whole. Kant's commercial cosmopolitanism is subordinated to his legal version: the 'spirit of commerce' and economic interaction may become means of progress, but they are not ends in themselves.

Kant's cultural cosmopolitanism is more hinted at (as in Wolff, see Chapter 2) than a full-blown theory (as in Herder).[25] There are passages which suggest that Kant perceived humanity – the middle term between animality and personality – as cultural agency, which is characterized by a certain amount of incommensurability and latitude of judgement, namely in those spheres which go beyond the 'essence' of the human race. Kant hints at this culturally sensitive and contextualized view when he assesses and tolerates China's and Japan's isolationist policies. The more important passages are those where he defends the ways of life of hunters and pastoralists like the Hottentots. Kant's anti-paternalism, the formal character of the categorical imperative and his theory of legitimate latitude with respect to cultivating one's capacities allow him to argue that judgements on forms of societies – hunting in comparison with commercial societies, for instance – are morally neutral.

Kant and the 'miserable comforters'

In a paragraph of the Second Definitive Article of *Perpetual Peace*, Kant characterizes the natural lawyers Grotius, Pufendorf and Vattel as *leidige Tröster* or 'miserable comforters'[26] (henceforth called 'the natural lawyers'). A proper understanding of Kant's passage helps us to solve the riddle of the Second Definitive Article. Kant's argument distinguishes between two different levels. *In thesi*, that is 'according to reason', he postulates a *Völkerstaat* or *Weltrepublik* (a state of nations, a world government or global state). States would have freely delegated their external sovereignty to a global world government. This level corresponds with the idea of international right.

Kant's second level is expressed with phrases and terms like *in hypothesi*, *Völkerrecht* (the right of nations) and 'surrogate'. States are in fact reluctant to abandon their external sovereignty. So the second-best option is a voluntary league of nations, a free federation, a surrogate, 'that reason must connect necessarily with the concept of the right of nations if this is to retain any meaning at all'.[27] Kant scolds the natural lawyers because they did not even propose this second-best option. Kant sees the right of nations as barbarous: like lawless and primitive savages, states were unwilling to renounce their wild freedom and exchange it for rightful, proper freedom under self-legislated laws. The natural lawyers did not challenge this; instead, they focused too much on limiting warfare, on rules of conduct and on the just war theory. For Kant, this is just preliminary work, not the main task of a proper international legal theory.

Leidig (which I translate as 'miserable') may mean *beschwerlich* (troublesome, but also tiresome) or *unangenehm* (unpleasant, inconvenient).[28] Thus Kant either wants to tell us that the doctrines of the natural lawyers are in fact only subtle justifications of more wars, and as such unconvincing. Or he intends to stress that their treatises are inconvenient insofar as they remind ruthless power politicians of the demands of morality and cause, at least occasionally, some pangs of remorse. Perhaps Kant wants to suggest that once these books had been written, the business of hypocrisy had become more tiresome. (Frederick the Great thought that he could do without the word *right* when he invaded Silesia in 1740. Later on he realized that this had been a mistake.[29])

The combination of the two words, of *leidig* and *Tröster*, shows that Kant does indeed attack and criticize the natural lawyers. Two examples illustrate the meaning of the terms: in March 1758, Johann Georg Hamann found himself in London, without any money and near a mental breakdown. He tried to find consolation and inner peace with his books, but it did not work. He called them *leidige Tröster*.[30] The second example is even more telling. Hamann refers to the Old Testament, the Book of Job, 16. 2–5: Job has lost his money, his family and his health. His friends try to comfort him. They use arguments that are not justified; they claim that he is to blame and that he must be a sinner, otherwise God would not punish him. They think that his complaints are blasphemous. Job replies:

> I have heard many such things. You are all miserable comforters! Shall vain words have an end? Or what provokes you that you answer? I also could speak as you do. If your soul were in my soul's place, I could join words together against you, and shake my head at you, but I would strengthen you with my mouth. The solace of my lips would relieve you.

The miserable comforters gloss over an intolerable situation. In their attempt to comfort Job they distort basic facts, for instance the moral fact that Job is not a blasphemous sinner. This is the background we should keep in mind when we read the passage. The passage from the book of Job would suggest that Kant intends to characterize the natural lawyers as miserable (*jämmerlich, erbärmlich*) in a rather negative sense, as authors who offer nothing but 'vain words'.[31]

What do the natural lawyers gloss over? Apparently Kant believes that they tend to paint a rosy picture of the state of nature, or international anarchy. For Kant, this is a condition of war, and he scolds the lawyers because they do not think it necessary to overcome this condition. A short comparison between Emer de Vattel and Jean-Jacques Rousseau, who were contemporaries, illustrates the point. For Vattel, the main aim of his textbook, and the ultimate end of the right of nations, is to limit and humanize warfare (Carl Schmitt has called this *Hegung des Krieges*).[32] The condition itself, where warfare is endemic, is taken for granted. Rousseau is different. He expresses his moral outrage at wars and the indifference of politicians in the face of it: 'I see a scene of murder, ten thousand butchered men, the dead piled in heaps, the dying trampled under horses' hooves, everywhere the face of death and agony.'[33] Rousseau tries to imagine the horrors of war, death, mutilation, destruction and agony. He develops ideas how to overcome this deadly condition, for instance in his commentaries on Saint-Pierre. This is apparently what Kant liked about Rousseau (and Saint-Pierre), and what he did not find in the natural lawyers.

Like Saint-Pierre and Rousseau, Kant believes that the juridical structure of international relations has to be changed. As Georg Geismann puts it: 'What is at stake for Kant, is not the elimination of a natural disposition in man to quarrel, but the elimination of possible juridical grounds for it.'[34] Changing the structure is a paradigm shift and amounts to what Thomas Hobbes postulated: *exeundum e statu naturali*, the state of nature has to be left. The starting point of Kant's analysis is the claim that states 'considered in external relation to one another' are in a natural condition, that this is 'a non-rightful condition (*nicht-rechtlicher Zustand*)', and therefore a state of war.[35] This assertion is utterly Hobbesian, and was not shared by the natural lawyers. They usually rejected Hobbes's identification of the law of nations and the state of nature, and believed it was too pessimistic and extreme. Kant, on the other hand, agrees with Hobbes: states are in fact in a condition of war, and this should not be glossed over (this is

KANT AND THE 'MISERABLE COMFORTERS' 73

exactly what the miserable comforters do). Kant parts company with Hobbes when he claims that also at the interstate level, a civil or rightful condition has to be established, as it is demanded by practical reason.[36]

This *exeundum* claim is the key difference between Kant and the natural lawyers; authors like Rousseau, Saint-Pierre or Christian Wolff were exceptions. In other words, Kant would have liked the natural lawyers to be more idealistic, to anticipate ideal international relations where wars are no longer part of the system. The theory of the right of nations, Kant asserts, needs what he calls 'visionaries of reason (*Phantasten der Vernunft*)' like Saint-Pierre and Rousseau, 'without whom nothing truly great would have ever been done in the world' (Kant apparently did not see, or preferred to overlook the fact, that both authors were Eurocentric in their approach; see the introduction to Chapter 3).[37]

Kant's criticism of the natural lawyers can be summarized as follows:

1. Their assessment of interstate relations is simply wrong. It is not a civil or public lawful condition, but still a state of nature where 'individual human beings, peoples and states can never be secure against violence from one another, since each has its own right to do *what seems right and good to it* and not to be dependent upon another's opinion about this'. Here, 'each follows its own judgment'. In the state of nature, we are legislator, judge and our own executive power all in one. There are natural laws, but no competent judges who apply them and there is no 'public lawful external coercion'.[38]
2. As a consequence, the natural lawyers play down international anarchy.
3. Furthermore, they do not believe that an original contract is necessary on the international level. However, they do think that this contract is indispensable for state right. Kant sees this as contradictory.
4. According to Kant, the miserable comforters mistakenly believe that a provisional condition (Kant assigns it to private right) is a peremptory or conclusive condition (Kant's public lawful condition).
5. A symptom of this mistaken concept of the right of nations is traditional just-war theory.

What Kant might have thought about Vattel's theory

A closer look at Vattel illustrates these five points. Of the three miserable comforters, Vattel was probably the most important influence. Let us start with classical just-war theory.[39] Vattel attempts to improve the doctrines of predecessors like Grotius, Pufendorf or Wolff (see Chapter 2), while not questioning the just-war theory itself. For him, war is a legitimate method to assert one's rights if the cause is 'apparently just'. These causes are listed in a separate chapter, and there are plenty.[40] In addition, various other passages of Vattel's major work mention legitimate reasons to go to war. For instance: 'Since a nation's renown is a very real advantage, it has the right to defend that renown as it would any other possession. He who attacks its honor does it a wrong, and reparation can be exacted even by force of arms.'[41] Like other natural lawyers from Hugo Grotius to Adam Smith, Vattel conceives war as a kind of lawsuit or trial, as the continuation of the course of law with different, that is military, means.[42] Like many others, Vattel believes that natural sociability, common interests and the concept of a 'European republic' (see below) would mitigate or even eliminate the shortcomings of the natural condition. There were at least two: first, if each state was its own judge, which interpretation was the correct one? Secondly, if in addition each state was its own executive power, what was the difference between brute force and legitimate coercion?

Vattel does not offer clear solutions to these problems. However, there are passages that can be read as attempts to give an answer. First, Vattel seems to believe that divergent interpretations or applications of general principles to specific cases, rarely occur and can easily be settled by agreement.[43] Secondly, Vattel's theory of formal or regular war (*guerre en forme*) tries to overcome the ambiguities and inconsistencies of just-war theory. Regular war, 'as regards its effects, must be accounted just on both sides'.[44] The 'justice of the cause' is irrelevant; what matters is 'the legality of the means', especially sticking to certain rules of conduct in times of war, a formal declaration of war and so on. A prince who wages an unjust war is guilty *in foro interno*, in terms of his conscience, but his acquisitions are legitimate, or 'legal in the sight of men', and he cannot be punished.[45]

Third, Vattel presents mid eighteenth-century Europe as 'a sort of Republic, whose members – each independent, but all bound together by a common interest – unite for the maintenance of order and the preservation of liberty.'[46] Means of maintaining this system are the balance of power and the habit of forming alliances against an overwhelming state. Kant made fun of this republic of 'order and liberty' – in a remark that is directed against champions of balance-of-power theories ('a mere fantasy' or *Hirngespinst*).[47] Again, Kant could have argued that Vattel glossed over international anarchy: while Vattel was working on his book, the Seven Years' War was fought, sometimes called the first world war, because it saw action in India, North America, Europe and at sea. The century had started with the Spanish War of Succession (1701–14); after 1740, more major wars followed.

Unlike Vattel, Kant attempts a paradigm shift in terms of the just war theory. It is rejected as a contradiction in terms ('war' and 'justice' cannot go together), but it is also kept in modified form in a new system of the right of nations, as a makeshift that should be overcome in due course. Here are the key elements:

1. No just war: wars in the state of nature cannot be just in a strict sense, they can only be a permitted, provisional institution.[48]
2. The right to go to war: Kant's key concept is that of an injury, or a violation of rights, and cases are extremely limited; Vattel tends to accept too many just causes.
3. Kant's republican peace proposition: Kant asserts that citizens 'as co-legislating members of a state . . . must . . . give their free assent, through their representatives, not only to waging war in general but also to each particular declaration of war'.[49]
4. A new emphasis: Unlike Vattel, Kant's theory of the right of nations emphasizes the *jus post bellum* (the right after war), not the *jus ad bellum* (the right to go to war).[50] Kant aims at a reform of the system of international relations after/between wars (see the Preliminary and Definitive Articles of *Perpetual Peace*).

The domestic analogy helps us to grasp the crucial differences between Vattel and Kant. This analogy is widespread among political philosophers and natural lawyers in early modern Europe.

Hobbes, for instance, is sure that domestic and interstate spheres can be compared: 'And the Elements of *natural law* and *natural right* which we have been teaching may, when transferred to whole *commonwealths* and *nations*, be regarded as the Elements of the *laws* and of the *right of Nations.* '[51] Hobbes and the natural lawyers immediately qualify this analogy. Vattel writes in a key passage of his preface:

> It is true that men, seeing that the Laws of Nature were not being voluntarily observed, have had recourse to political association as the one remedy against the degeneracy of the majority, as the one means of protecting the good and restraining the wicked; and the natural law approves of such a course. But it is clear that there is by no means the same necessity for a civil society among Nations as among individuals. It cannot be said, therefore, that nature recommends it to an equal degree, far less that it prescribes it.
>
> But these individual societies have, it is true, strong motives for mutual communication and intercourse; they have even an obligation to this effect, since without good reason no man may refuse his assistance to another. Ordinarily their resolutions are not taken nor their public policy determined by the blind rashness or the whim of an individual. Advice is taken and more calmness and deliberation shown; and in delicate or important situations arrangements are made and agreements reached by means of treaties. Moreover, independence is necessary to a state, if it is to fulfil properly its duties towards itself and its citizens and to govern itself in the manner best suited to it. Hence, I repeat, it is enough that Nations conform to the demands made upon them by that natural and world-wide society established among all men.[52]

Note the cosmopolitan overtones: Vattel refers to a 'worldwide society' based on natural law. He offers an updated and weak version of moral cosmopolitanism which is not egalitarian, but hierarchical (see Chapter 2). He rejects 'a civil society among Nations', which would be characterized by positive legislation and enforceable laws. Vattel admits right at the beginning that there are wicked people in this world and that the laws of nature are often not 'voluntarily observed'. This parallels Kant's conviction of human malevolence and the claim that 'in a condition under civil laws it is greatly veiled by the government's constraint'.[53] However, Kant sees international relations as a showroom of barbarism, brutality and savagery, whereas Vattel sees them as an example of moderate restraint and calm deliberation. Vattel qualifies the domestic analogy, as he believes – like Hobbes – that unlike individuals, states or political communities are self-sufficient and able to 'provide for most of their needs, and they find the help of other political societies not so necessary to them as the State itself is to individuals'. Communities have a natural obligation to communicate with each other, but 'this mutual intercourse can be sufficiently regulated by the natural law'.

Kant and Vattel do not only disagree in terms of interpreting eighteenth-century politics. 'Necessity' has a completely different meaning for them. For Vattel, it boils down to *pragmatic* necessity: unlike states, individuals are more dependent on others, especially as regards economic needs. Back in the eighteenth century, most states were still to a large extent autarkic; economic interdependence was not yet an issue.

Vattel's approach is empirical and pragmatic. There is an interesting shift from law (in the first sentence) to needs. Kant's methodology is very different. His 'completely isolated metaphysics of morals' eliminate empirical, for instance anthropological or pragmatic, elements.[54] Needs and possible features of politicians do not count; right (*ius*; the natural law) and nothing else matters in the first place if philosophical principles are established. For Kant, Vattel's considerations are therefore irrelevant, in terms of practical reason and the idea of international right. Kant focuses on the rightful (*rechtlich*) quality of relations among 'moral persons' or legal entities such as individuals and states. Instead of Vattel's nature, reason postulates: 'all humans who can mutually affect one another must belong to some civil constitution.'[55]

Summing up, we can say that there are three key differences between the miserable comforters and Kant. The first difference is the just-mentioned mixing of empirical and rational (*a priori*) arguments in Vattel and others. This leads to a second difference: Vattel distinguishes between two levels of the right of nations: the necessary right of nations (*droit des gens nécessaire*) and the voluntary right of nations (*droit des gens volontaire*). The former embodies the 'immutable commandments of justice', the latter applies these commandments. The result is a kind of juridical dualism. Remember that according to the voluntary right of nations, unjust conquests made during a formal war (*guerre en forme*) become legitimate.[56] It seems that Kant would have rejected this theory because it abandons the principle of justice. Kant also tries to apply abstract principles, but his permissive laws (*Erlaubnisgesetze*) are different. They are provisional. An unjust conquest, for instance, may be *provisionally* permitted, but only on condition that a public lawful condition is established in the future.[57]

The third difference is the transition from an individual to a collective line of reasoning in Vattel and other natural lawyers. Francis Cheneval has shown that, ever since Hobbes, international lawyers and political philosophers like Locke stayed clear of cosmopolitan conclusions: they started off with the survival of the *individual* in social contract theory, but they wound up with the survival of the *state* (see also Chapter 3). The ongoing condition of war was deemed irrelevant, as the collective entity of a state was able to survive.[58] Kant, but also authors like Wolff, Saint-Pierre or Rousseau, think that this transition is not legitimate. Social contract theory and normative individualism are taken to their logical, cosmopolitan conclusion. Wolff postulated the hypothesis (regulative idea in Kantian terms) of a *civitas maxima* (universal commonwealth) in his theory of the right of nations. Vattel's sentence 'It can not be said . . . that nature recommends [a civil society among nations] to an equal degree, far less that it prescribes it' is directed against Wolff. Kant sides with Wolff; his *civitas maxima* can be interpreted as an anticipation of Kant's *civitas gentium* (state of nations). Wolff is therefore not one of the miserable comforters.[59]

Is Kant's criticism justified? The idea of international right

Kant's judgement on the miserable comforters has to be qualified. My primary focus has been on Vattel. A first argument against Kant is that he sees the three authors Grotius, Pufendorf and Vattel as an entity. The differences among them get lost, and this is apparently unfair.

In favour of Grotius, we could say that he wrote his major treatise before Hobbes published his political philosophy. As a consequence, he did not share the conceptual tools of later authors. For instance, there is no clear division between 'inside' and 'outside' (domestic versus foreign affairs), or between the state of nature and a lawful condition. For Grotius, the right of nations (*ius gentium*) is by no means the right among sovereign states; even the concept of a state is very different. How can we explain this fact? For a long time, Grotius was seen as the founder of the modern theory of the law of nations. Recent research has turned this assessment more or less upside down: Grotius is now squarely rooted in the humanist, but also in the scholastic tradition.[60] Grotius, for instance, trusts that God will punish the wrongdoer. This line of thinking cannot be found in the more secularized Vattel. For Grotius, this belief partly answers the vexed question how the norms of natural law can become an accepted standard. Put in a nutshell, we could say that Grotius's world-view was still partly medieval. The problem of international anarchy did not pose itself for Grotius in full vigour, simply because he neither had a modern notion of 'international' nor of 'anarchy' (this is also the reason why Martha Nussbaum's interpretation of Grotius is utterly anachronistic; see Chapter 1). Finally, we should grant in all fairness that Grotius did perceive the relations among European communities or states as dangerous and precarious, and their continuous wars as horrible. In the introduction of his work, Grotius complains:

> Throughout the Christian world I observed a lack of restraint in relation to war, such as even barbarous races should be ashamed of; I observed that men rush to arms for slight causes, or no cause at all, and that when arms have once been taken up there is no longer any respect for law, divine or human; it is as if, in accordance with a general decree, frenzy had openly been let loose for the committing of all crimes.[61]

Written during the carnage of the Thirty Years' War, these sentences by no means paint a rosy picture of international relations.

In defence of Pufendorf, we can point out that he advocated a 'system of states' which would have partially overcome the Hobbesian state of nature, analogous to Kant's own proposal. Recent interpreters have seen these passages as anticipations of modern unions or federations such as the European Union.[62] He might have influenced Andrew Fletcher's vision of European confederations (see Chapter 3). Like Grotius, though, Pufendorf believes that interstate anarchy can be mitigated, but not really overcome.

Kant's assessment is probably most accurate in the case of Vattel. This is not surprising, because he seems to have been the only one of the three authors whose work Kant actually read. As argued above, Vattel's positivistic tendencies push him too close to political realities. His attempt to keep morality or the inner voice of conscience and natural law separated from and largely out of the right of nations invites his condemnation as a mere apologist of power politics and pragmatism, and as an accomplice of European colonialism (see Chapter 2).

A final argument in favour of all three authors is historical. The conceptual framework of many European authors especially in the eighteenth century was often limited, and shaped, by the binary opposition of the idea of a universal monarchy (*monarchia universalis*) on the one hand and the balance-of-power doctrine on the other. There was widespread consensus that a universal monarchy or the hegemony by one power was a bad thing, because it threatened or destroyed state independence. The fight against the universal monarchy took place both in the realm of ideas and in politics. It is no coincidence that a string of authors including Grotius and Pufendorf rejected Dante in this respect. In terms of European politics, the universal monarchy was perceived by many, especially by Protestants, as a real threat during the reigns of Charles V, Ferdinand II and Louis XIV. A balance-of-power system was then seen as the logical, desirable and only feasible alternative. In short, there was an absence of practical alternatives to the balance-of-power doctrine. Things changed after 1763, when balance-of-power practices led to a security crisis on the Continent, a crisis that was systemic and structural rather than contingent. Balance-of-power politics exacerbated the very problems they were supposed to solve. Most importantly, deficiencies of the system were perceived by politicians and writers alike, in stark contrast to the analyses of, say, Wolff, Hume or Vattel in the middle of the century.[63]

Last but not least, we should keep in mind that Kant calls the miserable comforters 'important men'. This is perhaps more than mere condescension. Kant believes that participants in a debate who disagree are not downright wrong. Like other philosophers during the Age of Enlightenment, he holds that absolute error is impossible, because humans as potentially rational beings share the same reason or common sense. If we follow this line of thought, then authors like Vattel are important because they anticipate what is fully rational for Kant (in this case, the idea of international right). It is fascinating to look for examples of this kind of anticipation in the writings of Vattel, for instance. Vattel states that 'a door is to be left at all times open for the return of peace'.

The context is a defence of his concept of a formal or regular war. The basic idea is Kantian in embryonic form: state actions are permitted if they do not hinder or, even better, if they make possible a future peaceful condition.[64] Vattel's 'natural and world-wide society established among all men' (quoted above) is another example. Taken over by Kant, the concept of an original community is transformed and adapted to critical philosophy.[65]

Suppose we accept that Kant's assessment of the miserable comforters is at least partly correct. What about Kant's own theory? Is it any better? Imagine a critic who argues: Well, Kant ultimately proposes a league of sovereign states, but this would make no difference for promoting peace. A free treaty among states will be honoured merely as long as none of those who signed it possess both the will and the power to break it; in other words, as long as peace, which the treaty is supposed to establish, would exist also without it. In short, Kant scolds the miserable comforters because they do not postulate that the state of nature has to be left. However, he himself does not offer a proper *exeundum*. So he is not any different. What makes it worse, his text is confusing, inconsistent and contradictory. All that we get is an arrogant and condescending attitude.[66]

So we have to dig deeper: What is Kant's message in the Second Definitive Article of *Perpetual Peace*? Did he propose a world republic or a limited, voluntary federation? What were his main arguments? Do they make sense? Did he condone or condemn state sovereignty? Was he squarely rooted in the natural law tradition or did he replace natural law by the will of states? Interpreters disagree on all these issues.[67] But it is crucial to understand the article, because it is the cornerstone of Kant's essay and the ultimate explanation why Kant scolds the natural lawyers.

The Second Definitive Article runs: 'The right of nations (*Völkerrecht*) shall be based on a *federalism* of free states.'[68] I will try to summarize its key elements. I have already pointed out that Kant distinguishes between two different levels: the right of nations is a surrogate and the second-best option; the idea of international right corresponds with reason, and leads to the postulate of a *Völkerstaat* or *Weltrepublik* (a state of nations, a world government or global state). The league of free states is the minimum standard; without it, the right of nations would keep its status as private right, and states would not move beyond a provisional condition.

As in state law, Kant advocates provisionally just institutions. The concept of the right of nations in turn presupposes sovereign states. Therefore, Kant excludes the ideal of a world government from his analysis of the right of nations. This exclusion has caused a lot of confusion, triggered by Kant's passage on the contradiction between the right of nations and the world federation. If we keep the two levels apart, we do not have to accuse Kant of any inconsistency.[69]

Four elements characterize this free federalism: 1) it is a non-aggression and defence alliance; 2) states respect each other as 'moral persons' or legal entities;[70] 3) this implies the duty not to interfere in domestic affairs of member states; 4) it is a federation encompassing republican and non-republican states (see below). The main function of this provisional federation is to initiate a process towards a full juridical state with public coercive laws. This dissoluble league of states is identical with what Kant also calls a 'permanent state congress'. For this reason, it seems, Kant praised (in a rather obscure passage) the loose European congress system in the first half of the eighteenth century.[71]

Bear in mind the critic's argument that this voluntary federation would make no difference. Kant admits that the surrogate cannot eliminate the possibility of wars. Still, the 'permanent congress of states' would offer an institutional framework for conflict mediation, arbitration and negotiation. The League of Nations and the United Nations have shown that, in addition, such institutions can fulfil tasks that go beyond the protection and promotion of peace. Pauline Kleingeld concludes: 'Such considerations shift the burden of proof onto those who imply that there is no value at all in creating channels for negotiation and mediation (and any other peace-promoting institutions that the league might provide for).'[72]

The league (and the resulting provisional right of nations) should be the first step on the road towards a world republic. In yet another confusing passage, Kant offers one main argument why the world government must not be instituted immediately. States, 'in accordance with their idea of the right of nations', reject what is demanded by reason: the idea of international right and the world federation. However, even if their concept is wrong (apparently modelled along the lines of the miserable comforters), they must not be *forced* into a state of states. As 'moral persons' with internally rightful constitutions, they have 'outgrown the constraint of others to bring them under a more extended law-governed constitution in accordance with their concepts of right'.[73] This line of reasoning looks very unKantian, because something empirical (the will of states) seems to matter. Charles Covell has even concluded that

> it was not to the idea of natural law that [Kant] appealed in order to explain the foundations of the laws that he believed were necessary to promote peace between states. On the contrary, it was Kant's conviction that the foundations of that part of the law of peace he saw as comprising the law of nations were to be looked for in the will and agreement of nations and states.[74]

According to Covell, this is the reason why Kant criticized the miserable comforters: they still stuck to natural law.

Why and in which respect does the will of states matter? Kant qualifies the analogy between the domestic and the interstate sphere with legal arguments. Like individuals, states ought to leave the state of nature. However, unlike individuals, states must not be coerced by others into a public lawful condition – simply because they are legal entities and politically autonomous, self-legislating units.[75] What ultimately matters is the road to peace, the way peace is established or founded (in German, there is a difference between *Frieden erzwingen* – by using force – and *Frieden stiften* by peaceful means). Will the world government ever be realized? Kant says no, but we can and should try to approach it. He offers two reasons why 'continual approximation' is possible. First, Kant hopes that states, even though they are reluctant to abandon their external sovereignty, might be willing to do this step by step. The German phrase *sich freiwillig bequemen* (to bring oneself to do something, to find oneself compelled, to accommodate oneself) is quite telling:[76] it combines free choice and the force of external circumstances. I am reluctant to do something, but I bring myself to do it because under the given circumstances (for instance the threat of nuclear war, global ecological problems) it is the lesser of two evils. In this respect, the future world federation with coercive powers would indeed be based on the will of states. Partly, it would be the result of self-interests and practical constraints. Here, the Second Definitive Article moves beyond pure legal analysis and enters the domain of the philosophy of history.

Kant's second hope is enlightenment, political and moral development. He hopes that in the future, our 'concept of the right of nations' might be modified and improved (the miserable comforters embodied these wrong concepts). In the long run, people would be enlightened enough to want to submit to a world federation as a peremptory juridical condition. The secret article might be read as an attempt to promote this process of enlightenment. It mentions philosophers but favours the freedom of expression of anybody who is in a position to speak up publicly.[77] Free intellectuals who look for 'true ideas' in legislation are contrasted with jurists, and perhaps it makes sense to assign Grotius, Pufendorf and Vattel to this second group: they 'only . . . apply existing laws' – and refine them –' but do not 'investigate whether such laws themselves need to be improved'.[78] Vattel and others seem to stand for ordinary, empirical jurisprudence. The result was a rather barbarous right of nations, and the natural lawyers did not challenge this element of barbarity. Kant hoped that the future would belong to the rational doctrine of international right.

5 • Late Eighteenth-century International Legal Theory: from *Cosmopolis* to the Idea of Europe

Narratives of late eighteenth-century international legal theory

I have tried to show in the previous chapter how Kant takes social contract theory and normative individualism to their logical, cosmopolitan conclusions. In this chapter, I want to take a closer look at some natural lawyers in the late eighteenth century. Kant apparently referred to lawyers and writers of his age with the cryptic remark that 'they' rejected the idea of international right and were happy with its 'surrogate', 'in accordance with their concept of the right of nations.'[1]

I start with a brief overview of the main trends of international legal theory at the end of the eighteenth century, contrasting it with previous approaches and focusing on various traditions. The next sections are each devoted to one particular author (Vattel, Martini, Moser and Martens), looking at their methodologies and their underlying assumptions. I am particularly interested in what they write about the relationship among natural, voluntary and positive law, about the balance of power, about Europe, about peace projects and about the right to war (their just-war theories). I conclude with a section on Robert Ward, the French Revolution and Cloots.

It has been fashionable among historians of international legal theory to distinguish among various 'schools' or 'traditions'. Arthur Nussbaum sees Hobbes and Spinoza as representative 'deniers of the law of nations'. They are distinguished from the naturalists of the natural law tradition, where three currents are discernible: the Suarezian/Grotian branch including the Oxford professor Richard Zouche (1590–1660), the German Samuel Rachel (1628–91), and the Dutch Cornelis van Bynkershoek (1673–1743); the Pufendorfian current encompassing Barbeyrac, Jean Jacques Burlamaqui and Thomasius, and finally the Wolffian current, with Emer de Vattel (1714–67) as the most important pupil. Sometimes Zouche, Rachel and Bynkershoek are assigned to the camp of early positivists, followed by authors such as Johann Jakob Moser (1701–85) and Georg Friedrich von Martens (1756–1821). Following Alfred Verdross, Wilhelm Grewe distinguishes the natural law current from the positivists and the 'synthetic school', which combined elements of the other two. Both Nussbaum and Grewe agree that by the end of the eighteenth century, positivism gradually got the upper hand, to triumph in the next century.[2]

Representatives from all 'camps' contributed to the various collections of state treaties since the middle of the seventeenth century. Gottfried Wilhelm Leibniz (1646–1716), Jacques Bernard (1658–1718), Jean Dumont (1666–1727), Friedrich August Wilhelm Wenck (1741–1810), Georg Friedrich von Martens (1756–1821) and Gabriel Bonnot de Mably (1709–85) were the most prominent authors. Their main focus was on the *droit public de l'Europe* and diplomatic practice.

In *Der Nomos der Erde* (1950), Carl Schmitt claims that by the eighteenth century, international legal theory had moved beyond the traditional, medieval focus on just war. The question of the justice of the cause was neglected, and war was seen as a political conflict among sovereign states which did not see each other as criminals but as '*justi hostes*', as potential enemies who (theoretically) shared equal rights. Balthasar de Ayala had made a promising start in 1582, using the term '*iustum*' in the sense of 'lawful' or 'legal', pointing out that only the sovereign had the right to wage war. According to Schmitt, '*guerre en forme*' or 'regular war' (Vattel), which had to fulfil certain formal criteria such as declaration of war or proper conduct, had triumphed over just-war doctrine by the middle of the eighteenth century. 'Justice' was a shorthand for 'according to certain rules belligerents and lawyers had agreed upon'.[3]

For various reasons, Schmitt's analysis is unconvincing. Ayala's formal war was a piece of propaganda, polemically directed against the Dutch insurgents, who, in Ayala's account, turned into criminals outside the legal sphere (and could thus be killed and enslaved at will). In addition, moderation in warfare prior to First World War was also caused by factors outside the legal sphere, like military developments and logistics. It cannot be explained by legal developments alone. Most importantly, Stephen Neff has shown that the formal-war doctrine was only one minor dissident theory: 'The just-war tradition, inherited directly from the Middle Ages, continued to be the dominant framework for legal analyses of war throughout the seventeenth and eighteenth centuries.'[4]

A more convincing picture is presented by Stephen Neff himself, in a recent and comprehensive study on *War and the Law of Nations* (2005). According to Neff, the Early Modern Age (1600–1815) was an era of transition, dominated by a mainstream just-war tradition, trying to strike a balance between natural law or the law of nature on the one hand and the (new) law of nations or voluntary law (sometimes also labeled 'volitional law') on the other. The source of the latter was the will of the states, or rather of political communities, it was based on explicit or implicit mutual consent and aimed at the promotion of the 'great society of commonwealths' or the human race. In short, older natural law was law 'from above', whereas voluntary law was the result of a bottom-up procedure. Martti Koskenniemi described its function in the following way:

> What these representatives of Enlightenment jurisprudence sought to achieve was precisely a distinction between themselves and their classical predecessors without having to ratify whatever it was sovereigns wished to do. They defined voluntary law to consist of the interpretations and 'modifications' which States have introduced into necessary natural law in order to apply it in practice. It was subjectively based and thus avoided the accusation of abstract utopianism (which Vattel threw at Berbeyrac, Hobbes and Grotius). But it was not apologist, either, as it was still natural law and maintained its connection with an objectively constraining morality. It was a mediating device to avoid, partially and temporarily, the immediate objections that contemporaries (and successors) directed upon pure naturalism (too objective) and pure positivism (too subjective).[5]

Voluntary law mediated (on this argument) 'between apology and utopia'; it was a clever, almost strategic move to fend off criticism. Thus international legal theory of the period was usually dualistic, striking a balance between the two types of law. Both 'co-existed and interwove to create what we now call international law'.[6]

In addition, two dissident schools emerged in the period. The Hobbesian school of thought rejected a key assumption of the natural law tradition, namely, that peace was the normal condition of 'international' relations. Instead, it claimed that the state of nature among states or communities was a condition of war. It also did away with the conventional idea of war as law enforcement and an instrument of justice. The state of nature, Hobbes claimed, was a 'conflict-of-rights situation' (Neff), where all parties involved had the same rights on their sides – especially the rights to self-preservation and self-defence. It was a situation that made talk about 'just causes' obsolete.[7] Hobbes's clear-cut distinction between the state of nature and a condition with public authority became notorious, but also crucial for understanding international relations. A public authority, Hobbes held, must be established to enforce judgments and interpretations in civil law, apply sanctions and coerce those who do not respect the reciprocal spheres of freedom: 'Covenants, without the Sword, are but Words.'[8] If there was no effective public authority, individuals would keep or regain their right to be their own judges and executioners, interpret the laws of nature and rely on their own strength. The coercive power compels individuals 'equally to the performance of their Covenants, by the terror of some punishment', and this threat must outweigh the benefits a possible transgressor might expect from breaking the covenant. The provision takes care of the free-rider problem: for calculating reason, transgression becomes an imprudent option.

The second dissident school was the contractual or duelling school, which rejected the image of war as law enforcement and instead saw it as a kind of duel or agreement to settle a dispute by force of arms. This dissident school further promoted the shift towards man-made voluntary law at the expense of natural law. Closely connected with this school was the new concept of war as 'lawful war in due form' (Vattel), which emphasized the codes conducting the hostilities and insisted on equal treatment of the belligerents, irrespective of the justness of their causes. The law of war was non-discriminatory, and peace-making was non-judgmental.[9] As mentioned before, formal-war doctrine was a subset of more comprehensive and traditional natural law and just-war theories. It only got the upper hand in the (late) nineteenth century, together with the Hobbesian tradition. After the Napoleonic Wars, and especially after the 1870s, positivist international legal theory came to see war as an element of state policy, while still keeping some elements of the just-war tradition.

Emer de Vattel: from the *civitas maxima* to the European republic

For various reasons, Vattel has become one of the classics of international law (on Vattel, see also Chapters 2 and 4). His work can be seen as the perfect synthesis of a refined natural law theory and actual state practice. In other words, his theory is both descending and ascending, combines a top-down with a bottom-up procedure. Vattel's 'Preface' of the *Law of Nations* (1758) contains an explicit and famous rejection of Wolff's postulate of the *civitas maxima*. I have tried to show in a previous chapter how Wolff arrived at a culturally sensitive international legal theory, did not grant exclusive rights for Europeans, claimed that religions are juridically equal, and criticized legal arguments based on the alleged superiority of European civilization. The overall result was a blend of epistemological, moral, political and cultural cosmopolitanisms (see Chapter 2). In Vattel, these cosmopolitan dimensions get lost. The reasons are manifold, and lead us back to Vattel's overall theory. He claims that the idea of a universal commonwealth is redundant, because Europe is already 'a sort of Republic' with a balance-of-power system.[10] Vattel holds that the main source of voluntary law is common practice and not some fictitious universal commonwealth. Unlike Wolff, Vattel equates *gentes* (nations or civil societies) with sovereign, that is, independent states (*états souverains*); and they tend to be European. With Vattel, state sovereignty becomes identical with independence and lack of 'submission to a higher legal order'.[11] States or nations thus cannot be conceived as being under the authority of some superior entity. Finally, Vattel rejects the idea of a universal commonwealth because he thinks that it undermines the indispensable distinction between voluntary law (*droit des gens volontaire*) and necessary law (*droit des gens nécessaire*, or the 'inner law of conscience'). This distinction must be kept 'so that we may never confuse what is just and good in itself with what is merely tolerated through necessity'.[12] With this distinction, natural or necessary law turns into what would later be called 'international morality'. For Vattel, voluntary law is natural law adopted to the actual practice of sovereign states composing the society of nations and based on their presumed consent. The voluntary law of nations respects the states' freedom and judgment; it is more flexible and adaptable than strict necessary law. Vattel does not abandon the idea of a 'worldwide society' based on natural law. We can still find cosmopolitan overtones; but they are nothing more than just that. He offers an updated and weak version of moral cosmopolitanism which is not egalitarian, but hierarchical.

Peter Remec has assessed Vattel's achievement in the following way:

> Actually, he roughly adapted the extent of his analogical deductions to the empirically observed practice of nations of his time. By this process he gave to the more acceptable principles of contemporary practice the respectable and fashionable cloak of a universally binding rational rule in contrast to practices which he personally abhorred and therefore effectively branded as illegal and irrational. The wide acceptance of Vattel's doctrine is due exactly to these reasons.[13]

According to this interpretation, Vattel mixed personal preferences with state practice and gave this hotchpotch the 'fashionable cloak' of 'universally binding' and 'rational rule'. This is probably an unfair assessment; Vattel did aim at a more coherent system of rights. He can be seen as the founding father of classical, nineteenth-century, state-centred and positivist international law. A plausible synthesis of natural and voluntary law, a well-ordered society of European states with a functioning balance-of-power system, formal war and the irrelevance of lofty cosmopolitan peace projects: all these elements made Vattel's approach appealing. It served as a point of reference for subsequent international legal theories.

Karl Anton Freiherr von Martini: a representative of the younger natural law theory after 1780

Recent historiography refers to the 'younger' natural law theory since 1780, with a new focus on the individuals and their rights, and a new function for natural/rational law: it defined a new role for the state (to protect these rights and spheres of freedom). More and more, natural law was merely supposed to replenish or complete positive legislation. Disciplinary demarcations were set up, for instance, between political science, moral philosophy, philosophical legal theory and natural law.[14]

Karl Anton Freiherr von Martini (1726–1800) can take the credit for the phrase 'anarchical society'. Following Moser, he also referred to 'external state law'. Influenced by Wolff, he was one of the liberal-minded Catholic reformers of the Habsburg monarchy during the reigns of Maria Theresia, Joseph II and Leopold II. He was co-author of the *Allgemeines Bürgerliches Gesetzbuch* (1811), the basic text of modern Austrian civil law, and spoke up in favour of toleration for Protestants and Jews.[15] Martini's works were based on his university lectures and served as textbooks for roughly forty years in the territories of the monarchy. The second part of his *Erklärung der Lehrsätze über das allgemeine Staats- und Völkerrecht* (1791) covers his international legal theory.

International legal theory at that time shared certain elements with Vattel and the tradition: the starting point was the concept of a state of nature; a system of rights and duties was constructed, tailored for this condition; the state of nature was seen as a condition of peace; war was considered as a sort of law enforcement; there were disputed questions, especially concerning the *ius in bello* (the right of war) and preventive war.[16]

In the state of nature, Martini claims, families formed anarchical societies to assist each other. There was no civil government, and human deficiencies undermined any attempt to achieve perfection. The heads of families thus submitted to a common authority, giving up their natural freedom and forming civil society.[17] In relation to each other, these societies are still in the natural condition, keeping their natural rights, such as equality, the right of self-preservation and independence.[18] Though Martini criticizes Hobbes, he concedes that the state of nature is more than deficient, definitely not a state of peace (Martini thus undermined a key assumption of traditional theory). Martini then proceeds to develop a system of rights and duties for the international state of nature, such as the rights of equality, freedom, independence and self-defence.[19]

So far, Martini has worked with the domestic analogy: relations among states are compared with and similar to relations among individuals before the establishment of civil society. For various reasons, however, natural duties among states are not as strict as those among individuals, and this applies to both perfect and imperfect duties. In terms of the right to go to war (*ius ad bellum*), the key concept is that of an injury, or *laesio*.[20] In case of an injury, for defence and for one's own safety, states are entitled to wage war. War is a form of law enforcement, for lack of a common authority (*Oberherrschaft*) among states.[21]

Again following conventional doctrine, Martini distinguishes between natural and positive law of nations. The natural law of nations is natural law 'applied to the business (*Geschäfte*) of nations'[22] – another familiar definition. As a member of the 'camp' of natural lawyers, Martini endorses the novel idea that there is no general (*allgemeines*) positive law of nations, only a particular, namely European, law of nations, which includes the American free states, presumably because they are of European descent.[23] What is missing is the category of voluntary law, so prominent in Vattel's system.

The main reason seems to be that Martini does not even endorse the minimalist notion of a European international community as Vattel did (which was, as it were, an extremely thinned-down version of Wolff's more daring *civitas maxima*). Martini criticizes both Wolff and Vattel in this respect. States do not have legal authority over other states, which are 'by nature' independent.[24] (Defensive) alliances and mediation are possible, but that is all. Saint-Pierre's peace project is rejected as impracticable and possibly useless – nations will probably never renounce their independence, and Saint-Pierre's device of arbitration is bound to fail.[25]

Martini's remedies for international anarchy are a sort of concert of Europe: mediation, alliances, meetings and congresses, diplomatic exchanges and so on – and the balance of power.[26] For Martini – as for Grotius, Vattel, Achenwall and others – the balance-of-power doctrine is closely connected with the following question: Do states have a right to maintain a balance of power, even if this should mean waging a preventive war against the so-called *potentia tremenda*, an overwhelming state arousing fear among its neighbours?[27]

Martini tries to distinguish among three different situations. First, if a state tries to increase its power with the help of unjust means, for instance by suppressing weaker nations, then preventive measures are legitimate. Secondly, if a nation or state tries to increase its power by using acceptable means, but others can assume that it is ready to injure others ('Kränkung von ihr zu fürchten'), displays pride and greed, and there is an opportunity to stop it, then other states may do so, as the state's behaviour amounts to an injury. Louis XIV, who was an 'unjust conqueror', is Martini's historical example. However – and this is his third situation – if the method of expansion is legitimate, and pride, thirst for power and signs of hostility are absent, then the state exerts its right to 'perfect itself', and preventive measures would constitute an injury.[28]

Martini concedes that general rules are difficult to establish: 'too much depends on arbitrary and collateral situations'.[29] The rules are apparently difficult to apply; single cases are above all a matter of judgement. This brings us back to the dilemma endemic in the state of nature: *Quis judicabit* – Who shall judge? Having dismissed any sort of international community and emphasizing state rights, Martini unintentionally winds up with an international legal theory that is closer to Hobbes than he might have liked. Martini has moved further down the path towards full-blown legal positivism. Cosmopolitan elements correspondingly disappear from the theory.

Johann Jacob Moser: Europe as a 'great political corporation'

Some have praised Johann Jacob Moser (1701–85) as the 'father of German state and international law'. He is usually assigned to the camp of positivists, basing the law of nations on contracts, actual practice (*Herkommen*) and equity law (*natürliche Billigkeit*), customary among civilized, that is European, sovereign states. He distinguishes his own inductive approach grounded on experience from the deductive school referring to abstract principles. He claims:

> I do not invent any system of the law of nations of the kind that scholars tend to form, each one according to their ideas and their passions, depending on what they want or consider to be best. Instead, my own system of the law of nations is based on what is common practice among European sovereigns and nations.[30]

Moser dismisses the idea of justice and both divine as well as natural law as legitimate sources of the law of nations – or rather he claims to dismiss them. In terms of justice, Moser holds that large sections of the law of nations have more to do with arbitrary conventions. Whenever justice is an issue, scholars and jurists are in no position to judge, and apart from that, their opinions are irrelevant and without impact. As a faithful Pietist, Moser reserves the capacity to judge with competence for God 'at the great general Day of Judgment'.[31]

Moser also dismisses natural law because he sees it as an unreliable source. Its principles are so abstract that they are of little use in specific situations. It leaves too much room for interpretation and even detached scholars hardly agree on fundamental principles. If they agree, this agreement alone matters, not its presumed convergence with 'right reason'. Dilemmas such as the problem of interpretation have been with the natural lawyers for a long time. However, there was widespread conviction that these difficulties could be overcome by one's own improved methodology or theory. Moser has lost this faith. Right springs from actual behaviour (*ex factis ius oritur*), and the relevant facts are treaties as well as *Herkommen*, custom and tradition.[32] With his focus on the European law of nations, Moser abandons with a stroke the cosmopolitan elements of his predecessors (often endorsed only half-heartedly). Little was left of these elements in writers like Martini anyway, if we take someone like Wolff as a yardstick.

Critics point at various shortcomings. First, despite his professed intention in the 'Introduction', Moser does in fact establish principles, proceeds deductively, but fails to justify these principles with his illustrations and examples. In short, Moser's methodology is internally inconsistent and thus unsatisfactory. His international legal theory is not a systematic whole, but a hotchpotch, 'an unstable mix of positives and principles, of political cynicism and the will to find a true order'.[33] Moser fails – or is reluctant – to get rid of all elements of natural justice: he refers to the 'generic and great truths' of natural law, contrasts violence with justice and probity, and writes about an 'impartial, reasonable human being'.[34] Secondly, in his attempt to avoid the normative utopianism of writers like Saint-Pierre, Moser winds up with an apology of the powers that be: might makes right.[35] More generally, Moser's positivism is exposed to a familiar logical circle. The distinction between the 'real' sources of the law of nations such as treaties and custom on the one hand and illegitimate ones on the other is itself normative, and implies a judgment on right and wrong that Moser claims we are not entitled to make. A related problem is that positivist assumptions cannot be justified by other positivist assumptions. As Hersch Lauterpacht would argue, state will cannot be the ultimate source of the law of nations, because this would require the normative assumption that states were bound by such law.[36]

Perhaps we should not be too harsh with Moser. We might say he distinguishes between two levels. On the one hand, there are the abstract principles of impartial justice (accessible for reasonable humans), and on the other hand there are more concrete rules applying these principles to specific situations. And Moser is sceptical about our judgements and ways of applying abstract principles, not about these principles themselves. Moser would not be a 'denier' of natural law, but would show 'reasonable doubt' about our capacity to judge in a competent fashion.

Like Martini, Moser rejects Saint-Pierre's peace proposal as 'empty, though sweet, dreams'. Significantly, Henry IV is mentioned, but not pacifists like Penn, Bellers or Rousseau.[37] Moser also rejects the idea of a universal monarchy in Europe. He thinks it impossible that European powers will ever accept 'a certain sovereign' above themselves, even if this sovereign had very limited functions. If there should ever be such an institution, it would not last.[38]

What is left? The balance of power comes to mind, which 'seems' to guarantee the freedom and sovereignty of most European powers. Moser presents the two opposing positions concerning the *potentia tremenda*: some say there is a right to preventive measures to keep the balance; others claim increasing one's power in a legitimate way is acceptable. Unlike Martini and other natural lawyers, Moser follows the Roman principle *non liquet* (it is not clear) and defers judgment. And he is probably right. The reasoning of previous authors showed that judgments invariably oscillated between legal, moral, pragmatic and political considerations. It had reached an impasse. Natural law indeed left too much room for interpretation. Conclusions seemed to be a matter of personal preferences. Moser the cynic does not fail to add that 'this alleged preservation of the balance of Europe is often a mere cloak to hide behind and achieve one's private aims'.[39]

Moser claims that the European states do not form a 'system'. However, there is some sort of 'unity' (*Verbundenheit*) among them. Above all, the Continent has developed its own (European) law of nations, thus forming a 'great political corporation'.[40] A corporation has a legal personality separate from its members, and can act in some respects like an individual. This reminds us of Saint-Pierre and others who asserted that Europe displayed some sort of coherence – cultural, religious, legal and economic. Moser does not develop this train of thought any further.

Georg Friedrich von Martens: refined legal positivism

Georg Friedrich von Martens (1756–1821) became famous for his collection of treaties, the *Recueil des principaux traités* (1791), which saw numerous editions and remained the standard collection well into the last century. His main work is *Précis du droit des gens moderne de l'Europe fondé sur les traités et l'usage* (1789), edited in German under the title *Einleitung in das positive Europäische Völkerrecht* (1796). Martens is usually seen as a positivist and was deeply influenced by Moser.[41]

Like Moser and Martini, Martens moves from generic *ius inter gentes* to the *European* law of nations and, like Moser, from natural and volitional law to positive law.[42] However, Martens does not deny that there is a 'pure natural law of nations' (*reines natürliches Völkerrecht*).[43] He claims that states have natural or 'fundamental' rights (*droit primitives, droits absolus*), such as the right to become more perfect, a concept apparently taken from Wolff. Other fundamental rights are equality, self-preservation, freedom and independence, among others. The natural and volitional law of nations more or less coincide with international morality (*Völkermoral*).[44]

If there is no voluntary law of nations, then there is no universal (*allgemeines*) positive law of nations, and Wolff's postulate of a *civitas maxima* (assuming presumed consent and so on) is an empty idea. This is exactly Martens's conclusion. He is no more lenient with more recent pacifist or cosmopolitan ideas or proposals. He calls the 'project of perpetual peace' (a reference to Saint-Pierre, Abbé Gregoire and Kant) a 'pleasant dream', a 'mere illusion (*Chimäre*)'. His key argument against these proposals is metaphysical: human nature is dominated by passions and selfishness, and we should not expect humans to change. He concludes in a manner reminiscent of Moser:

> It is neither to be expected nor is it desirable in every respect that the European peoples in their totality should decide to be united in a

universal monarchy or a republic in order to maintain perpetual peace. Parliaments and courts of law do not provide perpetual peace where the executive powers call for whole armies.[45]

The last sentence reminds us of Hobbes's 'covenants, without the sword, are but words', and shows how Hobbesian elements enter international legal theory through a back door. Martens's (and Moser's) scepticism concerning peace projects became standard in the nineteenth century. Bluntschli's correspondence with Moltke is the classical example.[46] The Hobbesian and the contractual school of thought dominated (see below).

Like Moser and so many writers before him, Martens holds that Europe forms some sort of community, based on Christianity, Roman law, common interests, similar morals, customs and other factors. Martens even calls Europe 'a nation consisting of states'. Martens also touches upon the balance of power in Europe and the problem of the *potentia tremenda*. It soon becomes clear that Martens offers a hotchpotch of legal, moral and political considerations, with a strong emphasis on pragmatics and politics. 'It is up to the politicians of the cabinets to assess if the balance of power is in danger, and what has to be done for its preservation.'[47]

Penser la guerre: how does Martens think about war? In his account, Vattel's 'lawful war in due form' predominates, in a way that Nussbaum has characterized as 'a rather perfunctory and thoughtless reiteration of traditional doctrine':[48] injuries or violations of perfect rights may be punished, states are their own judges, force may be repelled by force, war has to be considered 'externally just (*äusserlich gerecht*)' on both sides, and so on.[49] It is significant that just two paragraphs deal with the traditional *ius ad bellum*, whereas a whole book, more than sixty paragraphs, deals with the law of embassies. Here, Martens is obviously on safe ground, specifying, for instance, that 'there is no doubt that an embassy may end with the death of the ambassador. In this case, a decent funeral may be requested'.[50]

Nussbaum praised the *Précis* as 'the best systematic exposition of international law of Martens's time and for long afterwards', and claimed that it 'established what, up to the present time, has been the prevailing pattern of systematic treatment of international law.' Walter Habenicht called him one of the 'princes of positive law'.[51] We have seen that his main work is partly a muddy mixture of various traditions, of positivism, utilitarianism, natural law, even a bit of just-war theory. However, he is definitely more systematic than Moser, and his scientific standards (in terms of footnotes and bibliography) are impressive. Perhaps his most cunning move was avoiding the deep and dangerous waters of philosophical reasoning (about just wars, the nature of international relations or law and so on) and focusing on comparatively uncontroversial and harmless issues such as the rights of embassies, titles and honours of sovereigns, and the right of neutrality.

Robert Ward: emphasizing the historical dimension

Martens foreshadows many trends of the nineteenth century: the emphasis on sovereignty, the will and interests of states, legal positivism, the triumph of the *guerre en forme*, the distinction between international law and ethics, or the end of the natural law framework of the *ius ad bellum*. Most international lawyers accepted war as a means of state policy. Some just-war elements were kept. But all in all, the Hobbesian school of thought and the contractual school dominated.[52]

Jeremy Bentham (1789) and John Austin (1832) were crucial authors in the positivist transformation of the law of nations. Although Bentham asserted that he was simply replacing the term 'international law' for what had earlier been called 'the law of nations', he changed the boundaries of the discipline in two respects. First, he assumed that international law was only about the rights and obligations of states among themselves, and not about those including individuals. These would turn into mere objects of international law. Secondly, Bentham denied that cases involving foreign transactions adjudicated by local courts were decided by the norms of the law of nations. For him, they were a matter of internal rules.[53] Austin also drew a sharp distinction between international and domestic spheres. In a famous passage, he declared that international law was not really law in the strict sense.[54] Austin's main premise and challenge was that law is set by sovereign authority. As the norms regulating the conduct of sovereign states are by definition not regulated or enforced by an outside authority, international law is not really law at all. Sometimes legal positivism degenerated into sheer state voluntarism, the belief (or myth) that the will of the state was the only source of the law.

All these trends gained momentum in the nineteenth century, especially towards the end of it. There were some counter currents: the French Revolution; independent, pacifist thinkers with a clear cosmopolitan or truly European perspective; and the peace movement.

I want to start with a highly original and widely unknown independent thinker, Robert Plumer Ward (1765–1846). His main work *An Enquiry into the Foundation and History of the Law of Nations in Europe* (1795) is often mentioned as the first historical study of the law of nations.[55] Ward doubts that the law of nations is universal, as European codes are not. It becomes a historical phenomenon:

> if our principles are allowed, the Law in question, must not only be different in different districts of the Earth at present; but even in the same district, it must have varied in the course of time, in proportion as revolutions have happened in the religious and moral systems of its nations.

What is called for is an 'enquiry . . . into the history of Man'.[56] Ward is obviously influenced by the 'philosophical historians' of the Enlightenment such as Montesquieu, Adam Smith, Lord Kames, Adam Ferguson, Edward Gibbon or John Millar.[57] Along these lines, Ward claims that the balance-of-power system is a modern European phenomenon, that only modern Europe has formed a kind of commonwealth or republic, and that 'what is commonly called the Law of Nations' is not a universal phenomenon, but one exclusively related to European culture and history.[58]

Ward does think in historical terms, but he is not a moral or cultural relativist. In a manner reminiscent of Smith and Moser, he distinguishes between first principles (whose universality he does not doubt) and the process of applying them to specific situations, which are culturally relative.[59] Ward realizes that the law of nature, even if defended as part of a theory of moral minimalism, is too abstract and generic to provide a solid foundation of the European law of nations, or to 'bear the fabric that is erected upon them'.[60] Here, Ward clearly parts company with the natural law tradition and writers such as Vattel and Martini. Ward's balance between moral universalism and culturally sensitive relativism is definitely a precarious one: at times, he seems to move towards a full-blown relativist approach, as in a passage where he claims that what is morally right or wrong 'cannot be made binding *a priori*' upon others.[61]

If we now turn to our issues of cosmopolitanism and Europeanism, we could brutally press the consequences of Ward's historical approach into two statements: moral and legal cosmopolitanisms are 'out', Europeanism and Christianity are 'in'. Ward's cultural and historical sensitivity seems to lead to a kind of tolerance. For instance, Ward asserts that if we assume that the law of nations is a historical and modern European phenomenon, then it does not make sense to criticize or condemn 'other people as if they had broken a law, to which they had never submitted, which they had never understood, or of which they had probably never heard'. Therefore, Ward concludes, the Spaniards were 'not reasonable' when they accused the Mexicans or Peruvians of breaking the law of nations. The last sovereign emperor of the Tahuantinsuyu or Inca Empire, Atahualpa (executed by the Spaniards in 1533), was an 'innocent and unfortunate' monarch, while Francisco Pizarro (the conqueror of the empire) was 'ruthless'.[62] However, Ward's moderate relativism soon embraces the familiar distinction between civilized and savage nations, and asserts that only civilized people can be subsumed under the concept of 'mankind'. 'For when we talk of the world we shall then only mean the *civilized* world; and not only that, but the world civilized after our own ideas.'[63] With humans neatly divided into two groups of people, Ward proceeds with retelling familiar horror stories about non-European savages: about Tartars who eat their own parents, Arabs who plunder and kill travellers, or African kings who massacre their own subjects when ascending their throne. Muslims wage holy wars on Christians, Turks 'are taught by their religion to hate and despise the Christians', and so on.[64] Burke might have countered – as in the case of Montesquieu – 'that every word that he has taken from idle and inconsiderate Travellers is absolutely false'.[65] In all fairness, I should add that Ward is equally harsh with Europe's own past: the Middle Ages are seen as 'barbarous', and the Germanic law of nations as 'savage' and 'cruel'.[66]

Europeanism is 'in': like Saint-Pierre, Vattel, Moser and others, Ward sees Europe as a cultural unit, with communities and states belonging to the same 'class' because they share habits, customs (like the abolition of slavery), institutions (like permanent embassies) and, above all, the same religion. The law of nations is a European, Christian law, constituting a 'European republic'.[67] Outside Europe, it includes 'the Nations and Colonies that spring from us', especially in North and South America. Countries like Turkey and Russia are in a kind of 'twilight' state; they have the potential of becoming members of good standing of the European club.[68]

Ward sees the foundation of this particular, historically and culturally embedded law of nations in Christianity – 'in addition' to the more formal law of nature (this again points at Ward's compromise between relativism and universalism): 'With us in Europe, and the nations that spring from us, the moral system is founded upon REVEALED RELIGION. In other words, it is the same with CHRISTIANTY itself.'[69] Legal historians like Stephen Neff or Heiner Steiger do indeed emphasize the key role of Christianity in the formation of modern, Western law of nations – because of its propagation of universal moral principles and its pacifism.[70] Still, Ward's claim is perhaps one-sided: Christianity was one key factor *among others* in the process of formation. In addition, Ward tends to emphasize the presumed superiority of Christianity and Christian nations at the expense of non-Europeans like Muslims or the Chinese. Here, Ward clearly breaks with some of his predecessors and contemporary authors, and distorts historical facts. While writers like Gentili, Leibniz, Wolff, Vattel or Kant defended Chinese isolationism as a legitimate form of self-defence in the face of European aggression (see Chapters 2 and 4), Ward asserts that Chinese laws against strangers would demonstrate their 'barbarity' and the 'inferiority' of their concept of the law of nations.[71]

Nussbaum calls Ward's study a 'respectable accomplishment'[72] – Ward was a lawyer in London when he published the book and only thirty years old. His strengths are a philosophical mind and a historically and sometimes culturally sensitive approach. Too bad Ward became a politician later on and proceeded to write novels. At any rate, he reminds us that some issues need to be contextualized more.

Anacharsis Cloots: cosmopolitan republicanism

At the end of Chapter 3, I have mentioned the importance of the French Revolution as a turning point for European cosmopolitan attitudes. It is useful to distinguish between moderate and radical phases of the Revolution. In the early phase of the Revolution, French patriotism and moral as well as political cosmopolitanisms complemented each other. This synthesis was personified by Count Volney, Condorcet and, above all, by Anarcharsis Cloots, who addressed the national assembly as '*l'ambassadeur du genre humain*' in June 1790. For some time, cosmopolitan phraseology cloaked nationalist ambitions. After 1793, revolutionaries became increasingly xenophobic and nationalistic, criticizing the *cosmopolites* as enemies of the Revolution.[73]

Three traditions influenced French political writers of the early revolutionary period: the natural law tradition, the republican/democratic tradition and the tradition of cosmopolitan and European peace projects.[74] In line with the natural lawyers, they emphasized the natural rights of states, their equality and freedom, and their moral personality, which led to an emphasis on the free consent of states and ruled out intervention. Some proposals and suggestions, favouring some sort of international organization, hinted at political cosmopolitanism. In addition, these revolutionaries consciously returned to the – by then almost old-fashioned – just-war theory. As republicans, they spoke up in favour of popular sovereignty and the self-determination of peoples (as international lawyers would later call it). Of course they wanted to replace monarchies by republics (who were supposed to be more peaceful, see Montesquieu and others). From the tradition of cosmopolitan/European peace projects (see especially Saint-Pierre and Rousseau), they borrowed the ideas of collective security and the league of nations.

Critics outside France did not fail to point out that there was a tremendous split between noble theory and bloody practice, for instance in terms of the principle of non-intervention. They emphasized that for most revolutionaries, the political enemies turned into criminals or 'foes of the human race'. In short, certain French revolutionaries – especially after 1793 – adhered to a dangerous, dogmatic, ideological crusading mentality (Brissot spoke of a 'crusade for universal liberty'). Martens, when writing about the proposal of Abbé Grégoire (1795), pointed at the glaring contradiction between proclaimed 'freedom of nations' and an 'unlimited right to interfere in other nations'. He thought these were 'dangerous sentences'.[75]

Jean-Baptiste du Val-de-Grâce, Baron de Cloots (1755–94), better known under the name of Anacharsis Cloots, was born into a noble Prussian family and moved to Paris in 1789, becoming a politician and publishing a string of books, notably *La République universelle ou adresse aux tyrannicides* (1792) and *Bases constitutionelles de la République du genre humain* (1793). He was imprisoned and subsequently guillotined during the *terreur*.

Cloots develops a form of political cosmopolitanism, which can be labelled cosmopolitan republicanism or republican cosmopolitanism.[76] I will attempt to summarize its main features. Together with Nicolaus Vogt (1787) and John Oswald (1797), Cloots is a writer in the wake of the American and French Revolutions who is trying to reformulate republicanism, with a focus on large states (and no longer on the small city-states) and their peaceful relations (and not simply on statist defence). There were two versions of republican cosmopolitanism: authors like Jean-Jacques Rousseau, John Oswald or Friedrich Schlegel advocated alliances of republics, whereas Anacharsis Cloots was in favour of a world republic with departments, but without states.[77] According to Cloots, limiting the social contract to singular states contradicts the idea of a *volonté generale*, which is the basis of this very contract. As a consequence, the social contract should be global. In a similar vein, Cloots holds that human rights are by definition universal, and thus global in scope: 'Les droits de l'homme s'éntendent sur la totalité des hommes.'[78] State sovereignty is at best provisional; genuine sovereignty resides with the individuals of the global society. There seem to be some parallels with Kant's contractual cosmopolitanism (see Chapter 4).

In his highly influential book *Anarchical Society* (1977), Hedley Bull has claimed:

> The dominant theme of international relations, on the Kantian view, is only apparently the relationship among states, and is really the relationship among all men in the community of mankind – which exists potentially, even if it does not exist actually, and which when it comes into being will sweep the system of states into limbo.[79]

This is a gross misinterpretation of Kant's theory. For Kant, cosmopolitan right, at least initially, does not replace classical law among states or nations, but complements it. What Bull writes about Kant, though, is a perfect description of Cloots's design. There is no room for states, not even with a very limited form of sovereignty. There are just individuals and the world state with departments. In the words of Bull, Cloots's goal is 'the overthrow of the system of states and its replacement by a cosmopolitan society'.[80]

This design is truly revolutionary, but with the serious disadvantage that it does not attempt to mediate in any way between the existing modern states system and the ideal. Whereas Kant's legal cosmopolitanism is evolutionary, Cloots does not tell us how his project can be realized. There are some scattered hints, though, how this could be achieved, and here Cloots develops more conventional ideas: the world republic could take Europe as its starting point; global free trade could lead to, but would also be facilitated by, the world republic; as a republican, Cloots favours public discourses, tolerance and freedom of worship.[81]

I have already mentioned the xenophobic turn of the French Revolution after 1793, which became a turning point for European attitudes. Effects on European mentalities were tremendous. Cosmopolitan theories were increasingly identified with the goals and practices of the French Revolution, and rejected together with them. Many, among them even moderate thinkers, challenged the precarious balance between patriotism and cosmopolitanisms, and became increasingly nationalist.[82]

However, it would be an oversimplification to tell the simple story of a move from cosmopolitanisms to nationalism. The overall picture is, again, rather complex. There was a considerable diversity of reactions. Germany is a case in point. Johann Wolfgang von Goethe (1749–1832), for instance, developed what came to be called *cosmopolitisme littéraire*, a form of cultural cosmopolitanism (see Chapter 1). He did not share the national enthusiasm (or frenzy) of the German wars of liberation, and developed the concept of 'world literature (*Weltliteratur*)' in the 1820s instead. It encompassed the mutual perception, exchange and interaction of nations with the help of literature, and aimed at what was shared by all humans.[83] This intellectual or spiritual interaction, which includes translations, reviews and literary criticism across borders, encompasses a moral, cosmopolitan goal. 'The idea is not that nations shall think alike, but that they shall learn how to understand each other, and, if they do not care to love one another, at least that they will learn to tolerate one another.'[84] The concept of *cosmopolitisme littéraire*, coined by Sébastien Mercier in 1802, helped to eliminate the political and legal dimensions of cosmopolitanism, so dominant in Kant or Cloots. It became the basis of comparative literature in the nineteenth century and helped to keep the concept of cosmopolitanism alive for some time, in spite of growing nationalist tendencies.

Early German romantic thinking (which Kleingeld labels 'cosmopolitanism') was another development. While representatives shared some Enlightenment ideals, they criticized the emphasis on reason and stressed emotions, faith and spirituality, among others. A fine example is *Die Christenheit oder Europa*, a talk that Novalis (Friedrich von Hardenberg, 1772–1801) gave in 1799.[85] He painted a rather idealized picture of medieval Europe united by peace, faith and love. Like Ward, Novalis emphasizes the role of Christianity, but his ideal community is not restricted to Europe. 'The other parts of the world wait for Europe's reconciliation and resurrection to join with it and become fellow citizens of the kingdom of heaven.'[86]

We have seen that many late eighteenth-century international lawyers turned towards Europe, perceived either as a political or legal community, or as a cultural entity (or even as both). This trend is paralleled by the *cosmopolitisme littéraire*, which probably supported the trend towards Europeanism, as it referred to common European cultural traditions. There was another development, which mirrored the one in international legal theory. Up to the end of the eighteenth century, European thinkers had developed two distinct political roles for Europe. According to the group of the political cosmopolitans – Kant and Cloots are good examples – Europe was but the starting point of a truly global federation or world state. Authors like Saint-Pierre or Rousseau had designed plans of an exclusively European federation. It seems that after 1789, plans and ideas of this second type, and Europeanism in general, gained the upper hand. Friedrich Schlegel referred to a 'European Confederation (*Eidgenossenschaft*)', Adam Müller, admiring the glory of medieval Christianity, insisted on a 'great federation of the European peoples' (with some patriotic overtones), and Schelling believed in a coming European 'State of States'.[87] Even

Goethe's literary cosmopolitanism was hierarchical and Eurocentric rather than truly cosmopolitan, and Greek antiquity was the normative yardstick.[88]

The debate on cosmopolitanism in German-speaking countries revolved around two issues. First, intellectuals discussed the relationship between the French Revolution and cosmopolitanism. Secondly, they continued the familiar discussion how cosmopolitan and patriotic allegiances could be combined. Many came to identify cosmopolitanism with the Revolution, and rejected both. Patriotism, on the other hand, was subsequently replaced by forms of nationalism, and the latter declared incompatible with cosmopolitan sentiments.[89] An early and rather extreme example is Ernst Moritz Arndt (1769–1860), who turned chauvinistic, xenophobic and aggressive after Prussia's defeat in 1806.[90]

While some intellectuals tried to keep an uneasy balance and tried not to break with some kind of patriotic cosmopolitanism, the general trend was clearly favouring nationalism.[91] A splendid example is Friedrich Schiller (1759–1805), especially since he started off, in 1789, with the cosmopolitan universalism of a German *Weltbürger*, apparently deeply influenced by Kant (see Chapter 4).[92] The last decades of the eighteenth century had witnessed the development of a home-grown – and impressive – German culture, which led some Germans to adopt the concept of a German 'cultural nation (*Kulturnation*)'. Some time after 1797, after the first humiliating defeats against Napoleon, Schiller came up with the notion of 'German greatness', and tried to define it as 'ethical greatness'. He was clearly struggling to cope with the emotional consequences of military and political defeat. All of a sudden, Germany was supposed to be superior, and Schiller expressed his pride in *national* German culture. Jim Reed explains that:

> his argument had shifted from national consolation to national self-assertion, from national self-assertion to claims of a unique national value, and on to the edge of nationalistic aggression. In other words, perhaps he discerned the beginnings of demagogy in what he was writing.[93]

Like many other eighteenth-century authors, Burke did not think that patriotism, Europeanism and cosmopolitan sentiments were incompatible with each other (see Chapter 3). However, his attack on the French Revolution might also have inadvertently weakened cosmopolitan ideas, and his turn to historical reason probably helped to discredit the natural lawyers' standard reference to the worldwide community of humans.[94]

Finally, let me summarize some central features of late eighteenth-century international legal theory. First of all, the international lawyers tend to play down international anarchy. They claim – or imply – that the normal condition of human relations is one of peace and that the state of war is an exception. Even a positivist like Martens gives short shrift to the condition of war, indulging in extensive descriptions of peaceful interstate relations. They believe that a provisional condition is a peremptory or conclusive condition (Kant's public lawful condition). Secondly, the international lawyers see war as law enforcement, as an instrument of justice. Whereas Kant's motto is 'neither just war nor lawful war in due form, but juridical cosmopolitanism', the lawyers are happy with a more traditional approach. Third, the international lawyers do not believe that an original contract is necessary on the international level. Martini is a case in point: he divides his legal theory into two parts, state law and the law of nations. He knows a *pactum unionis* and a *pactum subjectionis* for state law, to overcome the 'anarchical society'. There is no corresponding contract on the interstate level. It is fascinating to see that representatives of different camps agree upon rejecting Saint-Pierre and other supposedly lofty dreamers of a European or cosmopolitan union. Vattel, Martini, Moser or Martens offer pretty identical arguments in spite of divergent methodologies. On top of that, they all endorse the balance-of-power doctrine, officially enshrined in the Peace of Utrecht documents (1713) and – together with sovereignty and denominational equality – one of the core principles of eighteenth-century European diplomacy and the *droit public européen*.[95]

The international lawyers believe in a common European and Christian culture, in a society of states which are politically independent but culturally, historically and economically related to each other. They seem to follow a general trend of the late eighteenth century, when *cosmopolis* and the *societas humanis generis* was gradually and partly replaced by the twin ideas of 'Europe' and 'civilization'.[96] Another surprising feature is that, in spite of their divergent methodologies, the natural lawyers and the positivists arrive at similar conclusions. Even the natural lawyers' methodologies are a rather shaky hotchpotch, lacking a consistent system, blending empirical with rational arguments.

Ward and Cloots are the two offbeat thinkers who do not fit into this overall picture: Ward with his turn to history and his – perhaps romantic – emphasis on Christianity, and Cloots with his continuation and radicalization of the traditions of moral and legal cosmopolitanisms.

6 • Immigration, Rights and the Global Community: Pufendorf, Vattel, Bluntschli and Verdross

It is often taken for granted that international law and legal theory have endorsed the right of states to exclude all aliens if they prefer to do so. A 1972 opinion of the US Supreme Court referred to 'ancient principles' in this respect.[1] It turns out that this was a gross distortion of historical data. Francisco de Vitoria (1486–1546), who is sometimes praised as the 'father of international law', argued for a very sweeping right to travel and to trade, the freedom of the seas and the right to immigration. He claimed that there is a right 'of natural partnership and communication' as part of the law of nations rooted in the notion of a global moral commonwealth:

> The whole world, which is in a sense a commonwealth, has the power to enact laws which are just and convenient to all men; and these make up the law of nations . . . No kingdom may choose to ignore this law of nations, because it has the sanction of the whole world.[2]

In the passage, Vitoria referred to voluntary law, which was somewhat precariously situated between natural law and positive legislation, and included an element of consent and (state) practice. Other members of the 'School of Salamanca' and subsequent international lawyers argued for a qualified right to immigration (see Chapter 2). For this reason, James Nafziger (1983) challenged the US Supreme Court's opinion, and pointed out that if there were any ancient principles, they suggested exactly the opposite, namely an obvious pattern of free movement. He suggested a qualified duty to admit aliens, provided they did not endanger 'public safety, security, general welfare, or essential institutions of a recipient state'.[3] Nafziger showed that extensive restrictions on immigration were a product of late nineteenth-century state practice.

Contemporary debates allow us to distinguish among three positions. First, there are those who follow the Vitorian approach and argue for open borders. Joseph Carens, at least at first sight, is a case in point (see Chapter 7). The second, diametrically opposed position endorses closed or controlled borders, and emphasizes state sovereignty and the right of political communities to exclude aliens. Michael Walzer is a fine example. Finally, there is a third, middle position, which tries to strike a balance between the first two: it is cosmopolitan like the first, but takes communitarian concerns into account. It is sceptical towards state sovereignty, but does not abandon it altogether. It holds that human rights (such as the right to free movement) are universal and should be global, but accepts that contexts and political realities have to be considered. In short, the third position speaks up for porous borders. Seyla Benhabib comes to mind.[4]

In this chapter, I will try to show that Nafziger's analysis is correct. All the authors I am going to deal with argue for a qualified right of free movement. They differ in their respective background theories. Some are natural lawyers, some move towards legal positivism, some offer an eclectic, all-inclusive theory. But all reject the theory of absolute state sovereignty, a theory that was widespread in European legal theory roughly between 1870 and the First World War. Instead, they endorse what Kelsen calls the primacy of international law over state law. In addition, some go on to argue for the primacy of some sort of natural law over positive legislation. We will see that they deal with a real problem concerning the right of immigration and the right of communities to determine who may come in and who not: where do we draw the line, and how can we justify drawing it? Implicitly, they accept that there is a fundamental asymmetry between those inside and those outside, and they see no reason to overcome this asymmetry. So they wind up with some sort of middle position, which tries to balance out divergent claims.

Samuel Pufendorf: a thin conception of immigration rights

I want to start my story with Hugo Grotius, who has for some time been seen as the father of modern natural law, of private law theory and of international law (together with Vitoria or instead of him). Hersch Lauterpacht referred to 'the Grotian tradition', claiming that the Dutch jurist had found a viable middle-ground between positivism and naturalism in his writings. Lauterpacht cherished his moral cosmopolitanism and his idea of a natural society of nations or communities (*societas gentium*).[5]

In a previous chapter, I have argued that this interpretation is rather flaky, especially in terms of Grotius' alleged cosmopolitanism, although it was widespread for a long time (see Chapter 2). At any rate, Grotius' idea of a natural society of communities was debated by his commentators, and the history of this debate can be interpreted as a gradual shift towards the novel concept of a society of states where *recta ratio* is progressively identified with the will of the sovereign prince. Samuel Pufendorf (1632–94) is usually considered as a crucial figure in this debate, one who favoured a development subsumed under concepts such as state sovereignty, princely absolutism and legal positivism. Pufendorf struggles hard to strike a balance between (his interpretations of) Grotius and Hobbes. Ultimately, his theory is more state-centred than previous ones, moving away from the Grotian idea of a moral community of humankind. State interests tend to predominate.

Pufendorf's emphasis on the state has repercussions on the notion of hospitality and the right of immigration. Unlike Francisco de Vitoria and Grotius, and even more than Alberico Gentili and Francisco Suárez, he stresses the right of any community to refuse visitors. Hospitality and trade belong to the imperfect duties of friendship which cannot be enforced.

According to Pufendorf, the following principles are based on natural law. First, he distinguishes between the right to visit and the right to settle permanently. The latter requires the consent of the state authorities.[6] Secondly, both strangers and natives have to stick to the principle of Roman jurisprudence to refrain from harming anyone (*neminem laedere*). In particular, strangers should be 'upright' people 'from whom no danger or disgrace will come'.[7] Thirdly, cases of distress, when the life of the stranger is at stake, trump the sovereign right of the state to refuse visitors. In cases of extreme necessity, for example if some shipwrecked traveller is in 'extreme want of food necessary to maintain life', they should be received, and might even violate property rights if 'unjustly attacked'.[8] Fourthly, there is the principle of formal reciprocity: states that grant to strangers the right to travel are entitled to expect the same policy from those communities where the strangers come from. If those communities close their borders, a tit-for-tat strategy is legitimate. In other words, Pufendorf holds that, by standards of reciprocity, it would be inconsistent to exclude foreigners while demanding hospitality rights for one's own citizens.[9]

Finally and most importantly, Pufendorf, building upon Grotius, distinguishes between perfect and imperfect rights. A perfect right (*ius perfectum*) is precise, enforceable and necessary if society is to exist at all. If a perfect right is violated in civil society, the injured person can go to court. In the international area, it justifies the use of force. Perfect rights are usually based on contract, promises or agreements. By contrast, an imperfect right (*ius imperfectum*) allows for some latitude, cannot be enforced, and goes beyond mere rules of coexistence, aiming at 'improved existence'. We are obliged 'by some moral virtue', but the obligation falls outside the sphere of strict justice. Pufendorf calls these obligations 'works of humanity or of love'. The imperfect duty to come to someone's aid and to offer shelter and hospitality are cases in point.[10] It is crucial to keep in mind that Pufendorf does not see imperfect rights as less important or qualitatively inferior to perfect ones.

Pufendorf considers all rights pertaining to hospitality or immigration to be imperfect ones. Provided they do not travel themselves, states, communities and nations have the right to refuse visitors; 'if any nation has no interest in visiting foreign peoples, there seems to be no law requiring it to admit those who come to it unnecessarily and without good reason.'[11] Though he does not state it explicitly, we can assume that the conception of the state as a moral person is the ultimate justifying principle for the alleged right to refuse visitors. Against Vitoria, Pufendorf holds that the perfect right of ownership trumps the imperfect right to visit and live in foreign countries. The property-holder simply has 'the final decision on the question, whether he wishes to share with others the use of his property'.[12] This is the modern principle of state authority.[13]

Pufendorf adds the pragmatic consideration that any unlimited influx of visitors who might stay for an unlimited period of time may have detrimental effects on the native community. In the language of natural law, this inflow could conflict with the community's duty of self-preservation. In addition, Pufendorf specifies that immigrants are obliged to recognize the government of the receiving country, must be willing to integrate and must be content with what has been assigned to them.[14] Pufendorf's reasoning repeatedly makes use of the domestic analogy. For instance, he argues that the relationship among communities can be compared to the owner of a garden who grants special privileges to one of his neighbours exclusively.

So far I have emphasized those elements in Pufendorf's theory that revolve around the modern principle of state authority. However, the complete picture is more complex. There are several factors in Pufendorf's theory that foster an attitude of hospitality and immigration. Like his predecessors, he holds that originally there was negative 'common dominion' among individuals. It was negative because without any preceding act, items or things 'belonged no more to one man than to another'.[15] He tells a story, reminiscent of Grotius, about how population pressure and social changes led to the introduction of private dominion or property. However, Pufendorf does not base hospitality rights on this doctrine of common dominion. It is his political anthropology and theory of sociability that become crucial in this respect. Pufendorf holds that more than other animals, humans are dependent on the help and assistance of others in order to survive and secure a good life. Their very self-love and desire to preserve themselves, combined with weakness (*debilitas*) and natural helplessness or feebleness (*imbecillitas*), urges humans to become sociable beings. From these observations, Pufendorf derives the first fundamental law of nature, the duty 'to cultivate . . . towards others a sociable attitude'.[16] If we have a duty to promote sociability, then it is not enough simply to abstain from injuring or harming others. In addition, we should confer some positive benefit upon others. More specifically, this implies granting things to others that we can give to them 'without loss, trouble, or labour on our part'. Examples include accepting foreign ships on our coast, admitting strangers, providing hospitality and allowing residence, innocent passage or passage for merchandise.[17]

How do these generous provisions go together with Pufendorf's emphasis on state sovereignty and reason of state? First of all, we have to keep the distinction between perfect and imperfect rights in mind: the mentioned generous provisions make a hospitable attitude more attractive, but do not invalidate the perfect rights of states or communities. Secondly, Pufendorf does not see a glaring contradiction between reasons of state and the precepts of humanity. He holds that long-term utility coincides with morality, that the morally good is usually also useful and rewarding.[18] Pufendorf's mixing of Christian and natural morality with a form of early utilitarianism was not uncommon. In short, Pufendorf does see a convergence of interests and duties at work in the real world, in a manner that explicitly anticipates the Scottish Enlightenment and Adam Smith, as scholars have discovered in recent years.

A fine example of this convergence of interests and duties is hinted at by Pufendorf when he writes that 'many states about us have grown immensely because they received foreigners and aliens with open arms, while others, who have repelled them, have been reduced to second-rate powers'.[19] Pufendorf probably refers to the 1580s, when over 100,000 refugees from the Catholic south Netherlands emigrated to the north, contributing to what has been called the economic 'miracle' at the onset of the Golden Age. Historians have noted the speed and comparative ease of integration into Dutch society and economy. In the 1590s, about 10 per cent of the total population of the United Provinces were immigrants from the south. They contributed to the subsequent Dutch dominance of the 'rich trades'.[20]

Summing up, we can say that for Pufendorf, denying or restricting immigration is not unlawful, in the sense of violating natural law, but may all the same be immoral, that is, contrary to the imperfect duty of humanity and love: 'no one can question the barbarity of showing an indiscriminate hostility to those who come on a peaceful mission . . . [T]o expel without probable cause guests and strangers, once admitted, surely savours of inhumanity and disdain.'[21] For the first time, we have a fully developed theoretical framework which distinguishes between perfect and imperfect rights. This framework is then used to solve a problem which has waited for a comprehensive solution since Francisco de Vitoria: how do we balance the perfect right of ownership with the imperfect right of hospitality? Pufendorf's answer to this question is that the admission of immigrants should become a matter of discretion. States exercise their discretion by considering how many immigrants can be absorbed, whether the state could be jeopardized and so on.

Emer de Vattel: an early triumph of state sovereignty

According to a widespread interpretation, Vattel's doctrine is state-centred, favours state sovereignty and turns natural law into something subjective by allowing each nation to decide 'what its conscience demands of it, what it can or cannot do; what it thinks well or does not think well to do'.[22] Vattel seldom moves away from the political realities of his age, brings the theory of the law of nations into line with state practice, and moves towards 'classical' nineteenth-century European international law with its emphasis on sovereign, independent states as the principal actors where individuals are mediated, and with clear distinctions between law and morality, perfect and imperfect duties, and international law and domestic jurisdiction. The ultimate outcome is a society of sovereign states regulating their interactions by customary law (see above Chapter 2).

Although Vattel is often assigned to the camp of the legal positivists, this assessment has to be qualified. Rooted in the natural law tradition, he develops a theory of inalienable rights and, like Rousseau, abandons Grotius' insistence on consent. This leads to a rejection of slavery and an endorsement of the right of revolution if the sovereign violates the 'sacred natural law'.[23] For Vattel, natural law is the foundation of the law of nations. However, the central principle of this natural law is the idea of the state as a moral person, its freedom and sovereignty. Natural law allows moral entities like the state a sphere of licence or liberty, while the exercise of this freedom may be diametrically opposed to the precepts of natural law. It is important to keep in mind that there is a trend towards this doctrine and that Vattel tries to keep a precarious balance between the conscience of sovereigns, necessary law and intrinsic justice on the one hand, and the 'external operation' of voluntary law and formal legality on the other.[24] Along with Pufendorf and other natural lawyers before him, Vattel distinguishes between perfect and imperfect duties and rights, between internal and external duties, and between duties towards oneself and towards others.[25]

Again following Pufendorf and Wolff, Vattel endorses the new paradigm of the state as a *persona moralis*, and the law of nations is the science of the rights and duties among these sovereign states.²⁶ Vattel defines sovereignty as the independence of any state from others. This state has its own public authority, government and laws. Sovereignty is inalienable, but resides with civil society rather than with the prince: 'The state is not, and cannot be, a patrimony, since a patrimony exists for the advantage of the possessor, whereas the prince is appointed only for the good of the state.'²⁷ This can be interpreted as a liberal defence of popular sovereignty, where the sovereignty of the prince is replaced by the sovereignty of the state and its moral personality. Following the Lockean version of the social contract theory, Vattel distinguishes between sovereignty, the public authority created by the social contract and residing in civil society or the nation, and the sovereign, the government set up by the will of the people in order to exercise public powers.²⁸ Given the sharp distinction between the realm of conscience and 'what is merely tolerated through necessity', Vattel has no problems in endorsing the concept of a *société humaine* while rejecting Wolff's *civitas maxima*. Humans are bound by conscience to assist each other as long as this imperfect duty of mutual assistance is compatible with the perfect duties towards oneself, and this moral obligation unites humans across the globe.²⁹

As states are sovereign, they have a right to refuse visitors. Legitimate reasons are 'evident danger', such as diseases, the possible corruption of morals and public disorder. Prudence and charity, the imperfect duties of humanity on the one hand, and the right of ownership on the other must be weighed against each other.³⁰ As in Pufendorf, we get the modern principle of state authority plus immigration as a matter of discretion. Once foreigners are admitted into the country, however, the sovereign has a duty to protect them.³¹ Vattel draws now widely accepted distinctions between natives, residents and permanent residents. Although natural law favours the *ius sanguinis* doctrine, specific problems, such as whether children of citizens born abroad are also citizens, are delegated to positive legislation in the respective countries, 'and such provisions must be followed'.³² The laws may differ from state to state, but are binding 'when enacted by the lawful authority'.³³ These specifications break new ground. There is a new shift away from the older question (Vitoria's): 'Is there a right to immigrate?' to the new: 'How should states treat immigrants?' The original Vitorian question becomes a matter of state practice.

Vattel repeatedly refers to 'the realm of conscience'. Is this mere embellishment? One might argue that it is, especially if we think of Vattel's statements on non-European peoples (see Chapter 2). Vattel's theory, revolving around the standards of effective occupation, of statehood and of civilization, clearly favours Europeans. European sovereign states decide where to draw the line. Vattel's popularity in the nineteenth century has so much to do with the fact that he anticipates that era.

Johann Caspar Bluntschli: the international legal theory of a Victorian gentleman

It is not difficult — and is sometimes done — to paint the dreadful picture of chauvinist, Eurocentric, imperialistic, militaristic, bellicose and positivist nineteenth-century European international law and legal theory, which ultimately prepared rather than helped to prevent the crisis of European civilization in the Great War. Conscientious historians often make an effort to qualify the picture. For instance, they distinguish among various periods of the century or point to the considerable differences among international lawyers.[34]

Johann Caspar Bluntschli (1808–81) was one of the most respected international lawyers of the late nineteenth century and one of the founders of the Institut de droit international at Ghent in 1873. Article I of the Institute's statutes defined its purpose: 'De favoriser le progrès du droit international, en s'efforçant de devenir l'organe de la conscience juridique du monde civilisé.'[35]

'Legal conscience' or 'consciousness' as well as 'the civilized world' are the key concepts of this passage. I will start with *la conscience* or, as Bluntschli calls it, the *(Rechts)bewusstsein*. If we translate *conscience* as 'conscience', we emphasize the moral and psychological dimension of this ambivalent term: Bluntschli, like other international lawyers of the Institute, wanted to codify the moral common sense of civilized contemporaries, the moral substrate or substance of diplomacy and state practice. Consciousness, on the other hand, points to the cognitive, rationalist dimension: in spite of nineteenth-century historicism, Bluntschli still endorsed enlightened, liberal rationalism and its universalism. Law was the effect of common European *Rechtsbewusstsein*. As a staunch believer in legal progress, Bluntschli held that his own work was a contribution to the gradual development of an international legal consciousness that would eventually overcome the last traces of barbarity.

This leads us to the second key concept, that of civilization: it bridged the growing gap between nascent historicism and fading natural law rationalism. The idea of civilization became the centre of attention and efforts in the course of the nineteenth century, culminating in John Stuart Mill's clear-cut distinction between civilized nations and barbarians.[36] Most international lawyers disagreed about minimum standards of civilization, but all shared a common belief in the superiority of European civilization, and in its inevitable spread across the globe. European arrogance and belief in progress reached a climax at the turn of the century. Bluntschli shared these convictions, but was rather moderate. His international legal theory described above all 'the development of the legal conscience of European *Kulturvölker*'.[37] However, he also dared to criticize the arrogant attitude of Europeans of his time: 'The arrogance of civilized peoples has always surely tended towards berating all other peoples as "barbarians". But this language smacks itself of barbarianism since it violates the human dignity of all people.'[38] On top of that, Bluntschli also doubted the widespread conviction among international lawyers that savage tribes did not belong to the society of nations.

Bluntschli's theory met two challenges. The first one was the qualified historicism of Friedrich Carl von Savigny (1779–1861) and his historical school that implicitly questioned universalist assumptions. Secondly, John Austin (1790–1859) challenged conventional doctrine when he declared that international law was not really law in the strict sense. Austin's main premise and challenge was that law was set by sovereign authority. As the norms regulating the conduct of sovereign states were by definition not regulated or enforced by an outside authority, international law was not really law at all (see the end of Chapter 5).

Bluntschli met these challenges with a compromise, an 'all inclusive', eclectic theory that combined historicism and rationalism, legal positivism and some natural law elements. International law was organic, dynamic, flexible and, cast in Bluntschli's own mind, basically liberal.[39] A brief look at *The Modern Law of Nations of Civilized States* (1868) shows that Bluntschli retained several natural law elements. For instance, he claimed that the basis of the law of nations was human nature shared by all (§§ 2 and 6), a generic sense of justice and the 'eternal principles of natural human right'.[40]

As already mentioned, civilized states had the right to spread the blessings of civilization and to educate and guide the savages, helping them to attain a higher level of legal consciousness. The latter did have some rights, and Bluntschli admitted abuse by the Europeans (§ 280). States that isolated themselves violated basic principles of the law of nations, and caused the 'disapproval (*Missbilligung*)' of the civilized world and could be 'called to account'. This probably hints at the practice of intervention by European powers. Unlike the majority of natural lawyers before him (including Pufendorf and Vattel), Bluntschli held that Europeans were justified in putting an end to Chinese and Japanese isolationist policies. Sometimes, he conceded, the exclusion of some foreigners was justified, for instance in order to protect public safety. Bluntschli obviously held that this did not apply to the Chinese or Japanese, because they rejected all foreigners indiscriminately 'without cause' and in an 'indecent manner'.[41] Bluntschli also had some sympathies for European practices to protect the rights of their citizens and ambassadors abroad by the use of force, especially on the 'dark' African continent (§§ 191–226, 380, 471f.).

Bluntschli held that complete isolation violated natural human right, the destiny of the human race, and contradicted the primacy of the international community over state sovereignty.[42] For him, sovereignty could definitely not be conceived as 'absolute', and this distinguished him from several international lawyers of his own time. He went beyond Pufendorf and Vattel in two respects. First, his argument based on the destiny of the human race was teleological and introduced some sort of philosophy of history into the legal discourse. Secondly, he conceptualized Francisco de Vitoria's first 'just title', the right to communicate and interact, as a perfect and enforceable right. Most natural lawyers after Vitoria had turned his first just title into an imperfect, unenforceable right (see Chapter 2). In Bluntschli, however, the value of civilization trumped the formal concept of impartial justice.

Bluntschli constructed the history of the law of nations as a history of legal progress, in theory as well as practice. He wrote on the rights of aliens: 'All this has become different and better. The aliens' human rights are respected in the civilized world and are given the same rights as the natives with respect to the most important parts of private law and commerce (*Verkehr*).'[43] This development towards the better was an ongoing process and was leading inexorably to the goal of a 'humane world law (*Weltrecht*)' and a 'humane world order'.[44]

Bluntschli's international legal theory and his liberal historicism invite historical contextualization. His unwavering belief in progress and teleology is a case in point. In the 1930s, British historian Herbert Butterfield called this Whig or whiggish historiography, where history became a story of teleological progress towards the glorious present.[45] The end of the nineteenth century witnessed two phenomena. On the one hand, members of the European society of states came to assert that no sovereign state had a legal duty to admit aliens (the modern principle of state authority). This was the era of restrictions on immigration, and Vattel was often quoted in support. Admission was usually denied to certain classes of aliens. Discriminatory exclusion laws were enacted in the United States and Canada, for instance, to stop oriental migration.[46] On the other hand, the majority of authors tacitly agreed with Vitoria's first just title: Europeans may travel, trade and settle down anywhere in the world. The doctrine of ownerless sovereignty conveniently provided a partial justification. Once European individuals had found their way into foreign territory, it was easy for their governments to intervene on their behalf if their rights had been infringed upon. It was assumed that territories whose natives were unfit or unwilling to protect white 'visitors' could be conquered, and chiefs 'forced to assume responsibility'. Most international lawyers roughly between 1871 and the First World War, but not all of them, supported European imperialism with their respective theories.[47]

Bluntschli's discussion about progress betrays a certain asymmetry in the right to immigration: this right must be upheld for Europeans when entering 'thinly populated' territories, but it does not hold for those who would enter European countries. If we had asked Bluntschli for the justifying principle behind this asymmetry, he would have referred to his twofold inclusion/exclusion theory. Recall that Pufendorf had implied that 'all humankind was one', and had drawn porous borders around separate communities.

Bluntschli moves beyond this position and draws an additional line between the community of civilized (European) states and those outside.

Alfred Verdross: a half-hearted return to natural law

While Bluntschli is a rather mainstream and moderate international lawyer of the mid nineteenth century, Alfred Verdross (1890–1980) stands for the 'new' science of international law after the Great War. When Robert Ward compared civil or municipal law and the law of nations in 1795, he argued that similarities were extensive.

> When however they come to be broken, the difference is far more serious. The breach of *municipal* law is attended only by the punishment of the offender (the law remaining still in force, strengthened perhaps by the very infraction); the breach of the other, can only be remedied by the refusal of those who are injured to comply with it any longer, and the law itself is totally destroyed.[48]

Ward points to the precarious character of international law, a result of the fact that it cannot be enforced in the way it is in civil law. His sentence is also a warning, mostly ignored by late nineteenth-century international legal theory. It was only after the carnage of the First World War that international lawyers attempted a new start, criticizing extreme legal positivism, the Hobbesian school of thought, the dogma of state sovereignty and the *'laissez-faire* approach to war' (Stephen Neff). They were more willing to learn lessons taught by 'utopian' writers, French revolutionaries or Kant, taking up just-war elements, favouring collective security, cooperation or an international enforcement organ like the League of Nations. The Pact of Paris (1928) even tried to outlaw war. At the end of the day, progress was rather limited, as 'the heady new wine of collective security and international organization was poured into old bottles'.[49] But a new start had been made: states should no longer be their own judges.

Imperialist mentality and European arrogance were partly abandoned, or at least eyed with scepticism. Together with an array of other scholars, Verdross aimed at overcoming late nineteenth-century international law (which was often referred to as 'classical' international law). For them, legal theory had been soaked with power politics, imperialism, nationalism, blunt legal positivism and an irresponsible reverence for the modern nation state. Above all, they challenged what they denounced as the dogma of sovereignty.

Verdross is a rather controversial figure in twentieth-century international legal theory. Bruno Simma has claimed that he shaped central European international legal thinking 'in a way unparalleled in the past'. Martti Koskenniemi, by contrast, has practically ignored him. One reason seems to be that, in Koskenniemi's own phrase, Verdross's political and ideological 'alignments were obscure'.[50] Verdross was a Catholic, conservative nationalist (first all-German, then Austrian) who supported the authoritarian, right-wing regime of the *Ständestaat* (but also argued that it was unconstitutional) and showed some sympathies for National Socialist ideas in the 1930s. Supporters point out that he was closely scrutinized after the *Anschluss*, and classified as 'politically unreliable'. He was no longer allowed to teach legal philosophy.[51]

Whatever his political outlook, in international legal theory Verdross was rather close to the pacifist, universalist and liberal branch, and thus also to Hans Kelsen.[52] In particular, Verdross supported and refined Kelsen's theory of the primacy of international law. He argued that, historically speaking, the majority of international lawyers up to Johann Jakob Moser had endorsed international law-monism.[53] Verdross's monism can be labelled 'moderate': unlike Kelsen, Verdross holds that domestic law contradicting international law cannot be rendered null and void. Domestic rules have a provisional quality:

> From this follows that while international law may have *normative* priority over domestic law, the full *effectiveness* of the primacy of international law can only be reached if the individual states are given the opportunity – even without the consent of their opponent – to assert and pursue their claims regarding international law in a process of arbitration or in legal proceedings.[54]

The provisional quality is a result of the decentralized nature of international law; the normative conflicts with the pragmatic dimension, with legal efficiency. In a full juridical condition, both dimensions would coincide.

Verdross follows a general trend of international legal theory after the First World War: some aspects of the natural law tradition were rediscovered, especially in connection with the modern doctrine of international human rights.[55] International legal theory moved away from a wholesale endorsement of legal positivism. Scholars like Hugo Krabbe, James Brown Scott, Hersch Lauterpacht, Josef Kunz or Charles De Visscher challenged the positivists' rejection of natural law as a source of international law. Verdross in particular 'returned' to the Spanish scholastics, especially Francisco de Vitoria and Francisco Suarez.[56]

Verdross distinguishes between absolute and relative sovereignty. Up to the nineteenth century, Verdross claims, international legal theory perceived sovereignty as self-rule and independence from other states, while accepting that sovereign states are subject to the norms of the necessary as well as the positive law of nations. For Verdross, Vattel is a case in point. The (late) nineteenth century distorted this understanding of relative sovereignty, claiming that states are sovereign in an absolute sense, even independent from moral and legal norms.[57]

The early Verdross follows conventional doctrine when emphasizing that individuals are in principle not subjects of international law. Thus they have no legitimate claims pertaining to the law of nations against states. The rights of aliens (*Fremdenrecht*) are the body of norms specifying the duties of states *among themselves* how to treat foreigners. Verdross's approach is state-centred: aliens who do not belong to another state are excluded by definition.[58] The international rights of aliens are distinguished from the domestic sphere. Most norms are specified in bilateral treaties. Systematically, three parts can be distinguished: the admission of aliens, their legal status once admitted and their expulsion. The general principles (*droit international commun des étrangers*) are but a few, especially in terms of admission. Although states may not isolate themselves completely in an arbitrary fashion, they are not obliged to admit aliens for permanent settlement. Entry (*Einreise*) can be linked to specific requirements or even be refused out of 'reasonable causes (*vernünftige Gründe*)'. These causes are not specified. However, it would amount to an abuse of right (*abus de droit*) if a thinly populated country refused any immigration.[59] Verdross is one of the first to offer a short history of hospitality rights in the writings of the natural lawyers. He holds that there was a turning point in Wolff and Vattel, who, in his account, both opted for state sovereignty and weakened the previous emphasis on the international community. Verdross finally discovers a nineteenth-century *renaissance vitorienne* in the writings of authors such as Bluntschli.[60] As far as Wolff is concerned, Verdross's interpretation is probably mistaken (see Chapter 2), and his claim of a renaissance of ideas traced back to Francisco de Vitoria seems to be rather far-fetched. Verdross emphasizes the Christian idea of personality as one of the sources of the rights of aliens. However, he neither establishes a connection with modern human rights nor follows Vattel's dualistic approach, which left room for the moral dimension. Verdross sometimes hints at his moderate monism, where both domestic and international law are part of one single 'universal legal order'. The minimum-standard treatment is a case in point.[61]

Bruno Simma has argued that Verdross's international legal theory encompasses two dimensions: one is empirical and practice-oriented, the other is philosophical. The combination of both dimensions makes his theory unique.[62] Verdross's theory of the rights of aliens definitely belongs to the empirical strand, not moving beyond the positive law of nations. As in Martini and other international lawyers since the 1780s (see Chapter 5), natural law is merely supposed to replenish or complete positive legislation, and to offer the philosophical underpinnings of a moderate form of legal positivism. However, we may assume that Verdross believed that one of the tasks of the international lawyer is to develop positive law in a way that undermines the dogma of absolute state sovereignty, secures peace, fosters international cooperation and contributes to the emergence of a cosmopolitan commonwealth, as sketched by Vitoria.

Concluding remarks

My brief survey of selected international legal theories shows a considerable continuity of some arguments alongside existing diversity. For example, most authors emphasize discretion or a qualified concept of sovereignty. The list can be continued: in a manner reminiscent of Vattel, Michael Walzer argued in the 1980s that there is a legitimate right to self-determination. 'Admission and exclusion are at the core of communal independence.'⁶³ To take another example, the *Human Development Report 2004* pointed out, with an argument reminiscent of Pufendorf, that '[n]o country has advanced by closing its borders. International migration brings skills, labour and ideas, enriching people's lives.'⁶⁴

My survey also shows a recurrent problem concerning the right of immigration: the authors do not find clear-cut dividing lines, they oscillate between community or state sovereignty and international human rights, between legal positivism and natural law, between the interests of those inside and those outside, between *polis* and *cosmopolis*. When they wind up with some sort of middle position, it seems as if this is little more than some kind of hotchpotch.

I think that from a historical perspective and the perspective of normative international legal theory, we can draw the following conclusions. What can be supported is a thin conception of natural justice, with central criteria or features such as universalizability, impartiality, the idea of free and universal consent, and equality. Thin justice entails the rejection of direct and indirect injury. It provides a framework within which judgements of appraisal (or appreciative judgements) are made. One device to find impartial rules is Rawls's veil of ignorance, which filters out arbitrary elements because the persons in that situation lack the relevant information. Justice as impartiality is best understood as a rational feature and the result of abstraction. It is inconsistent with claims to special privileges or advantages, and thus entails a commitment to the equality of all humans. In the modern language of subjective rights focusing on external juridical freedom, this means that '[e]ach person is to have an equal right to the most extensive total system of equal basic liberties compatible with a similar system of liberty for all'.⁶⁵

A thin conception of justice is indispensable for any rational discourse on international legal theory or immigration rights. This is why another pupil of Kelsen, Hersch Lauterpacht, has passionately defended the idea of natural law. He readily admits that natural law lends itself to abuse:

> However, exaggeration and abuse ought not to determine the fate of an otherwise beneficient idea. *Ab abusu ad usum non valet consequentia.* We would rather retain natural law with its possible abuses than cut

off the branch of law from the tree of justice. We would rather err in pursuit of a good life for all than glory in the secure infallibility of moral indifference. It is true that justice is invoked by selfish interests, but that is a poor reason for dispensing with it altogether.[66]

The idea of natural justice leads to two core arguments in favour of the right of immigration, one revolving around the idea of an original community and the second one based on the idea of impartiality. The idea of an original community, developed by thinkers such as Pufendorf and Vattel and taken up by lawyers such as Verdross, was refined by Kant, whose approach combined empirical with *a priori* elements. The empirical or *a posteriori* ones are but two. First, land is by nature continuous and limited. No section of land is absolutely separate from others; even water can be crossed. The earth has a spherical surface. Humans are thus 'enclosed . . . within determinate limits.'[67] Secondly, humans thus cannot avoid coming into contact with others, and their use of external freedom of choice may conflict with the use of others. Kant claims an inevitable conflict of unrestrained, 'wild' freedom, no matter how human nature is perceived. The universal element is expressed by the principles of equality, the innate right to freedom, and impartiality. No one has a right to determine unilaterally the limits of the land to which he or she is entitled. They must be determined by the united will of all, or their rational, hypothetical consent. Therefore, private ownership presupposes original collective possession, not as an empirical fact, but as a rational concept. In his preliminary work, Kant writes:

> Thus one has to *conceive* the idea of a general, united power of choice as an act of jurisdiction through which everyone's place is of necessity determined by a general will; that is to say a *universal property* (communio originaria) from which every possible ownership is derived.[68]

If we want to think of (individual) ownership consistently and universally, we have to conceptualize original collective possession. Kant argues for a form of legal cosmopolitanism that is rooted in his natural (or rational) law theory – and thus based on natural law cosmopolitanism (see Chapter 1). The crucial concepts are the general will, universal property, and the idea of justice. One might infer that this reasoning implies if not open then at least porous borders, as borders only have provisional legitimacy and state sovereignty is subordinated to the legislating authority of the original community.

The second argument in favour of the right of immigration runs as follows: if we understand Rawls's theory of the veil of ignorance as a method of arriving at rules based on the idea of natural justice, then we may wind up with a natural right to immigrate. 'Behind the "veil of ignorance", in considering possible restrictions on freedom, one adopts the perspective of the one who would be most disadvantaged by the restrictions, in this case the perspective of the alien who wants to immigrate.'[69] We might say that some of the authors dealt with in this chapter aim at adopting an impartial perspective when dealing with immigration rights, considering, among others, the rights of foreigners, non-Europeans or the disadvantaged.

The right to immigrate has to be qualified, in the first place because of what Carens calls 'public order restriction'. This argument leads to a qualified right of self-determination of communities, provided their institutional arrangements and their political cultures are compatible with the principles of natural justice. The international lawyers of this chapter integrated some form of 'public order restriction' into their theories. At the end of the day, it is a matter of discretion and judgement whether immigrants should be admitted or not. As Carens puts it: 'We have to weigh the claims of those trying to get in equally with the claims of those who are already inside, but to do that we have to know something about the nature of those claims.'[70] Pufendorf and other natural lawyers defended a similar position with different words. This does not mean that decisions are arbitrary. They have to reflect features of natural justice such as impartiality and equality.

7 • Conclusion

In this conclusion, I want to relate issues raised in previous chapters to present-day cosmopolitan discourses, and point to continuities. Past answers may not help us find solutions to contemporary problems, but they may encourage us to clarify our own thinking about problems, contexts and possible answers.

Chapter 2 argued for a nuanced assessment of several international lawyers. We may want to know why we do not get a coherent, uniform Western legal discourse, but a variety of positions and perspectives. Martine van Ittersum has offered a geographical argument, claiming that, in contrast to authors who belonged to maritime powers (Grotius or Locke), continental writers like Pufendorf or Wolff had no reason to justify colonialism, as they belonged to 'those parts of Europe that missed out on the riches of the Indies'. In addition, Ittersum asserts, these continental writers 'saw a clear connection between the dispossession of the native and recent events in German history', namely the Thirty Years' War.[1] The second claim is mere speculation; we do not have any evidence that Pufendorf or Wolff related colonial events to central European politics of their times. The first part of the argument is challenged by conflicting evidence: there were writers who were subjects of colonial powers and still they did not condone colonialism or nineteenth-century imperialism. Examples are Burke, Bentham, Diderot or Condorcet (see Chapter 3).[2]

I think that three reasons explain why the authors in the second chapter are so different from each other. First, it is plausible to claim that many – probably not all – authors who justified colonialism were too close to politics, or themselves involved in colonial practices. As Jennifer Pitts shows, John Stuart Mill, James Mill or Alexis de Tocqueville were 'active in the politics and administration of the British and French empires' – just like Locke or Grotius.[3] It seems that those deeply involved with colonial politics were unable to practise the kind of impartiality that is a precondition of intellectual and moral cosmopolitanisms. Secondly, the natural lawyers' interest in the idea of justice, natural rights and the social contract probably helped them to overcome their own bias, whereas more positivist lawyers like Vattel were looking at state and colonial practices rather than abstract principles, and tried to integrate these practices into their respective legal frameworks instead of criticizing them. Finally, I like to think that those who (partly) realized a cosmopolitan attitude practised the kind of autonomy in thinking that is intertwined with epistemological cosmopolitanism. I agree with Amanda Anderson who attacks the 'complacent hermeneutics of suspicion' so widespread among many contemporary historians, and their 'cynical certainty' that past authors necessarily failed in their attempts, whatever they may have been.[4] This complacent and perhaps arrogant attitude may turn into simple bias and ideology.

It is fascinating to see that a theologian like Francisco de Vitoria has succeeded in remaining partly relevant today, as an accepted legal source of indigenous rights.[5] In the words of one interpreter, 'a Christian cosmopolitanism' counterbalanced and corrected the colonial aspirations of the Castilian crown.[6] However, we should not become overly enthusiastic. The idea of a universal natural law was compatible with a hierarchy of races in the past. Moral or human rights cosmopolitanism was often imperfect, half-hearted or half-baked.

Philosophically speaking, human rights cosmopolitanism faces at least two major challenges. First, there are the cultural and historical relativists who claim that (moral) cosmopolitanism is Eurocentric rather than universal, and a product of European history.[7] Others vehemently deny the relativist challenge, among them so-called 'non-Europeans' (an unfortunate term, but I have no better) like Amartya Sen, Kwame Anthony Appiah or Ananta Kumar Giri. They point at cosmopolitan traditions beyond Europe and try to show that cosmopolitanisms are not necessarily Eurocentric.[8] Many believe that some, but not all forms of cosmopolitanisms are Eurocentric. Jan Nederveen Pieterse, for instance, puts it bluntly: 'The Eurocentrism of much cosmopolitanism is a familiar story (from Plato to NATO).' He looks for alternative forms of 'cosmovisions' beyond Europe, in the Islamic world or in the Chinese view 'All under Heaven', among others.[9] What he finds there seem to be additional versions of moral cosmopolitanism. Many opt for a critical, dialogic or emancipatory cosmopolitanism as a regulative principle which takes 'emergent multiversality' and worldwide pluralism into account.[10]

The second challenge is the functional ambivalence of human rights. As Costas Douzinas has shown, they can be a critical standard, a tool of opposing oppression, resisting domination or exploitation. In short: 'Human rights are part of a long and honourable tradition of dissent, resistance and rebellion against the oppression of power and the injustice of law.'[11] On the other hand, human rights can help to stabilize social organization, to conduct politics, or serve the interests of the leading classes. They can turn into an ideology. In spite of this functional deficiency, it seems that human rights discourses do not have a non-Western alternative. This statement implies that these discourses are intrinsically 'Western' – something that is not at all clear. Be that as it may, I assume that in the end the outcome is a very thin version of human rights or moral cosmopolitanism, if any.

If we try to summarize the third chapter in one sentence, we might say that commercial society and Adam Smith have won over Fletcher's modified civic humanism. It seems that forms of indirect, long-term economic cosmopolitanism have become more widespread in today's Britain than its contractual version. Even pro-European attitudes are rather marginal. Today most Britons side with *The Economist* which is happy that the European Union is not 'much more than just a free-trade area' and resents the idea of a European superstate: 'a headlong drive towards political and even military integration will be resisted'.[12]

The overall trend depicted in the chapter is in need of some clarification. Commercial cosmopolitanism in the eighteenth century was not a uniquely British phenomenon. Dietrich Hermann Hegewisch is a case in point. Like some British authors, he criticized mercantilism, advocated free trade, the free movement of labour and the right to emigrate. Economic cosmopolitans were not necessarily conservative or right-wing liberals, to use modern terminology. Cloots was, by contemporary standards, a left-wing revolutionary, but favoured global free trade.[13] Adam Smith was not the simpleton who had an unshakable belief in the self-regulative capacity of the free-market economy. His doctrine of an invisible hand can only be properly understood if it is seen within the wider framework of a deistic theology, where the market is part of and subordinated to a superior design of a pre-established harmony of ends. Smith was not a precursor of Manchester laissez-faire liberalism, a proponent of the minimal state and of functional, 'value-free' economics, but a moral philosopher who considered natural jurisprudence the 'most important' science, contributed to the eighteenth-century discourse of the 'science of a legislator', and attempted to combine ethics and economy in a comprehensive system. While Smith tried to eliminate the government's influence on market processes and outcomes, he advocated government intervention in many diverse areas. Smith's moral balance sheet of commercial society is subtle, mixing apologetic and critical elements, and forcefully exposes the ambivalences, paradoxes and negative side-effects of commercial progress.[14] Smith's commercial cosmopolitanism is embedded within a wider framework of weak moral cosmopolitanism.[15] It seems that only Bentham and later economists developed a full-blown utilitarian ethics, where expediency and efficiency are the ultimate justifying principles.

Contemporary globalization is often seen as a triumph of global free-marketeers. Strong economic cosmopolitanism is usually advocated by economists like Hayek or Friedman, and criticized by philosophers. Their key argument is that economic cosmopolitanism cannot guarantee (economic) justice or, more strongly, that the globalized market is (partly) the cause rather than the cure of international economic inequality. Pieterse, for instance, sees an imbalance between state, society and market forces in favour of the latter.[16] The process of this imbalance is called globalization, the corresponding background theory (or ideology) neo-liberalism. Emancipatory cosmopolitans like Habermas or Benhabib fight economic (or capitalist) cosmopolitanism – sometimes labelled worldwide neo-liberalism – with the help of moral and/or political cosmopolitanisms.

In an attempt to bring cosmopolitan ideals from the lofty heights of philosophy down to the everyday practice of ordinary life, Jeremy Waldron has pointed at the ancient *lex mercatoria* and the emergence of customary norms along trading routes and in commercial societies.

> The example of commerce ... is appealed to as a prototype of how the mundane growth of repeated contact between different humans and different human groups can lay the foundation for the emergence of cosmopolitan norms, in a way that does not necessarily presuppose a formal juridical apparatus.[17]

This repeats the arguments of indirect economic cosmopolitanism, offered by some authors in the Chapter 3. The advantage of this bottom-up approach is that it is fully compatible with local loyalties like patriotism, and assumes that it can do without political or legal cosmopolitanism. As Seyla Benhabib points out in her reply, the key disadvantage is that repeated contact alone 'is absolutely no guarantee of the spread of a cosmopolitan point of view that considers all human beings as individuals equally entitled to certain rights'.[18] This argument brings us back to moral cosmopolitanism, its asserted primacy over economic cosmopolitanism, and the question how it can be promoted (Nussbaum favours education, Benhabib democratic iteration). However, I do not think that Waldron's line of reasoning is proven invalid: economic cosmopolitanism may not guarantee moral cosmopolitanism, but it may prepare the ground for it. Benhabib in turn runs into the quandaries of human rights cosmopolitanism mentioned previously, especially cultural and historical relativism: if moral cosmopolitanism can be defended, then only a very thin version, which makes it difficult to back up criticism of contemporary global inequalities.

One may argue that these inequalities demand 'a formal juridical apparatus' – to use Jeremy Waldron's phrase – to combat them. In other words, moral cosmopolitanism would require institutionalization, legalization or 'juridification' of rights, and thus strong political cosmopolitanism. This leads us to Chapter 4. Remember that Kant argued that the lawless state of nature made a global social contract and a world republic 'logically necessary'. According to the modified argument, gross global economic inequalities as a state of moral lawlessness require cosmopolitan moral/social institutions that would overcome this very inequality.

I have already mentioned in the introduction that many, probably most, present-day cosmopolitans vehemently deny that they favour a world state.[19] Many also assert that Kant 'was against it'.[20] This is surprising, given the widespread admiration of Kant as one of the leading cosmopolitan philosophers, and given the fact that Kant not only advocated a world government but also asserted that it was the logical outcome of rational analysis. If we take Kant's ideal and compare it with contemporary world politics and international law, then we have at best just begun to realize his ideal, and the steps the international community has taken so far are rather meagre, to put it mildly.[21]

There are some voices who warn that present cosmopolitans should not neglect institutional concerns, or, as a bold thesis, that moral implies strong political or legal cosmopolitanism. Charles Jones, for instance, sees individuals as too weak to bring about change on a global scale, so they have an obligation to develop institutions or 'collectivities' which can do the job. Andrew Hurrell of the so-called English School claims that moral principles and ideas 'can be meaningfully and persuasively defended, justified, and criticized' worldwide only if three conditions are met, namely 'moral accessibility, institutional stability, and effective political agency'. As a consequence, keeping the present, state-based international system is 'extremely problematic'.[22]

Contemporary moral cosmopolitans would counter with the thesis that weak political cosmopolitanism will do, especially as there have been new developments since Kant's time which could be paraphrased as 'cosmopolitanism from below': the emergence of a global civil society and of transnational institutions, the new legal status of individuals in international law, a liberal understanding of sovereignty which emphasizes common values such as human rights and democratic principles, and so on.[23] In other words, the pragmatic argument against Kant is that the present international system works quite well without a world government, but with additional legal and quasi-legal arrangements. This takes us to the international lawyers of the fifth chapter.

First, let me emphasize again the complexity of the story: the seventeenth and eighteenth centuries should be seen as an era with multiple, overlapping discourses. We encountered, among others, the colonial discourses of Grotius, Locke and the like, which coincided with the rise of cosmopolitan thinking, reaching its peak around 1800. By that time, various sophisticated cosmopolitan theories had been developed. There was definitely no linear development from the cosmopolitan tendencies of the natural lawyers to the Eurocentrism of the 1850s and beyond. In fact, critics of empire were very outspoken in England and France especially in the 1780s; after that, 'imperial liberalism' (Jennifer Pitts) gradually gained the upper hand. Eurocentric theories were developed in the crucial period between 1780 and 1830.[24] Chapter 5 also followed the rise of legal positivism, which had yet another Eurocentric consequence: only European-style states were considered subjects of international law.

The reader might have seen from my tone that I have little sympathy for the mainstream international lawyers of the late eighteenth century and their positivist tendencies, and a lot of sympathy for Kant. Chapter 6 (in the section on Alfred Verdross) pointed at the half-hearted return to natural law elements in the new international legal theory after the First World War. Since then, more elements of this kind, such as the doctrine of international human rights or references to 'the common good' of the international community, have been incorporated into the body of international law. Lawyers, philosophers and historians alike do of course disagree how to assess these changes. Some argue that we have moved – even if only slightly – 'towards an international law of the world citizen'.[25] This becomes evident if we look at the new status of individuals in international law. The way in which a state treats its own citizens is no longer regarded as a purely internal matter, breaking down the former neat distinction between municipal and international laws. Individuals can be recognized actors in international law, for instance as war criminals. In 2003, the International Criminal Court was established, which some read as 'an implicit recognition that we are all world citizens in the sense of being bound by an embryonic world law and answerable for any transgressions'.[26]

As previously mentioned, these developments are open to divergent interpretations. However, one accepted approach is the 'international community school' (Bardo Fassbender), which rejects nineteenth-century emphasis on state sovereignty and the will and consent of states, and stresses instead the international community and 'certain common values' irrespective of state consent. Alfred Verdross and Bruno Simma have mentioned the theologians of the Second Scholastic and the natural lawyers before the advent of legal positivism as its founding fathers, Christian Tomuschat touched upon Francisco Suárez and Christian Wolff (see Chapter 2). In particular, 'elementary considerations of morality' are integrated into the legal framework, as Tomuschat put it, referring to the Corfu Channel judgment and other legal documents of the International Court of Justice.[27] This means that Hans Kelsen's project of a 'pure science of law' has been abandoned, in favour of what can be called a synthesis of legal, moral and political considerations, blending empirical with rational arguments (see Chapter 5). In the words of Tomuschat: '[A]ny system of governance, including the constitution of the international community, is rooted in certain values whose substance may oscillate between a purely political and, additionally, a legal dimension.'[28] Above all, this means that elements of moral cosmopolitanism are integrated into the design of international law.

This intrusion of 'international morality' (or the lip-service paid to it) becomes obvious in the case of humanitarian intervention and the return of just-war theorizing, especially in the wake of 9/11.[29] As usual, the relevant cases allow for divergent interpretations and political judgements. It is not at all clear if the interventions and wars have helped the case of moral or political cosmopolitanisms, or just brought an increase in humanitarian and cosmopolitan rhetoric. At any rate, they have often been carried out in the name of the international community, and intellectual debates have often relied on a cosmopolitan ethic. According to this perspective, humanitarian intervention is not just organized violence, but cosmopolitan law-enforcement to stop criminals from committing more crimes.[30] There may be some parallels between Thomas Paine's 'messianic interventionism' (Chapter 3) and the neo-interventionism of the Bush administration (2001–8).

All this implies that contemporary international legal theory has moved away from what Vattel, Martini, Moser or Martens wrote in the eighteenth century. They eyed interventions with scepticism, did not have any notion of international human rights, and favoured a cultural understanding of Europe over the concept of an international community. However, there is some continuity: an implicit defence of the balance of power and the rejection of a world government, the emphasis on the positive law of nations, the vague inclusion of elements of international morality, and a methodology which combines legal, moral and political elements.

In Chapter 6, I looked at international lawyers from Pufendorf to Verdross, who shared some similarities. If we brutally press their varieties into a unified picture, we might say that they offered a synthesis of legal positivism and natural law elements, displayed a pro-immigration attitude, but also emphasized the sovereign rights of communities. The admission of immigrants was seen as a matter of discretion. They posited an imperfect duty to promote friendship and sociability, but with ample leeway for communities. These specifications amount to a qualified right to immigrate, and this is what many contemporary authors argue for, among them Seyla Benhabib, Joseph Carens, Bernd Ladwig or Omid A. Payrow Shabani.[31] In spite of many differences, these authors, I think, agree that state sovereignty cannot be the ultimate justifying principle, but they aim at adopting an impartial, cosmopolitan perspective when dealing with immigration rights, they integrate some form of 'public order restriction' into their theories, imply that it is a matter of judgement whether immigrants should be admitted or not, but assert that these judgements should reflect universal features such as impartiality and equality. Most conclude in favour of borders which should be neither closed nor open, but porous.

I believe these are also considerations of the authors presented in Chapter 6. What has changed is the scale of migration, increasing almost sixfold from 1910 to 2000. Currently there are roughly 20 million refugees, asylum seekers and 'internally displaced persons' worldwide.[32] This has led to a string of new problems, from challenges to nation-based concepts of citizenship to problems of integration, the rise of populist anti-immigration parties and the looming fear that by the end of this century, for instance, Europe will be Islamic 'at the very latest', as Princeton historian Bernard Lewis put it. 'The battle lines are being drawn up between the mono- and multiculturalists and between nationalist and cosmopolitan views of the future.'[33]

Are there any 'lessons' we can draw from the cosmopolitan theories presented in this book? One lesson might be a general scepticism towards contemporary enthusiasm concerning cosmopolitanism. Many still do not seem to realize how deeply cosmopolitan currents were involved in colonialism and European expansion, that not all moral cosmopolitan theories were emancipatory, and how ambiguous the cosmopolitan heritage is. I have also pointed to historically uninformed recent studies in the Introduction. We do find some common themes reiterated or recycled since the eighteenth century: for instance, the thesis of compatibility of cosmopolitanism and patriotism, the concentric circles imagery or the problem of cosmopolitan rhetoric. When Brett Bowden claims that authors have 'rarely ... attempted to mediate' between patriotism, nationalism and cosmopolitanism and claims some originality for his own attempt, he fails to mention the many predecessors in this enterprise, from Basedow, Rebmann and Wieland to Goethe, Krug, Bouterwek, Fichte, Kant, Humboldt, Novalis and Herder, if we list only late eighteenth-century German thinkers. As Siegfried

Weichlein puts it: 'In Germany, cosmopolitan patriotism of all sorts empowered the state and its bureaucracy through its moral code and rhetoric.'[34] When Martha Nussbaum refers to the concentric circles imagery since Greek antiquity, she does so with full awareness of this popular picture, also and especially since the eighteenth century, and puts herself into this long tradition.[35] When Ulrich Beck, in an attempt to find traces of modernity's second cosmopolitan age, claims that 'former US Secretary of State Madeline Albright established a link between a very American, that is national, foreign policy and a human rights policy that is primarily guided by normative standards', we are reminded of Hugo Grotius and his very clever and successful effort to hide particularist interests behind the cloak of cosmopolitan rhetoric.[36] Albright herself, to her credit, was more self-critical when she later regretted her remarks on the UN sanctions regime – which led to the death of up to half a million Iraqi children – as indefensible. In 1996, Albright had asserted that her 'first responsibility' was towards the United States, even if that meant the death of children. In her autobiography (2003), she displayed the cosmopolitan attitude of a mournful sinner: 'Nothing matters more than the lives of innocent people. I had fallen into a trap and said something that I simply did not mean.'[37] This shows not only that cosmopolitanism lends itself to political abuse (of course it does), that those deeply involved with politics are often unable to practise the impartiality that is a precondition of intellectual and moral cosmopolitanisms (see above), it also illustrates that cosmopolitanism may be just an empty label for an academic agenda (in the case of Beck).

This takes me to another element of continuity: Rousseau attacked what could be labelled thick cultural cosmopolitanism – or, rather, Europeanism – that is, the belief that a single thick conception of the good life should spread all over the globe, swallowing existing cultures and traditions. Rousseau also dismissed economic or commercial cosmopolitanism, doubting that commerce is primarily beneficial, as Montesquieu, Adam Smith and others had claimed (see Chapter 3). Finally, Rousseau criticized the natural law cosmopolitanism of Samuel Pufendorf and Denise Diderot (as mentioned, natural law cosmopolitanism was an early form of moral cosmopolitanism). Rousseau's attack on the 'supposed cosmopolites' (who are merely hypocrites) apparently aimed at making room for genuine moral and political cosmopolitanisms.

One element of this theory is what can be labelled republican cosmopolitanism, which shares several features with Kant and Cloots (see Chapters 4 and 5), but especially with John Oswald or Friedrich Schlegel, as Rousseau advocated an alliance of republics. Like Appiah, Rousseau offers a version of thin, embedded cosmopolitanism.[38]

It is evident from this brief summary that several elements of this elaborate and early attack on forms of cosmopolitanism are reiterated in contemporary criticisms. Like Rousseau, some reject cosmopolitan theories from communitarian positions (but often without advancing to Rousseau's attempted synthesis).[39] Like Rousseau, the reluctant realist, neo-realist Danilo Zolo expresses his doubts about strong legal or political cosmopolitanism. He rehearses often-repeated arguments against a world government (which go back at least to Grotius), claiming that 'it could not emerge as anything other than a despotic totalitarian Leviathan'. The normative theories of weak political cosmopolitans such as David Held are derided as 'wishful thinking', as their goals are 'certainly unrealizable in the foreseeable future' and, in addition, 'of limited desirability'.[40] Finally, there are left-wing authors who attack globalization, neo-liberalism and US 'cultural imperialism', asserting that the current cosmopolitan discourse is mainly an imperial ideology tied to US and EU hegemony (Timothy Brennan, David Chandler, Peter Gowan) or runs the risk of 'becoming the normative gloss of globalised capitalism at its imperial stage' (Costas Douzinas).[41] The weapon of these attacks is often a weak form of moral cosmopolitanism. This is particularly obvious in the case of Douzinas, who offers in a concluding chapter the vision of a 'cosmopolitanism to come', which remains somewhat vague but contains the contours of a left-wing emancipatory cosmopolitanism revolving around cosmopolitan justice, a progressive understanding of human rights, normative individualism and the utopian tradition.[42] It would certainly be far-fetched and anachronistic to claim that Rousseau was a left-wing critic of capitalism, but his distrust of western commercial society and civilization, his assertion that both had destroyed moral potential, and his endeavours to find remedies, is a distant basis of these criticisms.

If I have stressed continuities since the eighteenth century, I do not want to suggest that contemporary debates merely recycle familiar themes. A lot is new under the sun. For instance, Toni Erskine has offered a creative and stimulating attempt to go beyond familiar dichotomies in her book *Embedded Cosmopolitanism*. She tends to decontextualize philosophy, for instance, when she claims that '[i]mpartialist cosmopolitanism denies that the state can have intrinsic moral value'.[43] I suppose that a historically sensitive approach would arrive at a different assessment. Wolff, Rousseau, Kant and some other mostly forgotten cosmopolitans of the late eighteenth century might be interpreted as offering impartialist versions of cosmopolitanism, while claiming that the state does have 'intrinsic moral value'. However, these are trifles compared with the overall thesis, which clearly goes beyond eighteenth-century attempts at a synthesis. Erskine contrasts 'embedded' and 'impartialist' cosmopolitanisms, and deliberately tries to avoid impartiality as the basis of her cosmopolitan position. Her starting point is situated or embedded, while the overall moral theory claims to be truly cosmopolitan. As her discussion of the cosmopolitan–communitarian dichotomy shows, Erskine wants to find a middle ground, beyond the conventional assumptions that genuine cosmopolitanism has to be impartial, while communitarianism is always embedded, parochial and state- or community-centred. According to Erskine, the traditional image of concentric circles is misleading and should be replaced by 'the figure of a web of intersecting and overlapping morally relevant ties'.[44]

It is significant that many critics of cosmopolitanism do not dismiss cosmopolitanism out of hand. There is a growing awareness that economic and cultural globalization, economic, ecological and pandemic crises, and the proliferation of weapons of mass destruction push societies away from nineteenth-century style nation-states. These and other forces have the power to 'foster the sense of connectedness with distant strangers', as Andrew Linklater puts it.[45] These historical developments raise questions of accountability and political agency across borders, and they may create a new sociocultural condition. In the end, the question may no longer run: 'cosmopolitanism, yes or no'? But: 'which type of cosmopolitanism, economic, cultural, political or moral, thick or thin'?[46] Or, more precisely: which form of cosmopolitanism should take the lead, which one should be supported?

This book has looked at several answers to these questions, in very different historical contexts. I do not claim that these answers help us to find our own solutions to contemporary problems, but they may help to clarify our own thinking about problems, contexts and possible answers. I chose the title 'imperfect cosmopolis' for several reasons. First, the cosmopolitans in this book were still the very small community of sages referred to in Greek antiquity (some argue that they have remained a tiny minority until today). Secondly, most of them defended a weak, moderate form of cosmopolitanism, not very different from the kind of 'third way' between the local, the rooted, the ethnos on the one hand and the global, the universal, the species on the other, something contemporary philosophers like Appiah are searching for.[47] Thirdly, their cosmopolitan theories probably deserve the label 'mono-cultural', in spite of all occasional openness towards non-European cultures. After all, this book also delineates the rise of Europeanism. There is the possibility that many did no more than pay lip-service to the idea of cosmopolitanism.

This book is part of and has contributed to a mainly western discourse; the wider and more complex genealogy of cosmopolitanism has not yet been fully researched. Therefore, fully aware of my own monocultural approach, I want to finish with a hint at this wider perspective, quoting from one of the articles of the Ghanaian cosmopolitan philosopher Kwame Anthony Appiah, who translates the Asante proverb *Kuro koro mu nni nyansa* as 'In a single *polis* there is no wisdom.'[48]

Notes

Introduction

1 Steven Vertovec and Robin Cohen, 'Introduction: conceiving cosmopolitanism', in *Conceiving Cosmopolitanism: Theory, Context, and Practice* (Oxford, 2002), pp. 1–22, David A. Hollinger, 'Not universalists, not pluralists: the new cosmopolitans find their own way', ibid., pp. 227–39, Gillian Brock and Harry Brighouse (eds), *The Political Philosophy of Cosmopolitanism* (Cambridge, 2005), Ananta Kumar Giri, 'Cosmopolitanism and beyond: towards a multiverse of transformations', *Development and Change*, 37, 6 (2006), 1277–92, James Brassett, 'Cosmopolitanism vs. Terrorism? Discourses of ethical possibility before and after 7/7', *Millennium: Journal of International Studies*, 36, 2 (2008), 121–47, Helen Dexter, 'The "New War" on terror, cosmopolitanism and the "Just War" revival', *Government and Opposition*, 43, 1 (2008), 55–78.
2 Gerard Delanty and Chris Rumford, *Rethinking Europe: Social Theory and the Implications of Europeanization* (London and New York, 2005), p. 84; Robert Frith, 'Cosmopolitan democracy and the EU: the case of gender', *Political Studies*, 56 (2008), 215–36.
3 Patricia Broser and Dana Pfeiferová (eds), *Der Dichter als Kosmopolit: Zum Kosmopolitismus in der neuesten österreichischen Literatur* (Wien, 2003), especially pp. 7–12.
4 John Cameron, 'Reflections on cosmopolitanism and capabilities', *Development and Change*, 37, 6 (2006), 1273-6, at p. 1274.
5 Vertovec and Cohen, 'Introduction', p. 21; Hollinger, 'Universalists', p. 228; Jan Nederveen Pieterse, 'Emancipatory cosmopolitanism: towards an agenda', *Development and Change*, 37, 6 (2006), 1247–57.
6 Daniel Chernilo, 'A quest for universalism: re-assessing the nature of classical social theory's cosmopolitanism', *European Journal of Social Theory*, 10, 1 (2007), 17–35, at p. 31.
7 Sheldon Pollock, Homi K. Bhabha, Carol A. Breckenridge and Dipesh Chakrabarty, 'Cosmopolitanisms', in Carol A. Breckenridge et al. (eds), *Cosmopolitanism* (Durham, NC and London, 2002), pp. 1–14, at p. 1.

8   See the overviews in Derek Heater, *World Citizenship: Cosmopolitan Thinking and its Opponents* (London and New York, 2002), pp. 7–25, Rebecka Lettevall and My Klockar Linder (eds), *The Idea of Kosmopolis: History, Philosophy and Politics of World Citizenship* (Huddinge, 2008), pp. 5–12, Andrea Albrecht, *Kosmopolitismus: Weltbürgerdiskurse in Literatur, Philosophie und Publizistik um 1800* (Berlin and New York, 2005), pp. 1–6.
9   David Held, *Democracy and the Global Order: From the Modern State to Cosmopolitan Governance* (Oxford, 1995), p. 233. See also pp. 270–5 and David Held, *Cosmopolitanism: A Defence* (Cambridge, 2003), Daniele Archibugi and David Held (eds), *Cosmopolitan Democracy: An Agenda for a New World Order* (Cambridge, 1995), Daniele Archibugi, David Held, and Martin Köhler (eds), *Re-imagining Political Community: Studies in Cosmopolitan Democracy* (Cambridge, 1998), and the publications listed in Frith, 'Democracy', pp. 233–6, Daniele Archibugi, 'Cosmopolitan democracy and its critics: a review', *European Journal of International Relations*, 10, 3 (2004), 437–73, at pp. 467–73, and Klaus Dingwerth and Philipp Pattberg, 'Global governance as a perspective on world politics', *Global Governance*, 12 (2006), 185–203.
10 Martha C. Nussbaum, 'Patriotism and cosmopolitanism,' in *For Love of Country?* ed. Joshua Cohen (Boston, 2002), pp. 3–17, the quotation at p. 4. See the excellent review essay by Veit Bader, 'For love of country', *Political Theory*, 27, 3 (1999), 379–97.
11 Seyla Benhabib, *The Rights of Others: Aliens, Residents, and Citizens* (Cambridge, 2004), p. 3, 'The philosophical foundations of cosmopolitan norms', in *Another Cosmopolitanism: With Commentaries by Jeremy Waldron, Bonnie Honig and Will Kymlicka*, ed. Robert Post (Oxford, 2006), pp. 13–44, at p. 20, 'Democratic iterations: the local, the national, and the global', ibid., pp. 45–82, at p. 49.
12 Kwame Anthony Appiah, *Cosmopolitanism: Ethics in a World of Strangers* (New York, 2007), pp. 151, XV and 163.
13 Jürgen Habermas, *The Inclusion of the Other: Studies in Political Theory*, ed. C. Cronin and P. De Greiff (Cambridge, MA and London, 1998), *Postnational Constellation: Political Essays*, trans. M. Pensky (Cambridge, MA and London, 2001), and *Postmetaphysical Thinking: Philosophical Essays*, trans. W. M. Hohengarten (Cambridge, MA and London, 1992). See the summary of Habermas's ideas in Michael Scrivener, *The Cosmopolitan Ideal in the Age of Revolution and Reaction, 1776–1832* (London, 2007), pp. 19–25.
14 The key work is Ulrich Beck, *The Cosmopolitan Vision* (Cambridge, 2006). The quotation is in Beck, 'The cosmopolitan society and its enemies', *Theory, Culture and Society*, 19, 1–2 (2002), 17–44, at

p. 18. See also Ulrich Beck, 'The cosmopolitan perspective: sociology in the second age of modernity', in Vertovec and Cohen, *Cosmopolitanism*, pp. 61–85.

15 Angelika Poferl and Natan Sznaider (eds), *Ulrich Becks kosmopolitisches Projekt: auf dem Weg in eine andere Soziologie* (Baden-Baden, 2004), Susanne Fuchs and Michael Zürn, 'Kosmopolitismus als Großtheorie?', *Zeitschrift für Internationale Beziehungen*, 13, 2 (2006), 247–54.

16 Jacques Derrida, *Of Hospitality: Anne Dufourmantelle Invites Jacques Derrida to Respond* (Stanford, California, 2000) and *Cosmopolitanism and Forgiveness* (Stanford, California, 2001); David J. Gauthier, 'Levinas and the politics of hospitality', *History of Political Thought*, 28, 1 (2007), 158–80; Kok-Chor Tan, *Justice Without Borders: Cosmopolitanism, Nationalism and Patriotism* (Cambridge, 2004); Massimo La Torre, 'Global citizenship? political rights under imperial conditions', *Ratio Juris*, 18, 2 (2005), 236–57; Robert Fine, *Cosmopolitanism* (London, 2007); Toni Erskine, *Embedded Cosmopolitanism: Duties to Strangers and Enemies in a World of 'Dislocated Communities'* (Oxford, 2008).

17 Albrecht, *Kosmopolitismus*, pp. 5–10.

18 Frith, 'Democracy', p. 218. See also Benhabib, 'Foundations', p. 23, Danilo Zolo, *Cosmopolis: Prospects for World Government* (Cambridge, 1997), p. IX, Deiniol Jones, 'The origins of the global city: ethics and morality in contemporary cosmopolitanism', *British Journal of Politics and International Relations*, 5, 1 (2003), 50–73, at p. 52, and Vertovec and Cohen, 'Introduction', pp. 2, 8, Beck, 'Perspective', p. 64.

19 Randall Lesaffer, 'Peace treaties from Lodi to Westphalia', in Randall Lesaffer (ed.), *Peace Treaties and International Law in European History: From the Late Middle Ages to World War One* (Cambridge, 2004), pp. 9–44, at p. 9 and, more extensively, Bardo Fassbender, 'Die verfassungs- und völkerrechtsgeschichtliche Bedeutung des Westfälischen Friedens von 1648', in Ingo Erberich et al. (eds), *Frieden und Recht. 38. Tagung der Wissenschaftlichen Mitarbeiterinnen und Mitarbeiter der Fachrichtung "Öffentliches Recht"*, Münster 1998 (Stuttgart, 1998), pp. S. 9–52.

20 Heinhard Steiger, 'From the international law of Christianity to the international law of the world citizen – reflections on the formation of the epochs of the history of international law', *Journal of the History of International Law*, 3 (2001), 180–93, especially p. 183.

21 Robert Wokler, 'The Enlightenment Project as betrayed by modernity', *History of European Ideas*, 24, 4–5 (1998), 301–13, at p. 302. Wokler claims that, with some justification, we can speak of an Enlightenment

Project, but that it was betrayed by modernity in the wake of the French Revolution. Sankar Muthu, *Enlightenment against Empire* (Princeton and Oxford, 2003), pp. 260–6, among others, drops the concept. Daniel Chernilo, 'A quest for universalism: re-assessing the nature of classical social theory's cosmopolitanism', *European Journal of Social Theory*, 10, 1 (2007), 17–35, at p. 32, refers to the 'cosmopolitan tradition', but without adequate conceptual clarification.

22   Rüdiger Görner, 'Kosmopolitismus contra Globalismus? Oder: Einleitende Weltbezüge', in Suzanne Kirkbright (ed.), *Cosmopolitans in the Modern World: Studies on a Theme in German and Austrian Literary Culture* (München, 2000), pp. 9–17, at p. 9 refers to the 'project' of Enlightenment cosmopolitanism. See also Walter D. Mignolo, 'The many faces of cosmo-polis: border thinking and critical cosmopolitanism', in Carol A. Breckenridge et al. (eds), *Cosmopolitanism* (Durham, NC and London, 2002), 157–87, at p. 157, Lee Harris, 'The cosmopolitan illusion', *Policy Review*, 118 (2003), 45-59, at p. 52–4 (a caricature of enlightened rationality and rational cosmopolitanism), and Scrivener, *Cosmopolitan Ideal*, p. 10.

23   Richard Price, *Political Writings*, ed. D. O. Thomas (Cambridge, 1991), pp. 146ff. The passage is quoted by Derek Heater, *World Citizenship and Government: Cosmopolitan Ideas in the History of Western Political Thought* (Basingstoke, UK, 1996), pp. 74 and 90.

24   See Price, *Writings*, pp. 122ff., 146, 147, 180 and 181–4.

25   Ibid., pp. 179, 147 (note), 184 and 188.

26   Rebecka Lettevall, 'The idea of *Kosmopolis*: two kinds of cosmopolitanism', in Letteval and Linder, *Kosmopolis*, pp. 13–30, with the quotation at p. 23; Gerd van den Heuvel, 'Cosmopolite, Cosmopoli(ti)sme', in Rolf Reichardt and Eberhard Schmidt (eds), *Handbuch politisch-sozialer Grundbegriffe in Frankreich 1680-1820* (Munich, 1986), 41–55, at pp. 45–6.

27   The debate is summarized (and a convincing solution to the riddle is offered) by Pauline Kleingeld, 'Kant's Second Thoughts on Race', *The Philosophical Quarterly*, 57 (2007), 573–92.

28   Albrecht, *Kosmopolitismus*, pp. 10 and 392.

29   Massimo La Torre, 'Global citizenship? Political rights under imperial conditions', *Ratio Juris*, 18, 2 (2005), 236–57, at p. 255.

30   Derek Heater, *A Brief History of Citizenship* (Edinburgh, 2004), pp. 36ff. Thus Nida-Rümelin is probably mistaken when he claims that the Antonine Constitution was the result of Stoic thinking: Julian Nida-Rümelin, 'Zur Philosophie des Kosmopolitismus', *Zeitschrift für Internationale Beziehungen*, 13, 2 (2006), 231–8, at p. 231.

31   Martha Nussbaum, 'Standing against despairing detachment', 21 June 2003, at *http://evatt.labor.net.au/news/234.html*, visited 18 April

2008; cf. Nussbaum, *Frontiers of Justice: Disability, Nationality, species Membership* (Cambridge, Mass. 2006), pp. 19–21, 36ff., 230 and 256. Also see the inaccuracies in Beck, 'Sociology', p. 65 and Peter Kemp, 'The cosmopolitan foundation of international law', in Lettevall and Linder, *Kosmopolis*, pp. 143–55, at p. 145.

32 Martha Nussbaum, 'Kant and Stoic cosmopolitanism' *Journal of Political Philosophy*, 5, 1 (1997), 1–25, at pp. 7 and 11, and *Cultivating Humanity: A Classical Defense of Reform in Liberal Education* (Cambridge, Mass., 1997), p. 59.

33 Pauline Kleingeld and Eric Brown, 'Cosmopolitanism', in Edward N. Zalta (ed.), *The Stanford Encyclopedia of Philosophy* (2002 edition), at *http://plato.stanford.edu/archives/fall2002/entries/cosmopolitanism*, visited 23 November 2007, pp. 2f.; John Sellars, 'Stoic cosmopolitanism and Zeno's Republic', *History of Political Thought*, 28, 1 (2007), 1–29; Eric Brown, 'Hellenistic cosmopolitanism', in Mary Louise Gill and Pierre Pellegrin (eds), *A Companion to Ancient Philosophy* (Oxford, 2006), 549-58; Jones, 'The origins of the global city', 50–73; Richard Tuck, *The Rights of War and Peace: Political Thought and the International Order From Grotius to Kant* (Oxford, 1999), pp. 22ff. and pp. 34–50.

34 Nussbaum, 'Kant', p. 3.

35 Pauline Kleingeld, 'Six varieties of cosmopolitanism in late eighteenth-century Germany', *Journal of the History of Ideas*, 60 (1999), 505–24, at p. 505; Kleingeld and Brown, 'Cosmopolitanism', p. 1; Albrecht, *Kosmopolitismus*, pp. 22-61; Benhabib, *Rights of Others*, p. 133: Patrick Hayden, *Cosmopolitan Global Politics* (Aldershot, 2005), p. 3; Heuvel, 'Cosmopolite'; H. J. Busch and Axel Horstmann, 'Kosmopolit, Kosmopolitismus', in Joachim Ritter (ed.), *Historisches Wörterbuch der Philosophie*, 4 (1976), 1155–67.

36 Neo-realist Danilo Zolo showers contemporary cosmopolitans with contempt in *Cosmopolis: Prospects for World Government* (Cambridge, 1997). Toni Erskine has offered a synthesis of communitarian and cosmopolitan approaches in her book, *Embedded Cosmopolitanism: Duties to Strangers and Enemies in a World of 'Dislocated Communities'* (Oxford, 2008). Heater, *World Citizenship*, pp. 14–25 conveniently summarizes the arguments of cosmopolitanism's enemies.

37 See Kleingeld, 'Varieties', Kleingeld and Brown, 'Cosmopolitanism', Samuel Scheffler, 'Conceptions of cosmopolitanism', in *Boundaries and Allegiances* (Oxford, 2001), 111–30, Charles Jones, 'Cosmopolitanism', in Donald M. Borchert (ed.), *Encyclopedia of Philosophy*, II (Detroit et al., 2006), 567–70.

38 Thomas Pogge, *World Poverty and Human Rights* (Cambridge, 2002), p. 169; cf. Andrew Dobson, 'Thick cosmopolitanism', *Political*

Studies, 54 (2006), 165–84, at p. 167 and Brett Bowden, 'Nationalism and cosmopolitanism: irreconcilable differences or possible bedfellows?', *National Identities*, 5, 3 (2003), 235–49, at pp. 241ff.

39 Hayden, *Global Politics*, pp. 6ff., Ingo K. Richter, Sabne Berking and Ralf Müller-Schmid (eds), *Building a Transnational Civil Society* (Houndmills, 2006). Daniele Archibugi and Mathias Koenig-Archibugi offer a very useful bibliography in: 'Globalization, democracy and cosmopolis: a bibliographical essay', in Daniele Archibugi (ed.), *Debating Cosmopolitics* (London, 2003), 273–91.

40 Kleingeld, 'Varieties', p. 515.

41 Cf. ibid., pp. 515–18.

42 Ibid., p. 518.

43 David T. Hansen, 'Curriculum and the idea of cosmopolitan inheritance', *Journal of Curriculum Studies*, 40, 3 (2008), 289–312, at p. 293; Amaryta Sen, *Development as Freedom* (New York, 1999).

44 Beck, *Cosmopolitan Vision* and Vertovec and Cohen, 'Introduction', p. 13.

45 Denis Cosgrove, 'Globalis and tolerance in early modern geography', *Annals of the Association of American Geographers*, 93, 4 (2003), 852–70, at p. 865. The term 'Christian cosmopolitanism' can be found in Mignolo, 'Faces', p. 167. See also Appiah, *Cosmopolitanism*, p. xiv and Heater, *Brief History*, pp. 105ff.

46 Anthony Langlois, 'Human rights and cosmopolitan liberalism', *Critical Review of International Social and Political Philosophy*, 10, 1 (2007), 29–45 offers an excellent discussion of liberal cosmopolitanism. See Heater, *World Citizenship*, p. 13 and Zolo, *Cosmopolis*, p. 167 on political, legal and judicial cosmopolitanism.

47 Jones, 'Cosmopolitanism', p. 567.

48 Scheffler, 'Conceptions', p. 115. Cf. Dobson, 'Cosmopolitanism' and Jones, 'Cosmopolitanism', p. 568.

49 Martha C. Nussbaum, 'Toward a globally sensitive patriotism', *Daedalus*, 137, 3 (2008), 78–93.

50 I have developed my own compromise in Cavallar, *The Rights of Strangers: Theories of International Hospitality, the Global Community, and Political Justice since Vitoria* (Aldershot, 2002), pp. 46–59. For an introduction, see the recent debate in *Journal of Philosophy of Education*, 43, 1 (2009), 1-29; Charles Jones, *Global Justice: Defending Cosmopolitanism* (Oxford, 1999); Heiner Bielefeldt, *Philosophie der Menschenrechte: Grundlagen eines weltweiten Freiheitsethos* (Darmstadt, 1998); or Sibylle Tönnies, *Der westliche Universalismus: Die Denkwelt der Menschenrechte*, 3rd edn (Wiesbaden, 2001).

51 See also Sharon Anderson-Gold, *Cosmopolitanism and Human Rights* (Cardiff, 2001); Breckenridge, *Cosmopolitanism*; Brock and

Brighouse, *Philosophy of Cosmopolitanism*; Pheng Cheah and Bruce Robbins (eds), *Cosmopolitics: Thinking and Feeling beyond the Nation* (Minneapolis, 1998).

52 Peter Uwe Hohendahl, *Patriotism, Cosmopolitanism, and National Culture: Public Culture in Hamburg 1700–1933* (Amsterdam and New York, 2003). See also Daniel L. Purdy, *The Tyranny of Elegance: Consumer Cosmopolitanism in the Era of Goethe* (Baltimore, Md. 1998), a study on the discourses on fashion and the designs of clothing; Michael Stanislawski, *Zionism and the fin-de-siècle: Cosmopolitanism and Nationalism from Nordau to Jabotinsky* (Berkeley, 2001), David Cesarani (ed.), *Jews and Port Cities, 1590-1990: Commerce, Community and Cosmopolitanism* (London, 2006).

53 Margaret C. Jacob, *Strangers Nowhere in the World: The Rise of Cosmopolitanism in Early Modern Europe* (Philadelphia, 2006); Michael Scrivener, *The Cosmopolitan Ideal in the Age of Revolution and Reaction, 1776–1832* (London, 2007). See also Jacob's short essay: 'The cosmopolitan as a lived category', *Daedalus*, 137, 3 (2008), 18–25. Peter Coulmas, *Weltbürger: Geschichte einer Menschheitssehnsucht* (Reinbek bei Hamburg, 1990) is a comprehensive cultural history of Europe since antiquity, which also deals with cosmopolitan themes. Elizabeth L. Eisenstein, *Grub Street Abroad: Aspects of French Cosmopolitan Press from the Age of Louis XIV to the French Revolution* (Oxford, 1992) researches the European-wide, decentralized and relatively autonomous discursive community of the francophone Republic of Letters.

54 Amanda Anderson, *The Powers of Distance: Cosmopolitanism and the Cultivation of Detachment* (Princeton, 2001), pp. 30 and 33. See also Suzanne Kirkbright (ed.), *Cosmopolitans in the Modern World: Studies on a Theme in German and Austrian Literary Culture* (München, 2000); Jessica Berman, *Modernist Fiction, Cosmopolitanism, and the Politics of Community* (Cambridge, 2001); Broser and Pfeiferová, *Der Dichter als Kosmopolit*.

55 Albrecht, *Kosmopolitismus*; Derek Heater, *World Citizenship and Government: Cosmopolitan Ideas in the History of Western Political Thought* (Basingstoke, UK, 1996), *World Citizenship: Cosmopolitan Thinking and its Opponents* (London and New York, 2002) and *A Brief History of Citizenship* (Edinburgh, 2004). See also Sigrid Thielking, *Weltbürgertum: kosmopolitische Ideen in Literatur und politischer Publizistik seit dem achtzehnten Jahrhundert* (München, 2000). Thomas J. Schlereth, *The Cosmopolitan Ideal in Enlightenment Thought: Its Form and Fuction in the Ideas of Franklin, Hume, and Voltaire, 1694–1790* (Notre Dame, 1977) offers an early study of the Enlightenment world-view and its republic of letters.

56 Simone Zurbuchen, *Patriotismus und Kosmopolitismus. Die Schweizer Aufklärung zwischen Tradition und Moderne* (Zürich, 2003), with a focus on patriotism, natural law and republicanism rather than cosmopolitan themes; Francis Cheneval, *Philosophie in weltbürgerlicher Bedeutung: Über die Entstehung und die philosophischen Grundlagen des supranationalen und kosmopolitischen Denkens der Moderne* (Basel, 2002). I have touched upon cosmopolitan themes in my own *The Rights of Strangers*.

57 Jan Nederveen Pieterse, 'Emancipatory cosmopolitanism: towards an agenda', *Development and Change*, 37, 6 (2006), 1247-57, at p. 1256.

58 One obvious omission of this study is Jean-Jacques Rousseau. See my essays 'Jean-Jacques Rousseau (1712–1778)', in Bardo Fassbender and Anne Peters (eds), *The Oxford Handbook of the History of International Law* (in preparation) and '"La société générale du genre humain": Rousseau on cosmopolitanism, international relations, and republican patriotism', in Paschalis M. Kitromilides (ed.), *From Republican Polity to National Community* (Oxford, 2003), pp. 89–109.

59 Chernilo, 'Quest for Universalism', p. 32.

60 Mignolo, 'Faces', p. 157; cf. ibid., pp. 168–74. See also Held, *Democracy*, p. 233; Giri, 'Cosmopolitanism', pp. 1279 and 1283f.; Kemp, 'Cosmopolitan Foundation', p. 147; Andrew Linklater, 'Cosmopolitanism', in Andrew Dobson and Robyn Eckersley (eds), *Political Theory and the Ecological Challenge* (Cambridge, 2006), 109–27, at pp. 109f.; Scrivener, *Cosmopolitan Ideal*, p. 19; or Nussbaum, 'Kant', pp. 12–25.

61 Michael Walzer, *Arguing about War* (New Haven and London, 2004), pp. 171ff.

Vitoria, Grotius, Pufendorf, Wolff and Vattel: accomplices of European colonialism and exploitation, or true cosmopolitans?

1 Henry Wheaton, *Elements of International Law* [1836], 8th edn (Oxford, 1936), pp. xv–xvi. This essay draws and elaborates on passages from my *The Rights of Strangers: Theories of International Hospitality, the Global Community, and Political Justice since Vitoria* (Aldershot, 2002).

2 Robert A. Williams, *The American Indian in Western Legal Thought: The Discourses of Conquest* (New York, Oxford, 1990), pp. 6–8 and p. 106.

3 Ibid., p. 107; cf. p. 103.

4 Antony Anghie, *Imperialism, Sovereignty and the Making of International Law* (Cambridge, 2005), pp. 1–31, quotation at p. 31.
5 Ibid., p. 30.
6 Brett Bowden, 'The colonial origins of international law: European expansion and the classical standard of civilization', *Journal of the History of International Law*, 7 (2005), 1–23, especially pp. 1, 3, 13 and 23; 'Civilization and savagery in the crucible of war', *Global Change, Peace and Security*, 19, 1 (2007), 3–16.
7 Paul Keal, '"Just Backward Children": International law and the conquest of non-European peoples', *Australian Journal of International Affairs*, 49 (1995), 191–206, at 192.
8 Paul Keal, *European Conquest and the Rights of Indigenous Peoples: The Moral Backwardness of International Society* (Cambridge, 2003), pp. 21, 88, 97 and 102.
9 Ibid., p. 107 and 85. See also pp. 21 and 84.
10 The key works I have consulted are: Jörg Fisch, *Die europäische Expansion und das Völkerrecht: Die Auseinandersetzungen um den Status der überseeischen Gebiete vom 15. Jahrhundert bis zur Gegenwart*, Beiträge zur Kolonial- und Überseegeschichte (Stuttgart, 1984), a brilliant and usually neglected study; Leslie Claude Green and Olive P. Dickason, *The Law of Nations and the New World* (Edmonton, 1989); James Muldoon, *The Americas in the Spanish World Order: The Justification for Conquest in the Seventeenth Century* (Philadelphia, 1994); Sharon Korman, *The Right of Conquest. The Acquisition of Territory by Force in International Law and Practice* (Oxford, 1996); W. J. Mommsen and J. A. De Moor (eds), *European Expansion and Law: The Encounter of European and Indigenous Law in 19th- and 20th-Century Africa and Asia* (Oxford, New York, 1992); the fine studies of Anthony Pagden, especially *European Encounters with the New World: From Renaissance to Romanticism* (New Haven and London, 1993), *The Uncertainties of Empire: Essays in Iberian and Ibero-American Intellectual History* (Aldershot, 1994), and *Lords of All the World: Ideologies of Empire in Spain, Britain and France, c.1500–c.1800* (New Haven and London, 1995). More recent articles by Pagden are: 'Stoicism, cosmopolitanism, and the legacy of European imperialism', *Constellations*, 7, 1 (2000), 3–22; 'Fellow citizens and imperial subjects: conquest and sovereignty in Europe's overseas empires', *History and Theory*, 44, 3 (2005), 28–46.
11 Williams, *American Indian*, p. 107.
12 Antonio Gómez Robledo, 'Le *ius cogens* international: sa genèse, sa nature, ses fonctions', *Recueil des Cours*, 172, 3 (1981), 23–5 and 189–91; Roberto O. Irigoyen, *Francisco de Vitoria y la Política Internacional Argentina de Hipolito Yrigoyen* (Buenos Aires, 1993),

p. 113. See also Marcelino Rodríguez Molinero, *La doctrina colonial de Francisco de Vitoria o el derecho de la paz y de la guerra: un legado perenne de la escuela de Salamanca* (Salamanca, 1993); Antonio Truyol Serra et al., *Actualité de la pensée juridique de Francisco de Vitoria* (Bruxelles, 1988); *Historia del derecho internacional público* (Madrid, 1998). More titles are listed in Francisco de Vitoria, *Political Writings*, eds Anthony Padgen and Jeremy Lawrance (Cambridge, 1991), pp. 383-7, and in Francisco Castilla Urbaño, *El Pensamiento de Francisco de Vitoria: Filosofía política e indio Americano* (Barcelona, 1992), pp. 347-62. The most recent publication available for me was: Salvador Castellote, 'Der Beitrag der Spanischen Spätscholastik zur Geschichte Europas', in Markus Kremer and Hans-Richard Reuter (eds), *Macht und Moral – Politisches Denken im 17. und 18. Jahrhundert* (Stuttgart, 2007), pp. 17-38. The term *inventis* in the title of Vitoria's lecture could either mean 'invention' or 'discovery' of the Americas; see the excellent essay of John Christian Laursen, 'De Indis Recenter Inventis: descubrimientos e invenciones legales y políticas en Vitoria, Las Casas y Fuentes', in Ana Maria Hernández de López (ed.), *Narrativa hispanoamericana contemporanea: entre la vanguardia y el posboom* (Madrid, 1996), pp. 102-4.

13 José Antonio Maravall, *Estado moderno y pensamiento social (Siglos XV a XVII)* (Madrid, 1972), vol. 1, pp. 193 and 212.

14 James Brown Scott, *The Spanish Origin of International Law: Francisco de Vitoria and his Law of Nations* (Oxford, 1934), pp. 281 and 283. For Josef Soder, *Die Idee der Völkergemeinschaft. Francisco de Vitoria und die philosophischen Grundlage des Völkerrechts* (Frankfurt am Main, 1955), Vitoria provided the perfect philosophical foundation of human rights and the international community, aiming at the welfare of all humankind.

15 J. A. Fernández-Santamaria, *The State, War and Peace: Spanish Political Thought in the Renaissance 1516–1559* (Cambridge, 1977), p. 111.

16 On the concept of the 'barbarian', see Keal, *Conquest*, pp. 67–75. In Vitoria, 'barbarian' usually equals 'non-Christian'.

17 Vitoria, 'On the American Indians', in *Political Writings*, eds Padgen and Lawrance, pp. 283ff.

18 Ibid., p. 291, italics in the original.

19 Ibid., p. 250.

20 Ibid., p. 271. The theological framework of Vitoria's Indian lecture is emphasized by Heinz-Gerhard Justenhoven, *Francisco de Vitoria zu Krieg und Frieden* (Köln, 1991), pp. 165ff. He also offers a very comprehensive list of secondary literature, ibid., pp. 188–213.

21 Vitoria, 'On the American Indians', pp. 270ff.

22 Vitoria, 'On the American Indians', p. 278.
23 Ibid., p. 291.
24 See, for instance, Ortega, 'Vitoria', 109, who sees this as a possible reason. The letter is quoted in Scott, *Spanish Origin*, pp. 84ff. and in Vitoria, *Relectio de indis o libertad de los indios*, ed. Luciano Pereña et al. (Madrid, 1967), pp. 152ff.
25 Letter to Miguel de Arcos, in Vitoria, *Political Writings*, pp. 331–3.
26 See my *Rights of Strangers*, pp. 80–4 and 90–8 for more extensive analyses.
27 Keal, *Conquest*, p. 93, quoting Pagden and Muldoon.
28 Sankar Muthu, *Enlightenment against Empire* (Princeton and Oxford, 2003), pp. 273–5; Vitoria, 'On the American Indians', pp. 250 and 290; Anthony Pagden, *The Fall of Natural Man: The American Indian and the Origins of Comparative Ethnology*, 2nd edn. (Cambridge, 1986), pp. 79–93.
29 Rosalyn Higgins, 'International law in the UN period', in Hedley Bull, Benedict Kingsbury and Adam Roberts (eds), *Hugo Grotius and International Relations* (Oxford, 1990), p. 278, and the quotation from B. V. A. Röling, 'Jus ad Bellum and the Grotian heritage', in Asser Instituut, *International Law and the Grotian Heritage* (The Hague, 1985), p. 122. See also idem, 'Are Grotius' ideas obsolete in an expanded world?', in Bull et al., *Grotius*, pp. 281–99, especially p. 296.
30 Karl-Heinz Ziegler, 'Die Bedeutung von Hugo Grotius für das Völkerrecht – Versuch einer Bilanz am Ende des 20. Jahrhunderts', *Zeitschrift für historische Forschung*, 23 (1996), 355–71; Norbert Konegen and Peer Nitschke (eds), *Staat bei Hugo Grotius* (Baden-Baden, 2005); Christoph A. Stumpf, *The Grotian Theology of International Law: Hugo Grotius and the Moral Foundations of International Relations* (Berlin and New York, 2006); Elke Tießler-Marenda, *Einwanderung und Asyl bei Hugo Grotius* (Berlin, 2002); Florian Mühlegger, *Hugo Grotius: ein christlicher Humanist in politischer Verantwortung* (Berlin and New York, 2007); Benedikt van Spyk, *Vertragstheorie und Völkerrecht im Werk des Hugo Grotius* (Hamburg, 2005). The critical group includes: Richard Tuck, *The Rights of War and Peace: Political Thought and the International Order from Grotius to Kant* (Oxford, 1999); Edward Keene, *Beyond the Anarchical Society: Grotius, Colonialism and Order in World Politics* (Cambridge, 2002); Martine Julia van Ittersum, *Profit and Principle: Hugo Grotius, Natural Rights Theories and the Rise of Dutch Power in the East Indies 1595–1615* (Leiden and Boston, 2006).
31 E.g. Hugo Grotius, *De Jure Belli ac Pacis Libri Tres* [1625; The Law of War and Peace], vol. II, trans. Francis W. Kelsey (Oxford, 1925),

2.20.44.4, p. 509. I have also used the on-line version edited by Richard Tuck, from the edition of Jean Barbeyrac (Indianapolis, 2005).

32 Grotius, *De Jure Belli*, 2.20.48–9, pp. 516–18.

33 Hugo Grotius, *Commentary on the Law of Prize and Booty* [1603], trans. by Gwladys L. Williams (Oxford, 1950, reprint New York, 1964), 12.97, pp. 221ff. See also ibid., 12.99, 12.103ff. and 12.104, pp. 226, 236 and 238. I have also used the on-line version edited by Martine Julia van Ittersum (Indianapolis, 2006). See Tießler-Marenda, *Einwanderung*, pp. 172 and 176. A brief introduction to the topic is Benedict Kingsbury and Adam Roberts, 'Introduction', in Bull et al., *Grotius*, pp. 42–7 on 'Grotius and the non-European world'.

34 Grotius, *Commentary*, 13.128, accessed from *http:/oll.libertyfund.org/title/1718/77251/1871412* on 15 February 2008. See Tuck, *Rights of War*, pp. 92–4 and Keene, *Anarchical Society*, p. 110.

35 Grotius, *Commentary*, 12.98, p. 222. On the arguments of the European 'thieves' in general, see ibid., 12.97–100, pp. 221–5, and *Jure Belli*, 2.22, pp. 546–56 on the unjust causes of wars, especially 2.22.13, pp. 551ff. on the Emperor's universal monarchy, and 2.22.14, pp. 553ff. on the papal donation. A reliable introduction into European thinking concerning the right to 'civilize the barbarians' is James Muldoon, *The Americas in the Spanish World Order: The Justification for Conquest in the Seventeenth Century* (Philadelphia 1994), ch. 2, pp. 38–65 and Gerrit W. Gong, *The Standard of 'Civilization' in International Society* (Oxford 1984).

36 Grotius, *De Jure Belli*, 2.22.12, p. 551.

37 Van Ittersum, *Profit and* Principle, pp. xix—lxii.

38 Keene, *Anarchical Society*, p. 51, van Ittersum, *Profit and Principle*, p. xxii.

39 Tuck, *Rights of War*, p. 79. Cf. van Ittersum, *Profit and Principle*, pp. 44, 483, 371–412, xxviii and passim.

40 Grotius, *De Jure Belli*, 1.3.7, p. 102. My interpretation follows Tuck, *Rights of War*, pp. 81–95 and van Ittersum, *Profit and Principle*, pp. xxiii, 43–52 and 490.

41 See the interpretation in Bowden, 'Colonial origins', pp. 4–8.

42 Grotius, *De Jure Belli*, 2.20.40, p. 506.

43 See the passages quoted in Cavallar, *Rights of Strangers*, pp. 128ff.

44 Grotius, *De Jure Belli*, 2.2.23, p. 205. See the detailed reconstruction in Tießler-Marenda, *Einwanderung*, pp. 163–84 and 200–6.

45 Grotius, *De Jure Belli*, 2.2.1, p. 187; 2.2.17, p. 202; 2.2.11, p. 196. Cf. Thomas Flanagan, 'The agricultural argument and original appropriation: Indian lands and political philosophy', *Canadian Journal of Political Science*, 22 (1989), pp. 589–602. Barbara Arneil, 'John

Locke, natural law and colonialism', *History of Political Thought*, 13 (1992), 588–94 holds that key elements of Locke's theory were anticipated by Grotius.

46 Grotius, *De Jure Belli*, 2.15.12, p. 403; Mühlegger, *Hugo Grotius*, p. 502; Christian Gellinek, 'Staat und Völkerrecht bei Hugo Grotius', in Konegen and Nitschke, *Hugo Grotius*, pp. 67–78, at p. 74.

47 Tuck, *Rights of War*, pp. 95 and 108; van Ittersum, *Profit and Principle*, p. lxi; Keene, *Anarchical Society*, pp. 3–6 and 97. I participated in Grotian hagiography with my own *Rights of Strangers*, pp. 138–55. Grotius's impact on subsequent international legal theory was tremendous. See David J. Bederman, 'Reception of the classical tradition in international law: Grotius' 'De jure belli ac pacis', *Emory International Law Review*, 10 (1996), 1–52; Frank Grunert, 'Von der Morgenröte zum hellen Tag: Zur Rezeption Hugo Grotius' *De iure belli ac pacis* in der deutschen Frühaufklärung', *Zeitschrift für neuere Rechtsgeschichte*, 25, 3 (2003), 204–21; Randall Lesaffer, 'The Grotian tradition revisited – change and continuity in the history of international law', *British Yearbook of International Law*, 73 (2002), 103–39; Michael Kempe, 'Der Anfang eines Mythos: Zum grotianischen Natur- und Völkerrecht in der europäischen Aufklärung', in: Konegen and Nitschke, *Hugo Grotius*, pp. 139–57.

48 Richard Waswo, 'The formation of natural law to justify colonialism, 1539–1689', *New Literary History*, 27, 4 (1996), 754–6.

49 Samuel Pufendorf, *The Law of Nature and Nations* [1672], trans. C. H. Oldfather and W. A. Oldfather (Oxford, 1934; reprint New York, 1964), 3.3.9, p. 364. Recent literature on Pufendorf is listed in: Klaus Luig, 'Samuel Pufendorf über Krieg und Frieden', in Norbert Brieskorn and Markus Riedenauer (eds), *Suche nach Frieden – Politische Ethik in der Frühen Neuzeit III* (Stuttgart, 2003), pp. 255–66. A succinct and excellent introduction is Francis Cheneval, *Philosophie in weltbürgerlicher Bedeutung: Über die Entstehung und die philosophischen Grundlagen des supranationalen und kosmopolitischen Denkens der Moderne* (Basel, 2002), pp. 270–86.

50 Pufendorf, *Law of Nature*, 3.3.9, p. 364. See ibid., pp. 364ff. for the following paragraph. There is a useful discussion of Pufendorf's position and his criticism of Vitoria in Barbara Arneil, 'John Locke, natural law and colonialism', *History of Political Thought*, 13 (1992), 594–600. See also Keal, *Conquest*, pp. 96–7.

51 Pufendorf, *Law of Nature*, 4.6.4, pp. 571. Cf. Tuck, *Rights of War*, pp. 155–8.

52 Pufendorf, *Law of Nature*, 8.6.5, p. 1297, my emphasis. See also Fisch, *Expansion*, pp. 250ff.

53 Pufendorf, *Law of Nature*, 3.2.8, pp. 340–4.
54 Christian Wolff, *Ius gentium methodo scientifica pertractatum* [1749] (New York, 1964), paras. 52–6, pp. 33–6.
55 Bowden, 'Colonial origins', p. 15. See Gerhard Biller (ed.), *Wolff nach Kant. Eine Bibliographie. Christian Wolff, Gesammelte Werke, Materialien und Dokumente vol.* 87 (Hildesheim, Zürich, New York, 2004) and Hans-Martin Gerlach (ed.), *Christian Wolff – seine Schule und seine Gegner* (Hamburg, 2001) on Wolff's philosophy in general.
56 Wolff, *Ius gentium*, para. 75 note, p. 44; para. 187 note, p. 98.
57 Ibid., para. 209, p. 109.
58 Ibid., para. 261, p. 133; para. 297, p. 150; Christian Wolff, *Institutiones juris naturae et genitum*, ed. Marcel Thomann, in *Gesammelte Werke*, vol. 26 (reprint Hildesheim: Georg Olms Verlag, 1969), para. 1131ff., pp. 705f; para. 1122, p. 699. See Fisch, *Expansion*, pp. 270–5 for Wolff's rejection of exclusive European rights, and especially pp. 271ff. on religion.
59 Wolff, *Ius gentium*, para. 263, p. 135.
60 Ibid., para. 309, p. 157.
61 Ibid., para. 312, p. 159.
62 Ibid., para. 309, p. 157, para. 310, pp. 157ff., para. 312, p. 159; para. 85ff., pp. 50ff., para. 282, p. 144.
63 Ibid., para. 313, p. 159.
64 Ibid.
65 Francis Cheneval, 'Auseinandersetzungen um die *civitas maxima* in der Nachfolge Christian Wolffs', *Studia Leibnitiana*, 33 (2001), 125–44; idem, *Philosophie*, pp. 132ff. and pp. 188–90; Nicholas Greenwood Onuf, *The Republican Legacy in International Thought* (Cambridge, 1998), pp. 60–70, and my own 'The law of nations in the Age of Enlightenment: moral and legal principles', *Annual Review of Law and Ethics*, 12 (2004), 213–29.
66 Cheneval, *Philosophie*, pp. 179ff.
67 Ibid., pp. 135, 138 and 162; Wolff, *Ius gentium*, para 20, p. 17.
68 Sankar Muthu, *Enlightenment against Empire* (Princeton and Oxford, 2003), pp. 71ff., 122ff. and 268–73.
69 Barbara Arneil, *John Lock and America: The Defence of English Colonialism* (Oxford, 1996), p. 2; cf. pp. 206–7; Arneil, 'John Locke', pp. 587–603; David Armitage, 'John Locke, Carolina, and the *Two Treaties of Government*', *Political Theory*, 32, 5 (2004), 602–27; Keal, *Conquest*, pp. 98–100 and the references in Cavallar, *Rights of Strangers*, p. 261. On Vattel in general, see Emmanuelle Jouannet, *Emer de Vattel et l'émergence doctrinale du droit international classique* (Paris,

1998), Stéphane Beaulac, *The Power of Language in the Making of International Law: The Word Sovereignty in Bodin and Vattel and the Myth of Westphalia* (Leiden, Boston, 2004), and, most recently, Karl-Heinz Ziegler, 'Emer de Vattel und die Entwicklung des Völkerrechts im 18. Jahrhundert', in Markus Kremer and Hans-Richard Reuter (eds), *Macht und Moral – Politisches Denken im 17. und 18. Jahrhundert* (Stuttgart, 2007), pp. 321–41. Both publications provide more secondary literature.

70 Emer de Vattel, *The Law of Nations or the Principles of Natural Law* (1758), trans. Charles G. Fenwick (Washington, 1916), 1.18.208, p. 85; cf. 207, p. 84: 'provided that actual possession has followed shortly after.' See Grewe, *Epochen*, pp. 466–70 for an analysis.

71 Vattel, *Law of Nations*, 1.18.208, p. 85; 1.18.209, pp. 85ff.; cf. Fisch, *Expansion*, pp. 275ff.

72 Vattel, *Law of Nations*, 1.7.81, pp. 37ff.; 2.7.97, p. 143; 2.7.97, p. 143; cf. Fisch, *Expansion*, pp. 276ff.

73 Vattel, *Law of Nations*, 1.7.81, pp. 37ff.; 1.18.209, p. 85; Flanagan, 'The agricultural argument', 589–602, at pp. 595ff.

74 Vattel, *Law of Nations*, 1.7.81, p. 38.

75 Peter Pavel Remec, *The Position of the Individual in International Law According to Grotius and Vattel* (The Hague, 1960), p. 189.

76 Anghie, *Imperialism*, pp. 9, 30ff., and 8; Bowden, 'Colonial origins', pp. 14–18.

77 P. G. McHugh, *Aboriginal Societies and the Common Law: A History of Sovereignty, Status, and Self-Determination* (Oxford, 2004), Ken MacMillan, *Sovereignty and Possession in the English New World. The Legal Foundations of Empire, 1576–1640*, Jörg Fisch, 'Law as a means and as an end. Some remarks on the function of European and non-European law in the process of European expansion', in Wolfgang J. Mommsen and Jap de Moor (eds), *European Expansion and Law. The Encounter of European and Indigenous Law in 19th- and 20th-century Africa and Asia* (Oxford, 1991), pp. 15ff., at p. 33.

78 Fisch, 'Law', pp. 16, 36–8.

79 Bernhard Hellig, *Chinas Außenpolitik am Vorabend des 'Opiumkrieges' (1839–1842)* (unpublished dissertation, Tübingen 1987) and Heinz Duchhardt, *Balance of Power und Pentarchie: Internationale Beziehungen 1700–1785* (Paderborn et al., 1997), pp. 227–32.

80 Martti Koskenniemi, *From Apology to Utopia: The Structure of International Legal Argument* (Helsinki, 1989), pp. 74–83 (on Grotius); idem, *The Gentle Civilizer of Nations: The Rise and Fall of International Law 1870–1960* (Cambridge, 2002), ch. 2, pp. 98–178.

British Enlightenment: the triumph of commercial cosmopolitanism

1 Michael Scrivener, *The Cosmopolitan Ideal in the Age of Revolution and Reaction, 1776–1832* (London, 2007), p. 19. See also Craig Calhoun, 'The class consciousness of the frequent travellers: towards a critique of actually existing cosmopolitanism', in Daniele Archibugi (ed.), *Debating Cosmopolitics* (London, 2003), pp. 86–116, at p. 89.
2 David Hume, 'Of the jealousy of trade' [1758], in Hume, *Political Essays*, ed. Knud Haakonssen (Cambridge, 1994), p. 153. See the interpretation in Richard F. Teichgraeber III, *'Free Trade' and Moral Philosophy: Rethinking the Sources of Adam Smith's Wealth of Nations* (Durham, NC, 1986), pp. 106 and 113ff. and John F. Berdell, 'Innovation and trade: David Hume and the case for freer trade,' *History of Political Economy*, 28 (1996), 116 and 119ff.
3 Hume, 'Of national characters' [1748], in *Political Essays*, p. 86 note. Cf. Richard H. Popkin, 'The philosophical bases of modern racism' and 'Hume's racism', in *The High Road to Pyrrhonism* (Indianapolis, 1993), pp. 79–102 and 267–76; idem, 'Eighteenth-century racism', in *The Columbia History of Western Philosophy* (New York, 1999), pp. 508–15, and David Boucher, *The Limits of Ethics in International Relations. Natural Law, Natural Rights, and Human Rights in Transition* (Oxford, 2009), pp. 208 and 210–12.
4 Abbé de Saint-Pierre, 'A project for settling an everlasting peace in Europe' [1713], in Esref Aksu (ed.), *Early Notions of Global Governance: Selected Eighteenth-Century Proposals for 'Perpetual Peace'* (Cardiff, 2008), pp. 52–65, at p. 52; Tomaz Mastnak, 'Abbé de Saint-Pierre: European Union and the Turk', *History of Political Thought*, 19 (1998), 570–98 and Francis Cheneval, *Philosophie in weltbürgerlicher Bedeutung* (Basel, 2002), pp. 326ff. On Saint-Pierre in general, see Olaf Asbach, *Staat und Politik zwischen Absolutismus und Aufklärung: Der Abbé de Saint-Pierre und die Herausbildung der französischen Aufklärung bis zur Mitte des 18. Jahrhunderts* (Hildesheim, Zürich, New York, 2005).
5 Voltaire, *Political Writings*, ed. and trans. David Williams (Cambridge, 1994), pp. 29, 26 and 27. The standard work on his political thought is Peter Gay, *Voltaire's Politics: The Poet As Realist*, 2nd edn (New Haven/London, 1988).
6 See also Gerd van den Heuvel, 'Cosmopolite, Cosmopoli(ti)sme', in Rolf Reichardt and Eberhard Schmidt (eds), *Handbuch politisch-sozialer Grundbegriffe in Frankreich 1680–1820* (Munich, 1986), pp. 41–55, at pp. 42 and 45.

7   Hans Peter Herrmann, '"Ich bin fürs Vaterland zu sterben auch bereit":
    Patriotismus oder Nationalismus im 18. Jahrhundert?', in Ortrud Gut-
    jahr et al. (eds), *Gesellige Vernunft: Zur Kultur der literarischen Auf-
    klärung* (Würzburg, 1993), pp. 119–44, especially pp. 141–4.
8   Herbert Rowland, 'The journal *Der Patriot* and the constitution of
    a bourgeois literary public sphere', in: Peter Uwe Hohendahl (ed.),
    *Patriotism, Cosmopolitanism, and National Culture: Public Culture in
    Hamburg 1700–1933* (Amsterdam and New York, 2003), pp. 55–70,
    at p. 55. Relevant and recent publications on eighteenth-century cos-
    mopolitanisms are, apart from Hohendahl and Scrivener, Andrea
    Albrecht, *Kosmopolitismus: Weltbürgerdiskurse in Literatur, Philos-
    ophie und Publizistik um 1800* (Berlin and New York, 2005); Mary
    Anne Perkins and Martin Liebscher (eds), *Nationalism versus Cosmo-
    politanism in German Thought and Culture, 1789–1914: Essays on
    the Emergence of Europe* (Lewiston, 2006); Margaret C. Jacob, *Stran-
    gers Nowhere in the World: The Rise of Cosmopolitanism in Early
    Modern Europe* (Philadelphia, 2006); Suzanne Kirkbright (ed.), *Cos-
    mopolitans in the Modern World: Studies on a Theme in German and
    Austrian Literary Culture* (München, 2000); and Pauline Kleingeld,
    'Six varieties of cosmopolitanism in late eighteenth-century Germany',
    Journal of the History of Ideas, 60 (1999), 505–24. The major older
    study is Thomas J. Schlereth, *The Cosmopolitan Ideal in Enlighten-
    ment Thought: Its Form and Function in the Ideas of Franklin, Hume,
    and Voltaire, 1694–1790* (Notre Dame, 1977).
9   See the excellent study by Jürgen Osterhammel, *Die Entzauberung Asiens:
    Europa und die asiatischen Reiche im 18. Jahrhundert* (München, 1998),
    pp. 289–96 at p. 290; Boucher, *The Limits of Ethics*, pp. 210–12 (on
    Hume's European critics).
10 Heuvel, 'Cosmopolite', pp. 43–4; Albrecht, *Kosmopolitismus*, pp. 29
    and 34; see also ibid., ch. 9, especially p. 299.
11 Albrecht, *Kosmopolitismus*, ch. 4, pp. 106–50; pp. 395ff.
12 This follows Kleingeld, 'Varieties', pp. 518–21.
13 See my interpretation in '"La société générale du genre humain":
    Rousseau on cosmopolitanism, international relations, and republi-
    can patriotism', in Paschalis M. Kitromilides (ed.), *From Republican
    Polity To National Community: Reconsiderations of Enlightenment
    Political Thought* (Oxford, 2003), pp. 89–109 and Albrecht, *Kosmo-
    politismus*, ch. 2, who points at Rousseau's profound ambivalence: the
    cosmopolitan Socrates is for an exclusive elite, the patriotic Cato for
    the ordinary people, ibid., p. 80.
14 Derek Heater, *World Citizenship: Cosmopolitan Thinking and its
    Opponents* (London and New York, 2002), pp. 40ff.; idem, *World*

Citizenship and Government: Cosmopolitan Ideas in the History of Western Political Thought (Basingstoke, UK, 1996), p. 74; H. J. Busch and Axel Horstmann, 'Kosmopolit, Kosmopolitismus', in Joachim Ritter (ed.), *Historisches Wörterbuch der Philosophie*, vol. 4 (1976), 1155–67, at 1159–62, and Albrecht, *Kosmopolitismus*, p. 393.

15 John Locke, *Two Treatises of Government*, ed. with an introduction by Peter Laslett (Cambridge, 1994), §§ 25, 26 and 128. All paragraphs refer to the second treatise. Useful introductions to Locke include Walter Euchner, *John Locke zur Einführung*, 2nd edn (Hamburg, 2004), James Tully, *An Approach to Political Philosophy: Locke in Contexts* (Cambridge, 1993) and John W. Yolton, *The Two Intellectual Worlds of John Locke: Man, Person, and Spirits in the 'Essay'* (Ithaca, NY, 2004). Howard Williams, 'John Locke and International Politics', in *International Relations and the Limits of Political Theory* (Houndmills et al., 1996), pp. 90–109 qualifies the standard account by Richard H. Cox, *Locke on War and Peace* (Oxford, 1960). I am much indebted to Francis Cheneval, *Philosophie in weltbürgerlicher Bedeutung: Über die Entstehung und die philosophischen Grundlagen des supranationalen und kosmopolitischen Denkens der Moderne* (Basel, 2002), pp. 286–303.

16 Locke, *Second Treatise*, § 14; cf. §§ 124, 183.
17 Ibid., § 145.
18 Ibid., §123.
19 Ibid., § 93; cf. §§ 11 and 159.
20 Ibid., § 14; cf. § 145.
21 Cf. ibid. § 13 and §§ 175–96.
22 Ibid., § 147.
23 Cheneval, *Philosophie*, p. 302 calls his theory 'contractualism which has not been settled'. Dietmar von der Pfordten defines normative individualism in political philosophy: the ultimate point of reference for questions relating to right or justice are the individual human beings; see his 'Normativer Individualismus', *Zeitschrift für philosophische Forschung*, 58 (2004), 321–46.
24 David Hume, *A Treatise of Human Nature* [1739–40], ed. with an analytical index by Sir Lewis Amherst Selby-Bigge, 2nd edn by Peter Harold Nidditch (Oxford, 1992), 3.2.11, pp. 568ff.; R. J. Glossop, 'Hume and the future of the society of nations', *Hume Studies*, 10 (1984), 46–58 and Frederick G. Whelan, 'Robertson, Hume, and the balance of power,' *Hume Studies*, 21 (1995), 315–32 are two of the rare studies on Hume's law of nations and international relations thinking. A recent introduction is Neil McArthur, *David Hume's Political Theory: Law, Commerce, and the Constitution of Government* (Toronto, 2007).

25 Hume, *Treatise*, 3.2.11, pp. 567ff.; cf. 'An enquiry concerning the principles of morals', section IV, p. 206.
26 David Hume, 'Of the balance of power' [1755], in *Political Essays*, ed. Knud Haakonssen (Cambridge, 1994), pp. 154–60, especially pp. 157ff. Recent publications on balance-of-power thinking are Stuart J. Kaufman, Richard Little and William C. Wohlforth (eds), *The Balance of Power in World History* (Basingstoke, 2007) and Richard Little, *The Balance of Power in International Relations: Metaphors, Myths and Models* (Cambridge, 2007).
27 David Hume, 'An enquiry concerning the principles of morals' [1777], in *Enquiries Concerning the Human Understanding and Concerning the Principles of Morals by David Hume*, ed. Sir Lewis Amherst Selby-Bigge, 2nd edn (Oxford, 1902), section V, part II, p. 225 note. For Razeen Sally, *Classical Liberalism and International Economic Order: Studies in Theory and Intellectual History* (London, 1998), pp. 56ff., Hume is patriotic and anti-cosmopolitan, whereas Schlereth, *Cosmopolitan Ideal*, pp. 97–103 views him as an internationalist or cosmopolitan.
28 See especially Andrew Wyatt-Walter, 'Adam Smith and the liberal tradition in international relations', *Review of International Studies*, 22 (1996), 5–6. Recent introductions to Smith include Jerry Evensky, *Adam Smith's Moral Philosophy: A Historical and Contemporary Perspective on Markets, Law, Ethics, and Culture* (Cambridge, 2005), Knud Haakonssen (ed.), *The Cambridge Companion to Adam Smith* (Cambridge, 2006), Gavin Kennedy, *Adam Smith's Lost Legacy* (Basingstoke, 2005), and Leonidas Montes, *Adam Smith in Context: A Critical Reassessment Of Some Central Components Of His Thought* (Basingstoke, 2005).
29 Adam Smith, *The Theory of Moral Sentiments* [1759], ed. D. D. Raphael and A. L. Macfie (Oxford, 1976), 3.3.42, pp. 154ff., 6.2.2.3 and 4, pp. 228ff.; idem, *An Inquiry into the Nature and Causes of the Wealth of Nations* [1776], ed. R. H. Campbell, A. S. Skinner and W. B. Todd (Oxford, 1976), 4.5.b.39, pp. 539ff.
30 Smith, *Theory of Moral Sentiments*, 6.2.2.6, p. 230; *Wealth of Nations*, 4.7.c.80, p. 626.
31 Smith, *Wealth of Nations*, 4.7.c.80, pp. 626ff. This passage is analysed at some length in Wyatt-Walter, 'Smith', pp. 23ff.
32 Jennifer Pitts, *A Turn to Empire: The Rise of Imperial Liberalism in Britain and France* (Princeton and Oxford, 2005), pp. 28–40; Georg Cavallar, *The Rights of Strangers: Theories of International Hospitality, the Global Community, and Political Justice since Vitoria* (Aldershot, 2002), pp. 238 and 252. The following passages are much indebted to Pitt's account, cf. *Turn to Empire*, ch. 2.

33 Pitts, *Turn to Empire*, p. 30.
34 Smith, *Theory of Moral Sentiments*, VI.ii.2.17, p. 275.
35 Pitts, *Turn to Empire*, p. 45.
36 Smith, *Wealth of Nations*, V.iii.92, pp. 946ff., IV.vii.c.103–8, pp. 637–41; V.i.e.26–31, pp. 746–56. There is an excellent analysis in Pitts, *Turn to Empire*, pp. 52–8.
37 The most important analysis is Thomas C. Walker, 'The forgotten prophet: Tom Paine's cosmopolitanism and international relations', *International Studies Quarterly*, 44 (2000), 51–72 (with more references), quotation at p. 51. Cf. ibid. pp. 52 and 69. See also David M. Fitzsimons, 'Tom Paine's new world order: idealistic internationalism in the ideology of early American foreign relations', *Diplomatic History*, 19 (1995), 569–82, Jack Fruchtman, *Thomas Paine: Apostle of Freedom* (New York and London, 1994), and Eric Foner, *Tom Paine and Revolutionary America* (Oxford, 2005). John Keane, *Tom Paine: A Political Life* (London, 1995) covers Paine's biography.
38 Thomas Paine, 'The Rights of Man' [1791/2], in *Political Writings*, ed. Bruce Kuklick (Cambridge, 1989), pp. 49–203, at p. 196; Fitzsimons, 'New world order', pp. 571–3 and 576–7; and Cavallar, *Rights of Strangers*, pp. 72–3.
39 Paine, 'Rights', p. 193.
40 Ibid., pp. 193, 153, 196 and 200. On Paine's concept of human rights, see ibid., pp. 75–9 and 120–8.
41 Cf. Walker, 'Prophet', pp. 59–60.
42 Paine, 'Rights', pp. 141 and 195. See also ibid., pp. 142 and 154; Thomas Paine, 'Common Sense' [1776], in *Political Writings*, pp. 1–38, at p. 8 and the analyses in Walker, 'Prophet', pp. 55–9 as well as Fitzsimons, 'New world order', pp. 577–9.
43 Paine, 'Rights', p. 158; cf. pp. 152ff.
44 Ibid., pp. 141, 143 and 194; Walker, 'The forgotten prophet', 51.
45 The two statements are contrasted with each other in Pitts, *Turn to Empire*, pp. 103ff.
46 Jeremy Bentham, 'Rid yourselves of ultramaria' [1793], in *Colonies, Commerce, and Constitutional Law: Rid Yourselves of Ultramaria and Other Writings on Spain and Spanish America*, ed. Philip Schofield (Oxford, 1995), p. 25; cf. p. 309 (on the moral aspect); pp. 10–22 include some of the tables and attached explanations; pp. 23–5 focus on domestic and military disadvantages.
47 Jeremy Bentham, 'Principles of international law' [1786/9], in *The Works of Jeremy Bentham*, ed. John Bowring (Edinburgh, London, 1843), vol. II, pp. 538, 546, 547–9. A fairly recent introduction to Bentham's political thinking is Wilhelm Hofmann, *Politik*

des aufgeklärten Glücks: Jeremy Benthams philosophisch-politisches Denken (Berlin, 2002). Pitts, *Turn to Empire*, ch. 4 offers a succinct and excellent analysis of Bentham's critique of colonialism.
48 Pitts, *Turn to Empire*, pp. 10, 112ff. and 246.
49 Jeremy Bentham, 'Constitutional code', book 1, ch. 6, in John Bowring (ed.), *The Works of Jeremy Bentham* (Edinburgh, 1843), vol. IX, p. 33, quoted in Pitts, *Turn to Empire*, p. 108.
50 Bentham, 'Emancipation Spanish: Philo-Hispanus to the people of Spain', in *Colonies, Commerce, and Constitutional Law*, pp. 197–276, especially pp. 205, 225, 247 and 265.
51 See especially Pitts, *Turn to Empire*, ch. 3.
52 Quoted in David Boucher, *Political Theories of International Relations* (Oxford, 1998), p. 320. Boucher offers an excellent introduction, see ibid., pp. 308–26. See also Boucher, *The Limits of Ethics*, pp. 180–6. Burke's postulate of a European community helped him to advocate intervention in revolutionary France.
53 Edmund Burke, *The Writings and Speeches of Edmund Burke*, ed. Paul Langford, textual ed. William B. Todd (Oxford, 1981–2000), vol. 8, p. 97ff.
54 Pitts, *Turn to Empire*, pp. 97 and 81–2; Boucher, *Theories*, p. 326.
55 Pitts, *Turn to Empire*, p. 78. See also ibid., pp. 72–3 and 77.
56 Burke, 'Speech on Fox's India Bill, December 1, 1783', in *Writings and Speeches*, vol. 5, p. 390.
57 Burke, 'Speech in reply, May 28, 1794', in *Writings and Speeches*, vol. 7, pp. 264ff. See Pitts, *Turn to Empire*, pp. 74–80.
58 Richard S. Dunn and Mary Maples Dunn (eds), *The World of William Penn* (Philadelphia, 1986) is a collection of useful essays. See also William R. Durland, *William Penn, James Madison and the Historical Crisis in American Federalism* (Lewiston, NY, 2000).
59 William Penn, 'An essay towards the present and future peace of Europe, by the establishment of an European dyet, parliament, or estates' [1693], in *The Peace of Europe: The Fruits of Solitude and Other Writings*, ed. Edwin B. Bronner (London, 1993), pp. 5–22, at 14, 20 and 9. The most relevant publication on the essay is Melvin B. Endy, 'William Penn's essay on the present and future peace of Europe: the proposal of a political pacifist', in Norbert Brieskorn and Markus Riedenauer (eds), *Suche nach Frieden: Politische Ethik in der Frühen Neuzeit III* (Stuttgart, 2003), pp. 373–405, especially pp. 390–400.
60 Endy, 'Penn's essay', pp. 398ff.
61 Penn, 'Essay', pp. 12 and 18. Franz Bosbach, *Monarchia Universalis: Ein politischer Leitbegriff der frühen Neuzeit* (Göttingen, 1988) portrays the career of the universal monarchy as a key concept of

European foreign policy from 1500 to 1800. See also by the same author, 'The European debate on universal monarchy', in David Armitage (ed.), *Theories of Empire, 1450–1800* (Aldershot, 1998), pp. 81–98.
62 Penn, 'Essay', pp. 6, 17–19.
63 Ibid., pp. 7ff. and 15.
64 Ibid., pp. 5, 12, 16 and 18.
65 Ibid., pp. 18, 12, 16.
66 Both quotations in Endy, 'Penn's essay', p. 383.
67 Eduard Berstein, *Cromwell and Communism* [1895], trans. H. J. Stenning (London, 1930), ch. 17, quoted in Aksu, *Early Notions*, p. 19.
68 John Bellers, 'Some reasons for an European state' [1710], in George Clarke (ed.), *John Bellers: His Life, Times and Writings* (London, 1987), pp. 132–53, at pp. 137 and 140.
69 Ibid., pp. 142–5, 148.
70 Ibid., pp. 135, 139, 147.
71 Ibid., p. 152. On Sully, see especially Klaus Malettke, 'Konzeptionen kollektiver Sicherheit in Europa bei Sully und Richelieu', in August Buck (ed.), *Der Europa-Gedanke* (Tübingen, 1992), pp 83–106, in particular pp. 84–95. Sully's plan, and the name of Henry IV, were cited in the works of Penn, Bellers, Saint-Pierre and others mainly because it suggested that the project was more than mere fantasy and wishful thinking.
72 Quoted in John Robertson, 'Introduction', in Andrew Fletcher, *Political Works*, ed. John Robertson (Cambridge, 1997), pp. ix–xxx, at pp. xviiff. See also the references ibid., pp. xxxvii–xl and especially John Robertson (ed.), *A Union for Empire: Political Thought and the British Union of 1707* (Cambridge, 1995); idem, 'Union by incorporation: England, Scotland and Ireland 1603–1801', in Thomas Fröschl (ed.), *Föderationsmodelle und Unionsstrukturen: Über Staatenverbindungen in der frühen Neuzeit vom 15. zum 18. Jahrhundert* (München, 1994), pp. 104–18; 'Andrew Fletcher's vision of union', in Roger A. Mason (ed.), *Scotland and England 1286–1815* (Edinburgh, 1987), pp. 203–25; Iain McLean and Alistair McMillan, *State of the Union* (Oxford, 2005), ch. 2, pp. 13–60.
73 See the 'Biographical notes' in Fletcher, *Works*, pp. xli–xlviii and Robertson, 'Union by incorporation', p. 112. According to Robertson, advocates saw incorporation as 'a mutual communication of rights and privileges, to the benefit of both parties' (ibid.).
74 Andrew Fletcher of Saltoun, 'An account of a conversation concerning a right regulation of governments for the common good of mankind' [1704], in *Selected Political Writings and Speeches*, ed. David Daiches (Edinburgh, 1979), pp. 106–37, at p. 128. A succinct summary of

Fletcher's proposal is offered by Cheneval, *Philosophie*, pp. 328–32. On Pufendorf's theory see Robertson, 'Union by incorporation', p. 111; Cavallar, *Rights of Strangers*, p. 200; and idem, 'Zwischen Integration und Abgrenzung: das Fremdenrecht als Teil der Europa-Ideen', in Markus Kremer and Hans-Richard Reuter (eds), *Macht und Moral: Politisches Denken im 17. und 18. Jahrhundert* (Stuttgart, 2007), pp. 143–60, at pp. 145–7.

75 Andrew Fletcher, 'A discourse concerning the affairs of Spain' [1698], in *Political Works*, pp. 83–117, at p. 99. In a passage that is most certainly ironical, Fletcher advises the future king of Spain to start his rule with the conquest of North Africa, since 'he cannot do anything more useful and convenient for Spain' (ibid., p. 113).

76 Fletcher, 'Account', pp. 129 and 135.

77 Ibid., pp. 117–22. The term 'incorporating union' can be found on p. 117, the quotations at pp. 121 and 122.

78 Ibid., pp. 108–10, the quotation at p. 110.

79 The standard study on the civic humanist paradigm is John Greville A. Pocock, *The Machiavellian Moment: Florentine Political Thought and the Atlantic Republican Tradition* (Princeton, 1975). Chapter XIV covers the eighteenth-century debates. See also 'Virtue and commerce in the eighteenth century', *Journal of Interdisciplinary History*, 3 (1972), pp. 119–34; Jack H. Hexter, 'Republic, virtue, liberty, and the political universe of J. G. A. Pocock', in *On Historians* (Cambridge, Mass., 1979), pp. 255–303. A useful definition of civic humanism can be found in John Robertson, 'The Scottish Enlightenment at the limits of the civic tradition', in Istvan Hont and Michael Ignatieff (eds), *Wealth and Virtue: The Shaping of Political Economy in the Scottish Enlightenment* (Cambridge, 1983), pp. 138ff. More references in Robertson, 'Bibliographical guide', pp. xxxviiiff. and Blair Worden, 'English republicanism', in James Henderson Burns and Mark Goldie (eds), *The Cambridge History of Political Thought 1450–1700* (Cambridge, 1991), pp. 443–75.

80 Adam Smith, *Inquiry*, 1.4.1, p. 37.

81 Fletcher, 'Account', pp. 134–6, the quotation at p. 136.

82 Ibid., pp. 130–1 and 134.

83 Ibid., pp. 113 and 115ff.; the quotation at pp. 129ff. The democratic peace proposition was widely discussed in the 1990s; as an introduction, see Georg Cavallar, 'Kantian perspectives on democratic peace: alternatives to Doyle', *Review of International Studies*, 27 (2001), 229–48.

84 Cf. Cheneval, *Philosophie*, pp. 328–30. On the standing army controversy in Britain, see Worden, 'Republicanism', p. 461.

85 Fletcher, 'Account', p. 132.

86 Ibid., p. 136.
87 Ibid., p. 130.
88 Immanuel Kant, *Gesammelte Schriften*, ed. Akademie der Wissenschaften zu Berlin (Berlin, Leipzig, 1900ff.), vol. VIII, p. 372. I have used the translation *Practical Philosophy*, trans. and ed. Mary J. Gregor (Cambridge, 1996).
89 Fletcher, 'Account', pp. 120–3 and 128. Worden, 'Republicanism', pp. 466ff. shows that, in general, some English republicans did not follow Machiavelli's clear preferences for a 'commonwealth for expansion'.
90 Cheneval, *Philosophie*, p. 332.
91 This is the argument of Robertson, 'Introduction', p. xxvii.
92 Fletcher, 'Account', pp. 124 and 113–15. Cf. Thomas Christopher Smout, *Scottish Trade on the Eve of the Union 1660–1707* (Edinburgh, 1963), who shows that the crisis of the Scottish economy was not caused by the union.
93 Robert Fine and Robin Cohen, 'Four cosmopolitanism moments', in Steven Vertovec and Robin Cohen (eds), *Conceiving Cosmopolitanism: Theory, Context, and Practice* (Oxford, 2002), pp. 137–62, at p. 138.
94 Anthony Pagden, *Lords of all the World. Ideologies of Empire in Spain, Britain and Frnace, c.1500–c.1800* (New Haven, London, 1995), pp. 160–3.
95 Endy, 'Penn's essay', p. 401.

Kant and the 'miserable comforters': contractual cosmopolitanism

1 Walter D. Mignolo, 'The many faces of cosmo-polis: border thinking and critical cosmopolitanism', in Carol A. Breckenridge et al. (eds), *Cosmopolitanism* (Durham, NC and London, 2002), pp. 157–87, at p. 166.
2 See Georg Cavallar, *The Rights of Strangers: Theories of International Hospitality, the Global Community, and Political Justice since Vitoria* (Aldershot, 2002), pp. 111ff., 274ff., 367ff., 328ff. and 367ff. Garrett Wallace Brown, 'Kantian cosmopolitan law and the idea of a cosmopolitan constitution', *History of Political Thought*, 27, 4 (2006), 661–84, at pp. 667–72, conveniently summarizes the 'five freedoms' of Kant's cosmopolitan right.
3 Abbé de Saint-Pierre, 'A project for settling an everlasting peace in Europe' [1713], in Esref Aksu (ed.), *Early Notions of Global*

Governance: Selected Eighteenth-Century Proposals for 'Perpetual Peace' (Cardiff, 2008), pp. 52–65, at p. 53.
4 See Cavallar, *Rights of Strangers*, p. 341 and especially Derek Heater, *World Citizenship and Government: Cosmopolitan Ideas in the History of Western Political Thought* (Basingstoke, 1996), pp. 65–70 and Heinz-Gerhard Justenhoven, *Internationale Schiedsgerichtsbarkeit: Ethische Norm und Rechtswirklichkeit* (Stuttgart, 2006), pp. 114–25 for more.
5 Immanuel Kant, *Gesammelte Schriften*, ed. Akademie der Wissenschaften zu Berlin (Berlin, Leipzig, 1900ff.), II, p. 253. I have used the translation: *Practical Philosophy*, trans. and ed. Mary J. Gregor (Cambridge, 1996). Occasionally, I have made changes.
6 A myriad of contemporary authors attacks, deplores, condemns or tries to explain Kant's racist statements, among them Robert Bernasconi, Thomas McCarthy, Robert Louden, Michael Scrivener and Charles Mills. The quotation is Robert Fine and Robin Cohen, 'Four cosmopolitanism moments', in Steven Vertovec and Robin Cohen (eds), *Conceiving Cosmopolitanism: Theory, Context, and Practice* (Oxford, 2002), pp. 137–62, at p. 145. See especially Michael Scrivener, *The Cosmopolitan Ideal in the Age of Revolution and Reaction, 1776–1832* (London, 2007), pp. 18ff.; Sharon Anderson-Gold, *Cosmopolitanism and Human Rights* (Cardiff, 2001), pp. 20–7; and Pauline Kleingeld, 'Kant's second thoughts on race', *The Philosophical Quarterly*, 57 (2007), 573–92, particularly pp. 575 and 582ff.
7 I suggested this interpretation in my *Rights of Strangers*, p. 349. It is fully developed in Kleingeld's excellent essay 'Thoughts on race'.
8 This follows Kleingeld, 'Thoughts on race', pp. 586–9.
9 Ibid., p. 580ff. and eadem, 'Six varieties of cosmopolitanism in late eighteenth-century Germany', *Journal of the History of Ideas*, 60 (1999), 505–24, at pp. 516ff. (on Forster); Mary Anne Perkins, *Christendom and European Identity: The Legacy of a Grand Narrative since 1789* (Berlin, New York, 2004), pp. 121–3 and 126, and Kleingeld, 'Thoughts on race', pp. 577ff. (on Herder), and Jürgen Osterhammel, *Die Entzauberung Asiens: Europa und die asiatischen Reiche im 18. Jahrhundert* (München, 1998), pp. 72–5 (on Justi).
10 Andrea Albrecht, *Kosmopolitismus: Weltbürgerdiskurse in Literatur, Philosophie und Publizistik um 1800* (Berlin and New York, 2005), pp. 391–9, Kant, *Schriften*, XVII, 2.1, p. 673, translated in Pauline Kleingeld, 'Kant's cosmopolitan patriotism', *Kant-Studien*, 94 (2003), 299–316, reprinted in Sharon Byrd and Joachim Hruschka (eds), *Kant and Law* (Aldershot, 2006), pp. 473–90, at p. 311.

11 Kant, *Schriften*, V, p. 295 and VII, pp. 219 and 228ff. See Scrivener, *Ideal*, pp. 36ff.; Carola Häntsch, 'The world citizen from the perspective of alien reason: notes on Kant's category of the *Weltbürger* according to Josef Simon', in Rebecka Lettevall and My Klockar Linder (eds), *The Idea of Kosmopolis: History, Philosophy and Politics of World Citizenship* (Huddinge, 2008), pp. 51–63, especially pp. 53–9.

12 Adam Smith, *The Theory of Moral Sentiments* [1759], ed. D. D. Raphael and A. L. Macfie (Oxford, 1976), 3.1.6, p. 113. Cf. Kant, *Schriften*, IV, p. 393. See Samuel Fleischacker, 'Values behind the market: Kant's response to the *Wealth of Nations*', *History of Political Thought*, 17 (1996), pp. 379–407 on the Smith–Kant connection.

13 Kant, *Schriften*, VII, pp. 83–5. Cf. Kant, *The Critique of Judgement*, trans. James Creed Meredith (Oxford, 1980), p. 153; V, pp. 294ff.; *Schriften*, IXX, pp. 184ff.

14 Kant, *Schriften*, VIII, p. 350 note.

15 Kant, *Schriften*, IV, p. 433; V, p. 128; *Religion within the Boundaries of Mere Reason and Other Writings*, trans. and eds Allen Wood and George di Giovanni (Cambridge, 1998), pp. 151ff.; VI, pp. 151–3.

16 Kant, *Schriften*, XXVII, 2.1, p. 673, translated in Kleingeld, 'Cosmopolitan patriotism', p. 479; Kant, *Schriften*, VIII, p. 99, translated in Kleingeld, 'Thoughts on race', p. 578.

17 Kant, *Schriften*, VI, p. 267; cf. VIII, p. 358.

18 Ibid., VI, p. 258 and VI, p. 352.

19 Ibid., VI, p. 258. Cf. VI, pp. 255–7 and VI, pp. 264–6. Wolfgang Kersting, 'Eigentum, Vertrag und Staat bei Kant und Locke', in Martyn P. Thompson (ed.), *John Locke und/and Immanuel Kan: Historical Reception and Contemporary Relevance* (Berlin, 1991), pp. 109–34 is a profound comparison between Locke's and Kant's theory of property.

20 Kant, *Schriften*, VI, p. 267. Cf. Kersting, 'Eigentum', pp. 127ff.

21 Karlfriedrich Herb and Bernd Ludwig, 'Naturzustand, Eigentum und Staat – Immanuel Kants Relativierung des "Ideal des Hobbes"', *Kant-Studien*, 84 (1993), 313ff. Pauline Kleingeld has pointed out that Kant's argument can only deliver a partial grounding for cosmopolitan right, and holds that the innate right to freedom provides a better and truly comprehensive justification. My point is that the two argumentative strategies are not mutually exclusive, but basically identical. See Pauline Kleingeld, 'Kant's cosmopolitan law: world citizenship for a global order,' *Kantian Review*, 2 (1998), 72–90.

22 Immanuel Kant, 'The metaphysics of morals Part I: Metaphysical first principles of the doctrine of right' [1797], in *Practical Philosophy*, trans. and ed. Mary J. Gregor (Cambridge, 1996), p. 435; Kant, *Schriften*, VI, p. 288. See Sigrid Thielking, *Weltbürgertum:*

Kosmopolitische Ideen in Literatur und politischer Publizistik seit dem 18. Jahrhundert (München, 2000) on eighteenth-century cosmopolitanism.
23 Kant, Immanuel, 'Toward Perpetual Peace' [1795], in *Practical Philosophy*, p. 330; Kant, *Schriften*, VIII, p. 360.
24 Ibid., p. 335ff.; Kant, *Schriften*, VIII, p. 368.
25 This paragraph summarizes Sankar Muthu's excellent 'Justice and foreigners: Kant's cosmopolitan right', *Constellations*, 7 (2000), 23–45, reprinted in Byrd and Hruschka (eds), *Kant and Law*, pp. 449–71. See also his *Enlightenment against Empire* (Princeton and Oxford, 2003). Thomas E. Hill, Jr., *Respect, Pluralism, and Justice: Kantian Perspectives* (Oxford, 2000), especially pp. 11–32 and 59–86 shows that Kantian ethics can be interpreted as pluralistic and endorsing cultural diversity, while avoiding the pitfalls of moral relativism.
26 Kant, *Schriften*, VIII, p. 355.
27 Ibid., VIII, p. 356.
28 Jacob and Wilhelm Grimm, *Deutsches Wörterbuch* (Leipzig, 1885), 6, p. 676.
29 See Georg Cavallar, *Pax Kantiana: Systematisch-historische Untersuchung des Entwurfs "Zum ewigen Frieden" (1795) von Immanuel Kant* (Wien, Köln, Weimar, 1992), pp. 136–42.
30 Johann Georg Hamann, *Londoner Schriften: Historisch-kritische Neuedition von Oswald Bayer und Bernd Weißenborn* (München, 1993), p. 342.
31 Knut Ipsen, 'Ius gentium – ius pacis? Zur Antizipation grundlegender Völkerrechtsstrukturen der Friedenssicherung in Kants Traktat "Zum ewigen Frieden"', in Reinhard Merkel and Roland Wittmann (eds), *'Zum ewigen Frieden': Grundlagen, Aktualität und Aussichten einer Idee von Immanuel Kant* (Frankfurt am Main, 1996), pp. 290–308; at p. 303 the phrase is 'translated' as 'unangenehme Schönredner'.
32 Carl Schmitt, *Der Nomos der Erde im Völkerrecht des Jus Publicum Europaeum* [1950], 3rd edn (Berlin, 1988), pp. 43ff. and 113–15.
33 Rousseau, 'The state of war' [1756], in Stanley Hoffmann and David P. Fidler (eds), *Rousseau on International Relations* (Oxford, 1991), p. 43. A brief introduction is Georg Cavallar, 'La société générale du genre humain: Rousseau on cosmopolitanism, international relations, and republican patriotism', in Paschalis M. Kitromilides (ed.), *From Republican Polity to National Community: Reconsiderations of Enlightenment Political Thought* (Oxford, 2003), pp. 89–109, and the recent essay by Maximilian Forschner, 'Jean-Jacques Rousseau über Krieg und Frieden', in Markus Kremer and Hans-Richard Reuter (eds), *Macht und Moral – Politisches Denken im 17. und 18. Jahrhundert* (Stuttgart, 2007), pp. 306–20.

34 Georg Geismann, 'On the philosophically unique realism of Kant's doctrine of eternal peace', in Hoke Robinson (ed.), *Proceedings of the Eighth International Kant Congress* (Milwaukee, 1995), vol. I, 1, pp. 273–89, at p. 282.
35 Kant, *Schriften*, VI, p. 344 and VIII, pp. 354ff.
36 Ibid. VI, p. 344; VI, p. 350; VIII, p. 354. See also Georg Cavallar, *Kant and the Theory and Practice of International Right* (Cardiff, 1999), pp. 46 and 54ff., Karlfriedrich Herb and Bernd Ludwig, 'Naturzustand, Eigentum und Staat – Immanuel Kants Relativierung des "Ideal des Hobbes"', *Kant-Studien*, 84 (1993), pp. 283–316.
37 Kant, *Schriften*, XV, p. 210 and II, p. 267.
38 Kant, 'Die Metaphysik der Sitten: Rechtslehre' § 44, in Kant, *Schriften*, VI, p. 312.
39 An introduction is Georg Cavallar, 'EU und USA: der Streit um die "gerechten Kriege"', in idem, *Die europäische Union – Von der Utopie zur Friedens- und Wertegemeinschaft* (Wien, 2006), pp. 118–36 (with more references).
40 Emer de Vattel, *The Law of Nations or the Principles of Natural Law* [1758], trans. by Charles G. Fenwick (Washington, 1916), book III, ch. III, §§ 379–94; Stéphane Beaulac, *The Power of Language in the Making of International Law: The Word Sovereignty in Bodin and Vattel and the Myth of Westphalia* (Leiden and Boston, 2004), pp. 127–83 and Cavallar, *Rights of Strangers*, pp. 306–17.
41 Vattel, *Law of Nations*, I, XIV, § 191.
42 See for instance Adam Smith, *Lectures on Jurisprudence*, eds R. L. Meek, D. D. Raphael and P. G. Stein (Oxford, 1978), (B) 340, 545.
43 Cf. Vattel, *Law of Nations*, III, IV, § 50.
44 Ibid., III, XII, § 190.
45 Ibid., § 192.
46 Ibid., III, III, § 47.
47 Kant, *Schriften*, VIII, p. 312.
48 For that reason I think it is misleading to see Kant as a 'just war theorist'; cf. Brian Orend, 'Kant's just war theory', *Journal of the History of Philosophy*, 37 (1999), 323–53.
49 Kant, *Schriften*, VI, pp. 345ff. This peace proposition is very different from what Doyle has claimed; cf. Georg Cavallar, 'Kantian perspectives on democratic peace: alternatives to Doyle', *Review of International Studies*, 27 (2001), 229–48.
50 Cf. Orend, 'Kant's just war theory', pp. 350–2.
51 Thomas Hobbes, *On the Citizen* [1641], in Richard Tuck and Michael Silverthorne (eds) (Cambridge and New York, 1998), ch. 14, section 4, p. 156; emphasis in the original. See Hidemi Suganami, *The Domestic Analogy and World Order Proposals* (Cambridge, 1989) and Francis

Cheneval, *Philosophie in weltbürgerlicher Bedeutung* (Basel, 2002), *passim* on the domestic analogy.
52 Vattel, *Law of Nations*, Preface, pp. 9ff. The following quotations ibid.
53 Kant, *Schriften*, VIII, p. 355.
54 Ibid., IV, p. 410.
55 Ibid., VIII, p. 349.
56 Vattel, *Law of Nations*, Preface, pp. 10ff. and III, XII, § 189. See Heinhard Steiger, 'Völkerrecht und Naturrecht zwischen Christian Wolff und Adolf Lasson', in Diethelm Klippel (ed.), *Naturrecht im 19. Jahrhundert. Kontinuität – Inhalt – Funktion – Wirkung* (Goldbach, 1997), pp. 48ff. and Emmanuelle Jouannet, *Emer de Vattel et l'émergence doctrinale du droit international classique* (Paris, 1998), pp. 229–50.
57 Kant, *Schriften*, VIII, pp. 347ff. See Reinhard Brandt, 'Das Problem der Erlaubnisgesetze im Spätwerk Kants', in Otfried Höffe (ed.), *Immanuel Kant: Zum ewigen Frieden* (Berlin, 1995), pp. 69–86 and Elisabeth Ellis, *Kant's Politics: Provisional Theory for an Uncertain World* (Yale, 2005), ch. 4.
58 Cheneval, *Philosophie*, p. 223.
59 Kant, *Schriften*, VIII, p. 357. An introduction to Wolff's international legal theory is Georg Cavallar, 'The law of nations in the Age of Enlightenment: moral and legal principles', *Annual Review of Law and Ethics*, 12 (2004), 6–10, and especially Cheneval, *Philosophie*, pp. 132–213. Dietmar von der Pfordten defines normative individualism in political philosophy: the ultimate point of reference for questions relating to right or justice are the individual human beings; see his 'Normativer Individualismus', *Zeitschrift für philosophische Forschung*, 58 (2004), 321–46.
60 Cf. Cavallar, *Rights of Strangers*, ch. 3, especially pp. 121–4; and Richard Tuck, *The Rights of War and Peace: Political Thought and the International Order from Grotius to Kant* (Oxford, 1999), ch. 3.
61 Hugo Grotius, *De Jure Belli ac Pacis Libri Tres* [1625; The Law of War and Peace], vol. II, trans. Francis W. Kelsey (3 vols., Oxford, 1925; reprint New York, 1964), prolegomena 28, p. 20.
62 Cf. Cavallar, *Rights of Strangers*, p. 200.
63 Cf. Paul W. Schroeder, *The Transformation of European Politics 1763–1848* (Oxford, 1994), pp. 46–52 and Hamish Scott, *The Birth of a Great Power System, 1714–1815* (Harlow, 2005), ch. 5, especially pp. 137–42 on the nature of international rivalry. Franz Bosbach, *Monarchia Universalis: Ein politischer Leitbegriff der frühen Neuzeit* (Göttingen, 1988) portrays the career of the universal monarchy as a key concept of European foreign policy from 1500 to 1800. See

also idem, 'The European debate on universal monarchy', in David Armitage (ed.), *Theories of Empire, 1450–1800* (Aldershot, 1998), pp. 81–98, and Derek Heater, *World Citizenship and Government: Cosmopolitan Ideas in the History of Western Political Thought* (Basingstoke, UK, 1996), pp. 60ff., 79 and 85ff.

Recent publications emphasize the achievements of the theory of the right of nations before Kant: Jan Schröder, 'Die Entstehung des modernen Völkerrechtsbegriffs im Naturrecht der frühen Neuzeit', *Jahrbuch für Recht und Ethik*, 8 (2000), 47–72; *Recht als Wissenschaft. Geschichte der juristischen Methode vom Humanismus bis zur historischen Schule (1500–1850)* (München, 2001); Karl-Heinz Ziegler, 'Die Ordnung der Welt in der Geschichte des Völkerrechts', in Johannes Müller and Johannes Wallacher (eds), *Weltordnungspolitik für das 21. Jahrhundert: historische Würdigung – ethische Kriterien – Handlungsoptionen* (Stuttgart, 2000), pp. 1–26 (with a list of his publications); Heinhard Steiger, 'Völkerrecht', in Otto Brunner, Werner Conze and Reinhart Koselleck (eds), *Geschichtliche Grundbegriffe. Historisches Lexikon zur politisch-sozialen Sprache in Deutschland* (Stuttgart, 1992), vol. 7, pp. 97–140.

64 Vattel, *Law of Nations*, p. 305; Kant, *Schriften*, VIII, p. 346.
65 Vattel, *Law of Nations*, Preface, pp. 9ff. and Kant, *Schriften*, VI, p. 258.
66 The sentence 'A free treaty among states . . .' is taken from Friedrich Gentz, 'Über den ewigen Frieden' [1800], in Kurt von Raumer, *Ewiger Friede: Friedensrufe und Friedenspläne seit der Renaissance* (Freiburg im Breisgau, 1953), pp. 461–97, at p. 479, trans. Pauline Kleingeld, 'Approaching perpetual peace: Kant's defence of a league of states and his ideal of a world federation', *European Journal of Philosophy*, 12 (2004), pp. 304–25, at p. 314. Gentz, one of Kant's pupils, later became secretary of the conservative Austrian state chancellor Metternich.
67 Recent publications on Kant's theory of the right of nations and *Perpetual Peace* are: Antonio Franceschet, *Kant and Liberal Internationalism: Sovereignty, Justice, and Global Reform* (New York, 2002); Katrin Gierhake, *Begründung des Völkerstrafrechts auf der Grundlage der Kantischen Rechtslehre* (Berlin, 2005); Wolfgang Kersting, *Kant über Recht* (Paderborn, 2004), ch. 4; Jörg Pannier, 'Das Geheimnis des zweiten Zusatzes: Ein historisch-kritischer Beitrag zu Kants Friedensschrift', *Politisches Denken Jahrbuch 2005* (Berlin, 2006), pp. 189–226; Howard Williams, 'Back from the USSR: Kant, Kaliningrad and world peace', *International Relations*, 20 (2006), pp. 27–48. More references in Cavallar, *Union*, p. 30, and Kleingeld, 'Peace', pp. 324–5.

I have been influenced by the following excellent studies: Cheneval, *Philosophie*, pp. 563–621; Ellis, *Kant's Politics*, ch. 3; Georg Geismann, 'Kants Weg zum Frieden: Spätlese von Seels "Neulesung" des Definitivartikels zum Völkerrecht', in Hariolf Oberer (ed.), *Kant: Analysen – Probleme – Kritik. Bd. III* (Würzburg, 1997), pp. 333–62; Otfried Höffe, *Kant's Cosmopolitan Theory of Law and Peace* (Cambridge, 2006; I have used the German original edition: *'Königliche Völker': Zu Kants kosmopolitischer Rechts- und Friedenstheorie* (Frankfurt am Main, 2001), especially part III); Kleingeld, 'Peace'; Rebecka Lettevall, 'Turning golden coins into loose change: philosophical, political and popular readings of Kant's *Zum ewigen Frieden*', *Jahrbuch für Recht und Ethik*, 17 (2009), 133–50, and Sharon Byrd and Joachim Hruschka, 'From the state of nature to the juridical state of states', *Law and Philosophy*, 27, 6 (2008), 599–641.
68 Kant, *Schriften*, VIII, p. 354.
69 Kant, *Schriften*, VIII, p. 354: 'This would be a *league of nations*, which, however, need not be a state of nations. That would be a contradiction'; Geismann, 'Kants Weg', p. 345; Kleingeld, 'Peace', pp. 312ff.; and Kant, *Schriften*, VIII, p. 367: 'The idea of the right of nations presupposes the *separation* of many neighboring states independent of one another.'
70 Sharon Byrd, 'The state as a "moral person"', in Robinson, *Proceedings*, I, 1, pp. 171–89.
71 Kant, *Schriften*, VIII, p. 350; cf. Byrd and Hruschka, 'State of nature', pp. 633 and 638–40; Peter van Krieken and David McKay (eds), *The Hague: Legal Capital of the World* (The Hague, 2005); and Heinhard Steiger, 'From the international law of Christianity to the international law of the world citizen – reflections on the formation of the epochs of the history of international law', *Journal of the History of International Law*, 3 (2001), 180–93, at p. 185.
72 Kant, *Schriften*, VIII, p. 357; VI, p. 350; the passage is based on Kleingeld, 'Peace', pp. 314ff., at p. 315.
73 Kant, *Schriften*, VIII, pp. 357 and 356.
74 Charles Covell, *Kant and the Law of Peace: A Study in the Philosophy of International Law and International Relations* (New York, 1998), p. 95. See also idem, *Kant, Liberalism and the Pursuit of Justice in the International Order* (Münster and Hamburg, 1994).
75 On the domestic analogy see Cheneval, *Philosophie*, pp. 570f, 593 and 606ff.; Kleingeld, 'Peace', p. 306–11; and Cavallar, *Kant and the Theory and Practice*, pp. 124–31.
76 Kant, *Schriften*, VI, p. 350; VIII, pp. 386, 313 and 357.
77 Volker Gerhardt, 'Der Thronverzicht der Philosophie', in Höffe, *Zum ewigen Frieden*, pp. 171–93, at p. 174.

78 Kant, *Kritik der reinen Vernunft*, A 316/B 373; Kant, *Schriften*, VIII, p. 369.

Late eighteenth-century international legal theory: from *cosmopolis* to the idea of Europe

1 Immanuel Kant, *Gesammelte Schriften*, ed. Akademie der Wissenschaften zu Berlin (Berlin, Leipzig, 1900ff.), VIII, p. 357.
2 Arthur Nussbaum, *A Concise History of the Law of Nations* (New York, 1954), pp. 144–85; Wilhelm G. Grewe, *Epochen der Völkerrechtsgeschichte* (Baden-Baden, 1984), pp. 412–19 and 'Vom europäischen zum universellen Völkerrecht: Zur Frage der Revision des "europazentrischen" Bildes der Völkerrechtsgeschichte', *Zeitschrift für ausländisches öffentliches Recht und Völkerrecht*, 42 (1982), 449–79; Karl-Heinz Ziegler, *Völkerrechtsgeschichte: Ein Studienbuch* (München, 1994), pp. 193–6. More secondary literature is listed in Stéphane Beaulac, 'Emer de Vattel and the exernalization of sovereignty', *Journal of the History of International Law*, 5 (2003), 237–92; C. F. Amerasinghe, 'The historical development of international law – universal aspects', *Archiv des Völkerrechts*, 39 (2001), 367–93; Karl-Heinz Ziegler, 'Zur Entwicklung von Kriegsrecht und Kriegsverhütung im Völkerrecht des 19. und frühen 20. Jahrhunderts', *Archiv des Völkerrechts*, 42 (2004), 271–93; and Georg Cavallar, *The Rights of Strangers: Theories of International Hospitality, the Global Community, and Political Justice since Vitoria* (Aldershot, 2002), pp. 306–7.
3 Carl Schmitt, *Der Nomos der Erde im Völkerrecht des Jus Publicum Europaeum* [1950], 4th edn (Berlin, 1997), pp. 122–9, 136–40; Emer de Vattel, *The Law of Nations or the Principles of Natural Law* (1758), trans. by Charles G. Fenwick (Washington, 1916), book III, ch. XII, § 190 (from now on: 3.12.190), p. 305.
4 Nussbaum, *History*, pp. 74ff.; Stephen C. Neff, *War and the Law of Nations: A General History* (Cambridge, 2005), p. 95. Interestingly, Carl Schmitt is never mentioned. See also the review of Karl Döhring, 'Carl Schmitt: Le nomos de la terre dans le droit des gens du Jus Publicum Europaeum', *Journal of the History of International Law*, 4 (2002), 374–6. As far as Ayala is concerned, see Balthazar de Ayala, *Three Books on the Law of War and on the Duties Connected with War And on Military Discipline* (Washington, 1912), for instance Book I, ch. 2, pp. 16–17 and ch. 6, pp. 61–4.
5 Martti Koskenniemi, 'Theory: implications for the practitioner', in Philip Allott et al. (eds), *Theory and International Law: An*

Introduction (London, 1991), p. 28, quoted in Beaulac, 'Emer de Vattel', p. 285.
6 Neff, *War*, pp. 85–7, at p. 86. See also Jan Schröder, 'Die Entstehung des modernen Völkerrechtsbegriffs im Naturrecht der frühen Neuzeit', *Jahrbuch für Recht und Ethik*, 8 (2000), 47–72; idem, *Recht als Wissenschaft: Geschichte der juristischen Methode vom Humanismus bis zur historischen Schule (1500–1850)* (München, 2001); and Heinhard Steiger, 'From the international law of Christianity to the international law of the world citizen – reflections on the formation of the epochs of the history of international law', *Journal of the History of International Law*, 3 (2001), 180–93.
7 Neff, *War*, pp. 92 and pp. 133–7, at p. 134. See also Kinji Akashi, 'Hobbes's relevance to the modern law of nations', *Journal of the History of International Law*, 2 (2000), 199–216 and Cavallar, *Rights of Strangers*, pp. 173–9.
8 Thomas Hobbes, *Leviathan* [1651], ed. Richard Tuck (Cambridge, 1991), ch. 17, p. 117.
9 Neff, *War*, pp. 92, 137–40; Vattel, *Law of Nations*, 3.3.66, p. 257; Neff, *War*, pp. 95–130; Randall Lesaffer, 'Paix et guerre dans les grands traités du dix-huitième siècle', *Journal of the History of International Law*, 7 (2005), 25–41.
10 Vattel, *Law of Nations*, 3.3.47, p. 251. Nicholas Greenwood Onuf, *The Republican Legacy in International Thought* (Cambridge, 1998), pp. 75–84 and Emmanuelle Jouannet, *Emer de Vattel et l'mergence doctrinale du droit international classique* (Paris, 1998), pp. 100–4 offer a comprehensive and excellent account of Vattel's rejection. Stéphane Beaulac, *The Power of Language in the Making of International Law: The Word Sovereignty in Bodin and Vattel and the Myth of Westphalia* (Leiden, Boston, 2004), 'Emer de Vattel', and Jouannet, *Emer de Vattel* are now the definitive studies on Vattel (with updated bibliographies).
11 Vattel, *Law of Nations*, 'Preface', p. 7a, note k; cf. Onuf, *Republican Legacy*, pp. 76ff. and Beaulac, 'Emer de Vattel', especially pp. 286 and 291, at p. 286.
12 Vattel, *Law of Nations*, 'Preface', p. 11a. See Heinhard Steiger, 'Völkerrecht und Naturrecht zwischen Christian Wolff und Adolf Lasson', in Diethelm Klippel (ed.), *Naturrecht im 19. Jahrhundert. Kontinuität – Inhalt – Funktion – Wirkung* (Goldbach, 1997), pp. 48ff. and Francis Stephen Ruddy, *International Law in the Enlightenment: The Background of Emmerich de Vattel's Le droit des gens* (Dobbs Ferry, NY, 1975), chs. 3 and 4 for a full analysis.
13 Peter Pavel Remec, *The Position of the Individual in International Law according to Grotius and Vattel* (The Hague, 1960), p. 189,

citing Carl Kaltenborn von Stachau, *Kritik des Völkerrechts nach dem jetzigen Standpunkte der Wissenschaft* (Leipzig, 1847), p. 85.

14 See the summary in Annette Brockmöller, *Die Entstehung der Rechtstheorie im 19. Jahrhundert in Deutschland* (Baden-Baden, 1997), pp. 36–42. The important historians are Diethelm Klippel and Jan Schröder: Diethelm Klippel (ed.), *Naturrecht im 19. Jahrhundert: Kontinuität – Inhalt – Funktion – Wirkung* (Goldbach, 1997), and Jan Schröder, *Recht als Wissenschaft: Geschichte der juristischen Methode vom Humanismus bis zur historischen Schule (1500–1850)* (München, 2001).

15 The two key works are: Karl Anton Freiherr von Martini, *Lehrbegriff des Natur-, Staats- und Völkerrechts* (1783; reprint Aalen, 1969) and *Erklärung der Lehrsätze über das allgemeine Staats- und Völkerrecht* (1791; reprint Aalen, 1969). The definitive study is Michael Hebeis, *Karl Anton von Martini (1726–1800): Leben und Werk* (Frankfurt am Main et al., 1996). See also Heinz Barta, Rudolf Palme and Wolfgang Ingenhaeff (eds), *Naturrecht und Privatrechtskodifikation: Tagungsband des Martini-Colloquiums 1998* (Wien, 1999), especially Michael Hebeis, 'Das juristische Werk des Karl Anton von Martini', in ibid., pp. 93–112, Heinz Barta and Günther Pallaver (eds), *Karl Anton von Martini: Ein österreichischer Jurist, Rechtslehrer, Justiz- und Bildungsreformer im Dienste des Naturrechts* (Wien and Berlin, 2007), and Aldo Andrea Cassi, *Il 'Bravo Funzionario' Absburgico tra Absolutismus e Aufklärung: Il Pensiero e l'Opera di Karl Anton von Martini (1726–1800)* (Milano, 1999). Martini refers to 'anarchische Gesellschaft' in *Erklärung*, for instance Erster Teil, paragraph 4 (from now on: I, § 4) and I, § 9; 'äusseres Staatsrecht' is mentioned in II, § 1. Hedley Bull became famous for the first concept: *The Anarchical Society: A Study of Order in World Politics* [1977], 2nd edn. (New York, 1995).

16 Diethelm Klippel and Michael Zwanzger, 'Krieg und Frieden im Naturrecht des 18. und 19. Jahrhunderts', in Werner Rösener (ed.), *Staat und Krieg: Vom Mittelalter bis zur Moderne* (Göttingen, 2000), pp. 136–55, at pp. 140–3.

17 Martini, *Erklärung* I, §§ 1–9; Hebeis, *Martini*, pp. 167ff. and 175. Martini's international legal theory is discussed ibid., pp. 195–204 and in Cassi, *Funzinario*, pp. 182–211.

18 Martini, *Erklärung*, II, § 27.

19 Ibid., I, § 1; II, §§ 5, 34.

20 Ibid., II, §§ 6–7; II, §§ 28–9, 40.

21 Ibid., II, §§ 184–7. Cf. Hebeis, *Martini*, pp. 201ff.

22 Martini, *Erklärung*, II, §§ 13–15; the quotation at II, § 17.

23 Ibid., II, § 22.

24 Ibid., II, §§ 19–20; II § 29.
25 Ibid., II, §§ 136 and 255–60; II, §§ 204 and 205.
26 Ibid., II, § 205.
27 On the 'overwhelming power' in Grotius, Vattel, Kant and others, see Georg Cavallar, *Kant and the Theory and Practice of International Right* (Cardiff, 1999), pp. 94–102.
28 Martini, *Erklärung*, II, § 198.
29 Ibid., II, § 198.
30 Johann Jakob Moser, *Versuch des neuesten europäischen Völkerrechts in Friedens- und Kriegszeiten*, 10 parts in 12 vols (Frankfurt am Main, 1777–80), vol. 1, pp. 11, 13, and 17ff. See also idem, *Grundsätze des Völkerrechts, aus 'Versuch des neuesten Europäischen Völker-Rechts in Friedens- und Kriegszeiten'* [1777] (Frankfurt am Main, 1959). A comprehensive study of Moser in English is Mack Walker, *Johann Jakob Moser and the Holy Roman Empire of the German Nation* (Chapel Hill, 1981). Recent publications are: Andreas Gestrich and Rainer Lächele (eds), *Johann Jacob Moser: Politiker, Pietist, Publizist* (Karlsruhe, 2002), a collection of excellent essays, and Sabrina-Simone Renz, *Johann Jacob Mosers staatsrechtlich-politische Vorstellungen* (Würzburg, 1998). According to Renz, Moser tried to find a balance between Enlightenment and pietism, between *landständische* freedom and enlightened absolutism. He aimed at a balance of ideas and of political powers (e.g. Emperor and estates; with a bibliography ibid., pp. 255–61). The quotation is from *Grundsätze*, p. 7.
31 Moser, *Versuch des Völkerrechts*, vol. 1, pp. 17–20, especially p. 20: 'dieses (Urteil) bleibet dem grossen allgemeinen Gerichtstage Gottes ... anheimgestellt.'
32 Walker, *Moser*, pp. 340ff. and Nussbaum, *History*, pp. 176ff.
33 Walker, *Moser*, p. 341.
34 Moser, *Grundsätze*, pp. 9, 10 and 25.
35 Walker, *Moser*, pp. 339 and 342; Nussbaum, *History*, pp. 177ff.
36 Martti Koskenniemi, *The Gentle Civilizer of Nations: The Rise and Fall of International Law 1870-1960* (Cambridge, 2002), p. 364. Lauterpacht's metanorm was: 'the principles of the universal commonwealth have to be observed' (*voluntas civitatis maximae est servanda*).
37 Moser, *Grundsätze*, p. 13.
38 Ibid., p. 16.
39 Ibid., p. 15.
40 Ibid., p. 13.
41 Nussbaum, *History*, pp. 139 and 172; Ziegler, *Völkerrechtsgeschichte*, pp. 201ff. Walter Habenicht, *Georg Friedrich von Martens* (Göttingen, 1934), pp. 100–5 lists his key works. Martens acknowledged the influence of Moser in *Einleitung in das positive europäische Völkerrecht*

auf Verträge und Herkommen gegründet (Göttingen, 1796), § 9. An English translation was published under the title *A Compendium of the Law of Nations, Founded on the Treaties and Custom of the Modern Nations of Europe*, trans. William Cobbett (London, 1785, 2nd edn 1802).

42 Martens, *Einleitung*, §§ 2–3; Nussbaum, *History*, pp. 172ff. and Habenicht, *Martens*, pp. 67–74.
43 Martens, *Einleitung*, VI, X; § 1.
44 Martens, *Einleitung*, § 117, §§ 122 and 136; § 5. See also Nussbaum, *History*, pp. 174ff. and Habenicht, *Martens*, pp. 77–81. Therefore, Martens is not a 'relativist' (a claim Habenicht infers from his writings in ibid, p. 54).
45 Martens, *Einleitung*, § 5, Vorbericht VII, and the quotation at § 13. Cf. Habenicht, *Martens*, p. 77.
46 Georg Cavallar, *Die europäische Union – Von der Utopie zur Friedens- und Wertegemeinschaft* (Vienna, 2006), ch. 3.
47 Martens, *Einleitung*, § 13, §§ 118–21.
48 Nussbaum, *History*, p. 174. See also Habenicht, *Martens*, p. 81–6.
49 Martens, *Einleitung*, §§ 258–60, the quotation at § 260.
50 Ibid., §§ 260–1, book 7, §§ 182–246, and § 238 with the quotation.
51 Nussbaum, *History*, p. 176; Habenicht, *Martens*, p. 58.
52 Neff, *War*, part III, especially pp. 161–72. Nineteenth-century international legal theory has gained widespread attention in recent years, not least because of its presumed role as an accomplice of European imperialism. As introductions, see especially Koskenniemi, *Gentle Civilizers*, ch. 2, pp. 98–178 and Brett Bowden, 'The colonial origins of international law: European expansion and the classical standard of civilization', *Journal of the History of International Law*, 7 (2005), 1–23.
53 Jeremy Bentham, *An Introduction to the Principles of Morals and Legislation* (1789), eds J. H. Burns and H. L. A. Hart (London, 1970), pp. 293–300. See the interpretation in Mark W. Janis, *An Introduction to International Law*, 2nd edn. (Boston et al., 1993), pp. 227–35.
54 John Austin, *The Province of Jurisprudence Determined* (1832), p. 208, quoted in Janis, *Introduction*, p. 4. See Roberto Ago, 'Positivism', in Rudolf Bernhardt (ed.), *Encyclopedia of Public International Law* (Amsterdam et al., 1997), vol. 3, pp. 1072–80 with more secondary literature and Ernst Reibstein, *Völkerrecht: Eine Geschichte seiner Ideen in Lehre und Praxis* (Freiburg and München, 1958), vol. 2, pp. 1–38.
55 Robert Ward, *An Enquiry into the Foundation and History of the Law of Nations in Europe from the Time of the Greeks and the Romans to the Age of Grotius*, 2 vols (London, 1795); Nussbaum, *History*,

p. 293; Amerasinghe, 'Development', p. 367. Apparently, Ward is rarely read: D. H. N. Johnson, 'The English tradition in international law', *The International and Comparative Law Quarterly*, 11 (1962), 416–45, at p. 438, gives Ward just a short paragraph and calls his work 'entertaining' and 'useful'. But he does not tell us why.

56 Ward, *Enquiry*, vol. 1, pp. 130 and 60. See also ibid., pp. XV, XX, XIIIff. and 131.

57 See Johnson Kent Wright, 'Historical writing in the Enlightenment world', in Martin Fitzpatrick et al. (eds), *The Enlightenment World* (London and New York, 2007), pp. 207–16, Karen O'Brien, *Narratives of Enlightenment: Cosmopolitan History from Voltaire to Gibbon* (Cambridge, 1997) and Cavallar, *Rights of Strangers*, pp. 230–53 for introductions (with more references).

58 Ibid., p. 147, vol. 2, pp. 478ff., p. XIII.

59 Ibid., pp. XII, XXXIff., and 35ff. Cf. Cavallar, *Rights of Strangers*, pp. 46–59. This is a distinction we can find in contemporary qualified universalists like Brian Barry, cf. *Justice as Impartiality: A Treatise on Social Justice*, Vol. II (Oxford, 1995).

60 Ward, *Enquiry*, p. 127.

61 Ibid., p. 58.

62 Ibid., p. X and 136.

63 Ibid., pp. 79, 102 and 106ff., the quotation at p. 106.

64 Ibid., pp. 81–4, 104ff., 139 and the quotation at p. 146.

65 Edmund Burke, *The Writings and Speeches of Edmund Burke*, ed. Paul Langford, textual ed. William B. Todd (Oxford, 1981–2000), vol. 7, p. 265.

66 Ward, *Enquiry*, pp. 211 and 265.

67 Ibid., pp. 139, 157ff., 160–1, 162, the quotation at pp. 163 and 478ff.

68 Ibid., pp. 162–4, 168.

69 Ibid., pp. XXXV, 95ff., 120, and the quotation at p. 128; cf. pp. 120–30 and 228.

70 Neff, *War*, pp. 34 and 45; Heinhard Steiger, 'From the international law of Christianity to the international law of the world citizen – reflections on the formation of the epochs of the history of international law', *Journal of the History of International Law*, 3 (2001), 180–93.

71 Ward, *Enquiry*, vol. 2, p. 4.

72 Nussbaum, *History*, p. 293.

73 See Gerd van den Heuvel, 'Cosmopolite, Cosmopoli(ti)sme', in Rolf Reichardt and Eberhard Schmidt (eds), *Handbuch politisch-sozialer Grundbegriffe in Frankreich 1680–1820* (München, 1986), pp. 41–55, especially pp. 47–50 and Gonthier-Louis Fink, 'Kosmopolitismus – Patriotismus – Xenophobie: Eine französisch-deutsche Debatte im

Revolutionsjahrzehnt 1789–1799', in Ortrud Gutjahr et al. (eds), *Gesellige Vernunft: Zur Kultur der literarischen Aufklärung* (Würzburg, 1993), pp. 23–42.

74 More extensive analyses are Grewe, *Epochen*, pp. 485–98 and Wolfgang Martens, 'Völkerrechtsvorstellungen der Französischen Revolution in den Jahren 1789–1793', *Der Staat*, 3 (1964), 295–314.

75 Martens, *Einleitung*, pp. XIVff., the quotation at p. XV. See Grewe, *Epochen*, pp. 488, 496 and 489 on Grégoire and his *Déclaration*. Alan Cassels, *Ideology and International Relations in the Modern World* (London and New York, 1996), pp. 18–40 describes the ideological zeal of the revolutionaries, with the quotation from Brissot at p. 22.

76 Francis Cheneval, 'Der kosmopolitische Republikanismus erläutert am Beispiel Anacharsis Cloots', *Zeitschrift für philosophische Forschung*, 58, 3 (2004), 373–96. Cheneval's excellent essay is my main source. See also the bibliography ibid., pp. 394–6 and François Labbé, *Anacharsis Cloots le Prussien Francophile: Une philosophe au service de la Révolution française et universelle* (Paris, 1999).

77 Nicolaus Vogt, *Über die europäische Republik* (Frankfurt am Main, 1787); John Oswald, *Le Gouvernement du Peuple ou Plan de constitution pour la République universelle* (Paris, 1797); Anacharsis Cloots, *La République universelle ou Adresse au Tyrannicides* (Paris, 1792) and idem, *Bases constitutionnelles de la République du genre humain* (Paris, 1793).

78 Cloots, *Bases constitutionnelles*, p. 3, quoted in Cheneval, Republikanismus, p. 379.

79 Hedley Bull, *The Anarchical Society: A Study of Order in World Politics* [1977], 2nd edn. (New York, 1995), p. 24.

80 Cheneval, 'Republikanismus', pp. 384 and 392ff. and Bull, *Society*, p. 25.

81 Cheneval, 'Republikanismus', pp. 386–92.

82 Katherine B. Aaslestad, 'Old visions and new vices: republicanism and civic virtue in Hamburg's print culture, 1790–1810', in Peter Uwe Hohendahl (ed.), *Patriotism, Cosmopolitanism, and National Culture: Public Culture in Hamburg 1700–1933* (Amsterdam and New York, 2003), pp. 143–66, at pp. 147 and 152.

83 Rüdiger Görner, 'Goethe's cosmopolitanism', in Suzanne Kirkbright (ed.), *Cosmopolitans in the Modern World: Studies on a Theme in German and Austrian Literary Culture* (München, 2000), pp. 33–40; Pheng Cheah, 'What is a world? On world literature as worldmaking activity', *Daedalus* 137, 3 (2008), 27–38; Andrea Albrecht, *Kosmopolitismus: Weltbürgerdiskurse in Literatur, Philosophie und Publizistik um 1800* (Berlin and New York, 2005), pp. 299–318; Jim Reed, 'Before the storm: internationalism before German-ness',

in Mary Anne Perkins and Martin Liebscher (eds), *Nationalism versus Cosmopolitanism in German Thought and Culture, 1789–1914: Essays on the Emergence of Europe* (Lewiston, 2006), pp. 35–48, at pp. 47ff.

84 Johann Wolfgang Goethe, 'Some passages pertaining to the concept of world literature', translated in Cheah, 'World literature', p. 28.

85 My summary follows Pauline Kleingeld, 'Six varieties of cosmopolitanism in late eighteenth-century Germany', *Journal of the History of Ideas*, 60 (1999), 505–24, at 521–4. See also Mary Anne Perkins, *Christendom and European Identity: The Legacy of a Grand Narrative since 1789* (Berlin, New York, 2004), pp. 27–35.

86 Novalis, *Schriften*, eds. Paul Kluckhohn and Richard Samuel (Stuttgart, 1960), III, 524, translated in Kleingeld, 'Varieties', p. 522.

87 All quotations and references in Mary Anne Perkins, 'Introduction', in Perkins and Liebscher, *Nationalism*, pp. 1–34, at pp. 5–10.

88 Cheah, 'World literature', p. 31.

89 Albrecht, *Kosmopolitismus*, pp. 169–92.

90 Ibid., pp. 319–22 and Sigrid Thielking, *Weltbürgertum: Kosmopolitische Ideen in Literatur und politischer Publizistik seit dem 18. Jahrhundert* (München, 2000), pp. 48ff.

91 See the overviews in Thielking, *Weltbürgertum*, pp. 38–83, Albrecht, *Kosmopolitismus*, *passim*, especially pp. 319–52; Siegfried Weichlein, 'Cosmopolitanism, patriotism, nationalism', in Tim Blanning and Hagen Schulze (eds), *Unity and Diversity in European Culture c.1800* (Oxford, 2006), pp. 77–99; and, among many others, Maurizio Viroli, *For Love of Country: An Essay on Patriotism and Nationalism* (Oxford, 1997), ch. 4 and 5.

92 This paragraph follows Jim Reed's excellent article 'Before the storm'.

93 Reed, 'Before the storm', p. 46.

94 Jennifer M. Welsh, *Edmund Burke and International Relations: The Commonwealth of Europe and the Crusade against the French Revolution* (New York, 1995).

95 Beaulac, 'Emer de Vattel', pp. 277–9 (with extensive references); Dieter Wyduckel, 'Recht, Staat und Frieden im Jus Publicum Europaeum', in Heinz Duchhardt (ed.), *Zwischenstaatliche Friedenswahrung in Mittelalter und Früher Neuzeit* (Köln, Wien, 1991), p. 199; Lesaffer, 'Paix et guerre', pp. 25–8.

96 Georg Cavallar, 'Cosmopolis: Supranationales und kosmopolitisches Denken von Vitoria bis Smith', *Deutsche Zeitschrift für Philosophie*, 53 (2005), 49–67.

Immigration, rights and the global community: Pufendorf, Vattel, Bluntschli and Verdross

1   Kleindienst vs. Mandel, 408 US 753, 765 (1972), with the full text at *http://supreme.justia.com/us/408/753/case.html*, visited 14 September 2007. This chapter builds upon Georg Cavallar, *The Rights of Strangers: Theories of International Hospitality, the Global Community, and Political Justice since Vitoria* (Aldershot, 2002). I want to thank the participants of a conference at the University of Tilburg, especially Hans Lindahl.
2   Francisco de Vitoria, 'On Civil Power', in Anthony Padgen and Jeremy Lawrance (eds), *Political Writings* (Cambridge, 1991), p. 40.
3   James A. R. Nafziger, 'The general admission of aliens under international law', *American Journal of International Law*, 77 (1983), 804–47, especially pp. 808ff. and 805 (with the quotation).
4   The distinction is suggested by Joseph H. Carens, 'Aliens and citizens: the case for open borders', in Will Kymlicka (ed.), *The Rights of Minority Cultures* (Oxford, 1995), pp. 331–49, at p. 331, note 1. Cf. *Michael Walzer, Spheres of Justice: A Defence of Pluralism and Equality* (New York, 1983) and Seyla Benhabib, *The Rights of Others: Aliens, Residents, and Citizens* (Cambridge, 2004).
5   Hersch Lauterpacht, 'The Grotian tradition in international law' (1946), in Elihu Lauterpacht (ed.), *International Law, Being the Collected Papers of Hersch Lauterpacht* (Cambridge, 1975), vol. 2, pp. 307–65.
6   Samuel Pufendorf, *The Law of Nature and Nations* [1672], trans. C. H. Oldfather and W. A. Oldfather (Oxford, 1934; reprint New York, 1964), 3.3.9, pp. 363, 365 and 366.
7   Ibid. 3.3.8, p. 363.
8   Ibid., 2.6.5, pp. 302ff.; 3.3.5, p. 354.
9   Ibid. 3.3.9, p. 364.
10 Samuel Pufendorf, *On the Duty of Man and Citizen According to Natural Law*, ed. James Tully, trans. Michael Silverthorne (Cambridge and New York, 1991), 1.9, pp. 68–76 is a very succinct introduction. See also idem, *Law of Nature*, 1.1.19 and 20, pp. 18–20; 1.7.7, pp. 118ff.; 1.7.9, p. 119; 3.4.1, p. 379; Stephen Buckle, *Natural Law and the Theory of Property: Grotius to Hume* (Oxford, 1991), pp. 85ff.; and Ernst Reibstein, 'Pufendorfs Völkerrechtslehre,' *Österreichische Zeitschrift für öffentliches Recht*, 7 (1956), 43–72, pp. 61ff. Emmanuelle Jouannet, *Emer de Vattel et l'émergence doctrinale du droit international classique* (Paris, 1998), pp. 164–219 offers the most comprehensive analysis on perfect and imperfect duties and rights in Grotius, Hobbes, Pufendorf, Wolff and others. My interpretation is

much indebted to Jerome B. Schneewind, *The Invention of Autonomy: A History of Modern Moral Philosophy* (Cambridge, 1998), pp. 133ff.
11 Pufendorf, *Law of Nature*, 3.3.9, p. 364. Cf. 8.9.2, p. 1330.
12 Ibid., 3.3.9, p. 364. See ibid., pp. 364ff. for the following paragraph in the text.
13 David A. Martin, 'The authority and responsibility of states', in T. Alexander Aleinikoff and Vincent Chetail (eds), *Migration and International Legal Norms* (The Hague, 2003), pp. 31–45, at p. 31; Ines Sabine Roellecke, *Gerechte Einwanderungs- und Staatsangehörigkeitskriterien: Ein dunkler Punkt der Gerechtigkeitstheorien* (Baden-Baden, 1999), p. 240 calls it the 'Zugehörigkeitsbestimmungsrecht'.
14 Pufendorf, *Law of Nature*, 3.3.10, p. 366.
15 Pufendorf, *Law of Nature*, 4.4.13, p. 554 and 4.4.5, p. 537. See ibid., 4.4: 'On the origin of dominion', pp. 532–57 for the following paragraph in the text. Buckle, *Natural Law*, ch. 2, esp. pp. 77–86 and 91–107 covers Pufendorf's theory of property.
16 Pufendorf, *Law of Nature*, 2.3.15, p. 208. See also Schneewind, *Invention*, p. 130 and the essays by Craig L. Carr and Michael J. Seidler, 'Pufendorf, sociality and the modern state', *History of Political Thought*, 17 (1996), 354–78 and Istvan Hont, 'The language of sociability and commerce: Samuel Pufendorf and the theoretical foundations of the "Four-Stages Theory"', in Anthony Pagden (ed.), *The Languages of Political Theory in Early-Modern Europe* (Cambridge, 1987), especially p. 274 for more.
17 Pufendorf, *Law of Nature*, 3.3.1, p. 346; 3.3.3, p. 350; 3.3.8–10, pp. 361–8. A short analysis of the 'general duties of humanity' can be found in Thomas Behme, *Samuel von Pufendorf: Naturrecht und Staat. Eine Analyse und Interpretation seiner Theorie, ihrer Grundlagen und Probleme* (Göttingen, 1995), pp. 93ff.
18 Pufendorf, *Law of Nature*, 2.3.10, pp. 195ff.
19 Ibid., 3.3.10, p. 366.
20 Jonathan Irvine Israel, *The Dutch Republic: Its Rise, Greatness, and Fall 1477–1806* (Oxford, 1995), pp. 308ff. and 310ff.
21 Pufendorf, *Law of Nature*, 3.3.9, p. 365.
22 Emer de Vattel, *The Law of Nations or the Principles of Natural Law* [1758], trans. by Charles G. Fenwick (Washington, 1916), 'Introduction', p. 6. For the following list of features see Andrew Hurrell, 'Vattel: pluralism and its limits', in Ian Clark and Iver B. Neumann (eds), *Classical Theories of International Relations* (Houndmills et al., 1996), pp. 233–55, at p. 234. Hurrell himself wants to 'unsettle' but not overthrow this conventional picture with his article. For an introduction to Vattel, see especially Jouannet, *Vattel* and the more recent essay of Karl-Heinz Ziegler, 'Emer de Vattel und die Entwicklung

des Völkerrechts im 18. Jahrhundert', in Markus Kremer and Hans-Richard Reuter (eds), *Macht und Moral – Politisches Denken im 17. und 18. Jahrhundert* (Stuttgart, 2007), pp. 321–41.

23 Vattel, *Law of Nations*, 3.13.201, pp. 310ff.; 1.4.54, pp. 25ff. See Jeremy Rabkin, 'Grotius, Vattel, and Locke: An older view of liberalism and nationality', *The Review of Politics*, 59 (1997), pp. 302ff. for more.

24 Vattel, *Law of Nations*, 3.12.189; Jouannet, *Vattel*, pp. 229ff. There is an extensive reference to Vattel's predecessors and their own attempt to modify the law of nations when applied, ibid., pp. 230–50.

25 Vattel, *Law of Nations*, 'Introduction', § 17, p. 7; 1.2.17–18, p. 14, and *passim*. See Jouannet, *Vattel*, pp. 151–60 for a comprehensive analysis.

26 See Vattel, *Law of Nations*, 'Introduction', §§ 2–4, and *passim*; see also Knut Ipsen, 'Ius gentium - ius pacis? Zur Antizipation grundlegender Völkerrechtsstrukturen der Friedenssicherung in Kants Traktat "Zum ewigen Frieden"', in Reinhard Merkel and Roland Wittmann (eds), *'Zum ewigen Frieden': Grundlagen, Aktualität und Aussichten einer Idee von Immanuel Kant* (Frankfurt am Main, 1996), pp. 299ff.

27 Vattel, *Law of Nations*, 1.5.61, p. 29. See Frederick G. Whelan, 'Vattel's doctrine of the state' [1988], in Knud Haakonssen (ed.), *Grotius, Pufendorf and Modern Natural Law* (Dartmouth, Aldershot et al., 1998), pp. 403–34, at pp. 404 and 409–20, and Rabkin, 'Grotius, Vattel, and Locke', pp. 301–4 on Vattel's liberalism.

28 Vattel, *Law of Nations*, 1.1, p. 11 and Whelan, 'Vattel's doctrine,' p. 411.

29 Vattel, *Law of Nations*, 'Preface', p. 11a; 'Introduction', §§ 10–13, pp. 5ff.; 3.12.189, pp. 304ff.

30 'Introduction', § 16, pp. 6ff.; 1.19.230, p. 92; 2.10.135–7, pp. 154ff.

31 Ibid., 2.8.100, p. 144; 2.8.104, p. 145.

32 Ibid., 1.19.212–14, p. 87; 1.19.215, p. 87.

33 Ibid., 1.19.222, pp. 89ff.

34 See for instance Stephen C. Neff, *War and the Law of Nations: A General History* (Cambridge, 2005), pp. 159–214 and Martti Koskenniemi, *The Gentle Civilizer of Nations: The Rise and Fall of International Law 1870–1960* (Cambridge, 2002).

35 'Promoting the progress of international law, by trying to become the mouthpiece of the legal conscience of the civilized world'. Quoted in Koskenniemi, *Gentle Civilizer*, p. 41. This section follows ibid., pp. 39–97, Betsy Baker, 'The "Civilized Nation" in the work of Johann Caspar Bluntschli', in Markus Kremer and Hans-Richard Reuter (eds), *Macht und Moral – Politisches Denken im 17. und 18. Jahrhundert* (Stuttgart, 2007), pp. 342–58, and Georg Cavallar, *Rights of*

Strangers, pp. 377–9. See also idem, *Die europäische Union – Von der Utopie zur Friedens- und Wertegemeinschaft* (Wien, 2006). The Institute proposed its own *International Regulations on the Admission and Expulsion of Aliens* in 1892; cf. Satvinder Singh Juss, *International Migration and Global Justice* (Aldershot, 2006), pp. 3–4.

36 John Stuart Mill, 'A few words on non-intervention' [1859], in *Essays on Equality, Law, and Education*, ed. by John M. Robson, introduction by Stefan Collini (University of Toronto Press, 1984), p. 119; Wilhelm G. Grewe, 'Vom europäischen zum universellen Völkerrecht: Zur Frage der Revision des "europazentrischen" Bildes der Völkerrechtsgeschichte', *Zeitschrift für ausländisches öffentliches Recht und Völkerrecht*, 42 (1982), pp. 449–79, at pp. 465–75, on Mill p. 471; Jörg Fisch, *Die europäische Expansion und das Völkerrecht: Die Auseinandersetzungen um den Status der überseeischen Gebiete vom 15. Jahrhundert bis zur Gegenwart*, Beiträge zur Kolonial- und Überseegeschichte Bd. 26 (Stuttgart, 1984), pp. 293–5.

37 Baker, 'Civilized Nation', pp. 342–58, the quotation in Koskenniemi, *Gentle Civilizer*, p. 84.

38 Johann Caspar Bluntschli, 'Civilisation', in Bluntschli and Karl Brater (eds), *Deutsches Staats-Wörterbuch* (Stuttgart und Leipzig, 1864), p. 510, trans. in Baker, 'Civilized Nation', p. 352.

39 Koskenniemi, *Gentle Civilizer*, pp. 42–7 and 95–7.

40 Johann Caspar Bluntschli, *Das moderne Völkerrecht der civilisirten Staten* [1868], 3rd edn. (Nördlingen, 1878), Introduction, pp. 1ff. Bluntschli divided the text into paragraphs.

41 Bluntschli, *Völkerrecht*, pp. 26–8 and §§ 382 and 384.

42 Ibid., pp. 27ff. and § 381.

43 Johann Caspar Bluntschli, *Die Bedeutung und die Fortschritte des modernen Völkerrechts* (Berlin, 1866), p. 35. See also his account of the history of the law of nations ibid., pp. 17–63 and Bluntschli, *Völkerrecht*, pp. 12–55.

44 Ibid., p. 55 and Bluntschli, *Bedeutung*, p. 63.

45 Herbert Butterfield, *The Whig Interpretation of History* [1931] (New York, London, 1965). A brilliant parody of Whig historiography is Walter Sellar and Robert Yeatman, *1066 and all that* [1930] (London, 1985).

46 Nafziger, 'The general admission', pp. 815ff.

47 An excellent recent introduction (which also offers more secondary literature) is Koskenniemi, *Gentle Civilizer*, ch. 2 (pp. 98–178).

48 Robert Ward, *An Enquiry into the Foundation and History of the Law of Nations in Europe from the Time of the Greeks and the Romans to the Age of Grotius*, 2 vols (London, 1795), pp. 33ff.

49 Neff, *War*, pp. 279–304, the quotations at pp. 294 and 297; Wilhelm G. Grewe, *Epochen der Völkerrechtsgeschichte* (Baden-Baden, 1984),

part 5, pp. 677–746; Karl-Heinz Ziegler, *Völkerrechtsgeschichte: Ein Studienbuch* (München, 1994), ch. 10, pp. 240–63.

50 Verdross's work is evaluated in a special issue of *European Journal of International Law*, 6 (1995), in Herbert Miehsler, Erhard Mock, Bruno Simma and Ilmar Tammelo (eds), *Ius Humanitatis: Festschrift zum 90. Geburtstag von Alfred Verdross* (Berlin, 1980) and in Anke Brodherr, *Alfred Verdross' Theorie des gemäßigten Monismus* (München, 2004). The quotations are in Bruno Simma, 'The contribution of Alfred Verdross to the theory of international law', *European Journal of International Law*, 6 (1995), 33–54, at p. 54, and Koskenniemi, *Gentle Civilizer*, pp. 246ff. Comprehensive bibliographies are included in *European Journal of International Law*, 6 (1995), 103–14 and in Brodherr, *Theorie*, pp. XI–XXIII.

51 Anthony Carty, 'Alfred Verdross and Othmar Spann: German romantic nationalism, National Socialism and international law', *European Journal of International Law*, 6 (1995), 78–97; Brodherr, *Theorie*, pp. 13–19 and 225–30; Simma, 'Contribution', pp. 36–7.

52 See, for instance, Verdross's role in formulating Article 4 of the Constitution of the Weimar Republic in 1919, reported by Simma, 'Contribution', pp. 42ff.

53 Alfred Verdross, *Die Einheit des rechtlichen Weltbildes auf Grundlage der Völkerrechtsverfassung* (Tübingen, 1923), pp. 13–29.

54 Alfred Verdross, *Völkerrecht*, 3rd edn (Vienna, 1955), pp. 71ff. I want to thank Karl-Heinz Ribisch for this and the following translations. The primacy of international law in Verdross is discussed by Simma, 'Contribution', pp. 44–7, Brodherr, *Theorie*, especially pp. 54–7 and Jochen von Bernstorff, *Der Glaube an das universale Recht: Zur Völkerrechtstheorie Hans Kelsens und seiner Schüler* (Baden-Baden, 2001), pp. 85–8.

55 See Paul Gordon Lauren, *The Evolution of International Human Rights: Visions Seen* (Philadelphia, 1998) and, among many others, Norbert Brieskorn, *Menschenrechte: Eine historisch-philosophische Grundlegung* (Stuttgart, Berlin, Köln, 1997) as well as Robert P. George, *In Defense of Natural Law* (Oxford, 1999). The true watershed came in 1945; see Bardo Fassbender, 'Idee und Anspruch der universalen Menschenrechte im Völkerrecht der Gegenwart', in Josef Isensee (ed.), *Menschenrechte als Weltmission* (Berlin, 2009), pp. 11–41, in particular pp. 14–17.

56 Simma, 'Contribution', pp. 38ff.; Josef L. Kunz, 'Natural-law thinking in the modern science of international law,' *American Journal of International Law*, 55 (1961), 951–8; Heinrich Rommen, *Die ewige Wiederkehr des Naturrechts* [1936], 2nd edn. (München, 1947);

Christopher R. Rossi, *Broken Chain of Being: James Brown Scott and the Origins of modern international Law* (The Hague et al., 1998).

57 See Verdross, *Völkerrecht*, pp. 7ff. and the analysis in Brodherr, *Theorie*, pp. 75–9 and 127ff.

58 Verdross, *Völkerrecht*, pp. 285–95. This late nineteenth-century approach is modified after 1945; see Alfred Verdross and Bruno Simma, *Universelles Völkerrecht: Theorie und Praxis*, 3rd edn (Berlin, 1984), pp. 798ff.

59 *Völkerrecht*, p. 287.

60 Alfred Verdross, 'Les règles internationales concernant le traitement des étrangers', *Recueil des Cours*, 37 (1931), III, 327–412, at pp. 338–40.

61 Ibid., pp. 330 and 337.

62 Simma, 'Contribution', p. 33.

63 Walzer, *Spheres of Justice*, p. 62.

64 *Human Development Report 2004, Cultural Liberty in Today's Diverse World* (Oxford, 2004), p. 47, quoted in Juss, *International Migration*, p. 75.

65 John Rawls, *A Theory of Justice* (Cambridge, 1971) p. 302, his first principle of justice. See Cavallar, *Rights of Strangers*, pp. 46–59 for a more extensive discussion.

66 Hersch Lauterpacht, 'Kelsen's pure science of law' [1933], in Elihu Lauterpacht (ed.), *International Law, being the Collected Papers of Hersch Lauterpacht* (Cambridge, 1975), vol. 2, part 1, pp. 404–30, at p. 428. The Latin sentence in the quotation means: 'It is wrong to derive a right from abuse.'

67 Immanuel Kant, 'The metaphysics of morals Part I: Metaphysical first principles of the doctrine of right' [1797], in Mary J. Gregor (ed.), *Practical Philosophy* (Cambridge, 1996), pp. 365–506, at pp. 414ff. (Kant, *Schriften*, VI, p. 262) and p. 489 (Kant, *Schriften*, VI, p. 352). My analysis is much indebted to Leslie Arthur Mulholland, *Kant's System of Rights* (New York, 1990), pp. 273–8 and Wolfgang Kersting, *Wohlgeordnete Freiheit: Immanuel Kants Rechts- und Staatsphilosophie* (Frankfurt am Main, 1993), pp. 267–72.

68 Immanuel Kant, 'Vorarbeiten zur Rechtslehre', in Deutsche Akademie der Wissenschaften zu Berlin (ed.), *Kant's Gesammelte Schriften* (Berlin and Leipzig, 1955), vol. 23, pp. 207–370, at p. 322.

69 Carens, 'Aliens and citizens', p. 336.

70 Joseph H. Carens, 'Migration and morality: a liberal egalitarian perspective', in Brian Barry and Robert E. Goodin (eds), *Free Movement: Ethical issues in the Translational Migration of People and of Money* (New York, 1992), pp. 25–47, at p. 37.

Conclusion

1. Martine Julia van Ittersum, *Profit and Principle: Hugo Grotius, Natural Rights Theories and the Rise of Dutch Power in the East Indies 1595–1615* (Leiden and Boston, 2006), p. xxix.
2. See also Sankar Muthu, *Enlightenment against Empire* (Princeton and Oxford, 2003).
3. Jennifer Pitts, *A Turn to Empire: The Rise of Imperial Liberalism in Britain and France* (Princeton and Oxford, 2005), p. 2.
4. Amanda Anderson, *The Powers of Distance: Cosmopolitanism and the Cultivation of Detachment* (Princeton, 2001), pp. 65ff.
5. Felix S. Cohen, 'The Spanish origin of Indian rights in the law of the United States', *The Georgetown Law Journal*, 31, 1 (1942), 1–21; Antonio-Enrique Pérez Luño, *La polémica sobre el nuevo mundo: Los clásicos españoles de la flosofia del derecho* (Madrid, 1992); Walter D. Mignolo, 'The many faces of cosmo-polis: border thinking and critical cosmopolitanism', in Carol A. Breckenridge et al. (eds), *Cosmopolitanism* (Durham, NC and London, 2002), pp. 157–87, at p. 164.
6. Mignolo, 'Faces', p. 167. Cf. ibid., pp. 158ff. and 161.
7. Examples are Gertrude Himmelfarb, 'The illusions of cosmopolitanism', in Martha C. Nussbaum et al., *For Love of Country?* ed. Joshua Cohen (Boston, 2002), pp. 72–7, at p. 75; Harald Müller, 'Liberaler Kosmopolitismus: Eine partikularistische Emanation mit Unverträglichkeiten und Nebenwirkungen', *Zeitschrift für Internationale Beziehungen*, 13, 2 (2006), 239–45, at pp. 239–41, who equates cosmopolitanism with liberal cosmopolitanism.
8. Amartya Sen, 'Humanity and Citizenship', in Nussbaum et al., *Love of Country*, pp. 111–18; Kwame Anthony Appiah, 'Cosmopolitan patriots', *Critical Inquiry*, 23, 3 (1997), 617–39, at pp. 636–8; Ananta Kumar Giri, 'Cosmopolitanism and beyond: towards a multiverse of transformations', *Development and Change*, 37, 6 (2006), 1277–92. Anthony Langlois, 'Human rights and cosmopolitan liberalism', *Critical Review of International Social and Political Philosophy*, 10, 1 (2007), 29–45 offers a short, but profound discussion of the Asian values debate and shows why moral cosmopolitans are liberals with good reasons.
9. Jan Nederveen Pieterse, 'Emancipatory cosmopolitanism: towards an agenda', *Development and Change*, 37, 6 (2006), 1247–57, at p. 1255.
10. Pieterse, 'Cosmopolitanism', pp. 1247ff..; Mignolo, 'Faces', p. 182, Giri, 'Cosmopolitanism', p. 1284; David A. Hollinger, 'Not universalists, not pluralists: the new cosmpolitans find their own way', in Steven Vertovec and Robin Cohen (eds), *Conceiving Cosmopolitanism: Theory, Context, and Practice* (Oxford, 2002), pp. 227–39, at pp. 228–33.

11 Costas Douzinas, *Human Rights and Empire: The Political Philosophy of Cosmopolitanism* (Abingdon and New York, 2007), p. 13. See also 'Part I: The paradoxes of human rights' in this book for a full analysis.
12 'Turkey belongs in Europe', *The Economist*, 5 December 2002.
13 Pauline Kleingeld, 'Six varieties of cosmopolitanism in late eighteenth-century Germany', *Journal of the History of Ideas*, 60 (1999), 505–24, at pp. 519–20; Francis Cheneval, 'Der kosmopolitische Republikanismus erläutert am Beispiel Anacharsis Cloots', *Zeitschrift für philosophische Forschung*, 58, 3 (2004), 373–96, at pp. 387ff.
14 Dennis Rasmussen, *The Problems and Promise of Commercial Society: Adam Smith's Response to Rousseau* (University Park, PA, 2008). See also Georg Cavallar, *The Rights of Strangers: Theories of International Hospitality, the Global Community, and Political Justice since Vitoria* (Aldershot, 2002), pp. 235 and 249–52.
15 The primacy of moral cosmopolitanism is suggested by Adam Smith's parable of the earthquake in China and the man who was to lose his little finger the following day, which culminates in a praise of 'the man within, the great judge and arbiter of conduct', the 'impartial spectator': see Adam Smith, *The Theory of Moral Sentiments* [1759], ed. D. D. Raphael and A. L. Macfie (Oxford, 1976), pp. 157ff. Significantly, the story is retold by Kwame Anthony Appiah, *Cosmopolitanism: Ethics in a World of Strangers* (New York, 2007), pp. 156–7.
16 Kleingeld, Pauline, and Eric Brown, 'Cosmopolitanism', in Edward N. Zalta (ed.), *The Stanford Encyclopedia of Philosophy* (2002 edition), at *http://plato.stanford.edu/archives/fall2002/entries/cosmopolitanism*, visited 23 November 2007, pp. 8 and 10; Pieterse, 'Cosmopolitanism', p. 1248; Sharon Anderson-Gold, *Cosmopolitanism and Human Rights* (Cardiff, 2001), pp. 102ff.; Friedrich August Hayek, *The Constitution of Liberty* (London, 1960); Milton Friedman, *Capitalism and Freedom* (Chicago, IL, 1962). A profound critique of nineteenth-century globalization was of course provided by Karl Marx, who in turn has influenced many left-wing contemporary critics of the world market, for instance Hardt and Negri. See David Boucher, *Political Theories of International Relations* (Oxford, 1998), pp. 364ff.
17 Jeremy Waldron, 'Cosmopolitan norms', in Seyla Benhabib, *Another Cosmopolitanism. With Commentaries by Jeremy Waldron, Bonnie Honig, and Will Kymlicka*, ed. Robert Post (Oxford, 2006), pp. 83–101, at p. 94.
18 Seyla Benhabib, 'Hospitality, Sovereignty, Democratic Iterations', in ibid., pp. 147–85, at p. 153.
19 Martha Nussbaum, *Frontiers of Justice: Disability, Nationality, Species Membership* (Cambridge, Mass., 2006), pp. 313–15; Appiah,

Cosmopolitanism, p. 163; Kleingeld and Brown, 'Cosmopolitanism', p. 9. See also Danilo Zolo, *Cosmopolis: Prospects for World Government* (Cambridge, 1997), pp. IX, XIV and 153 and Cavallar, *Rights of Strangers*, pp. 345ff.

20 Charles Jones, 'Cosmopolitanism', in Donald M. Borchert (ed.), *Encyclopedia of Philosophy*, vol. 2 (Detroit et al., 2006), pp. 567–70, at p. 569; Michael Scrivener, *The Cosmopolitan Ideal in the Age of Revolution and Reaction, 1776–1832* (London, 2007), p. 20; Nadia Urbinati, 'Can cosmopolitical democracy be democratic?', in Daniele Archibugi (ed.), *Debating Cosmopolitics* (London, 2003), pp. 67–85, at p. 76.

21 See most recently especially Sharon Byrd and Joachim Hruschka, 'From the state of nature to the juridical state of states', *Law and Philosophy*, 27, 6 (2008), 599–641, at pp. 640ff.

22 Charles Jones, *Global Justice: Defending Cosmopolitanism* (Oxford, 1999), pp. 68ff. and 227ff.; Andrew Hurrell, *On Global Order: Power, Values, and the Constitution of International Society* (Oxford, 2007), p. 12 (with the quotation) and pp. 314ff. See also Andrew Dobson, 'Thick cosmopolitanism', *Political Studies*, 54 (2006), 165–84, at pp. 181ff.; Lea L. Ypi, 'Statist Cosmopolitanism', *Journal of Political Philosophy*, 16, 1 (2008), 48–71.

23 Steven Vertovec and Robin Cohen, 'Introduction: conceiving cosmopolitanism', in Vertovec and Cohen, *Conceiving Cosmopolitanism*, pp. 1–22, at p. 11; Seyla Benhabib, 'The philosophical foundations of cosmopolitan norms', in *Another Cosmopolitanism*, pp. 13–44. See also Cavallar, *Rights of Strangers*, pp. 361–3, with more literature.

24 The key studies are: Francis Cheneval, *Philosophie in weltbürgerlicher Bedeutung: Über die Entstehung und die philosophischen Grundlagen des supranationalen und kosmopolitischen Denkens der Moderne* (Basel, 2002); Muthu, *Enlightenment against Empire*; Pitts, *Turn to Empire*; Jürgen Osterhammel, *Die Entzauberung Asiens: Europa und die asiatischen Reiche im 18. Jahrhundert* (München, 1998); and Andrea Albrecht, *Kosmopolitismus: Weltbürgerdiskurse in Literatur, Philosophie und Publizistik um 1800* (Berlin and New York, 2005).

25 Heinhard Steiger, 'From the international law of Christianity to the international law of the world citizen – reflections on the formation of the epochs of the history of international law', *Journal of the History of International Law*, 3 (2001), 180–93, at pp. 183 and 193. For the following, see Derek Heater, *World Citizenship: Cosmopolitan Thinking and its Opponents* (London and New York, 2002), ch. 4 and *A Brief History of Citizenship* (Edinburgh, 2004); Anderson-Gold, *Cosmopolitanism*, ch. 3 and 5; Bardo Fassbender, 'Idee und Anspruch der universalen Menschenrechte im Völkerrecht der Gegenwart', in

Josef Isensee (ed.), *Menschenrechte als Weltmission* (Berlin, 2009), pp. 11–41 and 'Der Schutz der Menschenrechte als zentraler Inhalt des völkerrechtlichen Gemeinwohls', *Europäische Grundrechte-Zeitschrift*, 30, Heft 1–3 (2003), 1-16.

26 Heater, *Brief History*, p. 111. See also and particularly David Boucher, *The Limits of Ethics in International Relations: Natural Law, Natural Rights, and Human Rights in Transition* (Oxford, 2009), pp. 311–29, who concludes: 'The International Criminal Court represents one of the most significant achievements for a universal moral order' (ibid., p. 329).

27 Alfred Verdross and Bruno Simma, *Universelles Völkerrecht: Theorie und Praxis*, 3rd edn. (Berlin, 1976), pp. 29–34; Christian Tomuschat, 'Obligations arising for states without or against their will', *Recueil des Cours*, 241, 4 (1993), 195–374, at p. 304. See Fassbender, 'The United Nations Charter as constitution of the international community', *Columbia Journal of Transnational Law*, 36 (1998), 529–619 and Fassbender, 'Schutz', pp. 4ff. on the 'international community school'.

28 Tomuschat, 'Obligations', p. 314.

29 Véronique Zanetti, 'Nach dem 11. September: Paradigmenwechsel im Völkerrecht?', *Deutsche Zeitschrift für Philosophie*, 50, 3 (2002), 455–69; the review essay in *Political Studies Review*, 6, 3 (2008), 327–39; and Georg Cavallar, 'EU und USA: der Streit um die "gerechten Kriege"', in *Die europäische Union – Von der Utopie zur Friedens- und Wertegemeinschaft* (Wien, 2006), pp. 118–36.

30 Helen Dexter, 'The "new war" on terror, cosmopolitanism and the "just war" revival', *Government and Opposition*, 43, 1 (2008), 55–78.

31 Seyla Benhabib, *The Rights of Others: Aliens, Residents, and Citizens* (Cambridge, 2004); Joseph H. Carens, 'Aliens and citizens: the case for open borders', in Will Kymlicka (ed.), *The Rights of Minority Cultures* (Oxford, 1995), pp. 331–49; Bernd Ladwig: 'Gibt es ein Recht auf Einwanderung?', in *Politisches Denken Jahrbuch 2002*, (Stuttgart and Weimar), 18–40; Ines Sabine Roellecke, *Gerechte Einwanderungs- und Staatsangehörigkeitskriterien: Ein dunkler Punkt der Gerechtigkeitstheorien* (Baden-Baden, 1999); and Omid A. Payrow Shabani, 'Cosmopolitan justice and immigration. A critical theory perspective', *European Journal of Social Theory*, 10, 1 (2007), 87–98. More publications are listed in Georg Cavallar, 'Zwischen Integration und Abgrenzung: das Fremdenrecht als Teil der Europa-Ideen', in Markus Kremer and Hans-Richard Reuter (eds), *Macht und Moral – Politisches Denken im 17. und 18. Jahrhundert* (Stuttgart, 2007), pp. 143–60. Carens starts off with the bold claim – also indicated in the title of his essay – that we should 'commit ourselves to open borders', but later qualifies it in many respects.

32 Benhabib, *Rights of Others*, p. 5, based on a United Nations report.
33 Christopher Caldwell, 'Islamic Europe? When Bernard Lewis speaks', *Weekly Standard*, 4 October 2004; Vertovec and Cohen, 'Introduction', p. 19.
34 Brett Bowden, 'Nationalism and cosmopolitanism: irreconcilable differences or possible bedfellows?', *National Identities*, 5, 3 (2003), 235–49, at p. 236; H. J. Busch and Axel Horstmann 'Kosmopolit, Kosmopolitismus', in Joachim Ritter (ed.), *Historisches Wörterbuch der Philosophie*, vol. 4 (1976), 1155–67; Siegfried Weichlein, 'Cosmopolitanism, patriotism, nationalism', in Tim Blanning and Hagen Schulze (eds), *Unity and Diversity in European Culture c.1800* (Oxford, 2006), 77–97, the quotation at p. 87.
35 Martha Nussbaum, 'Patriotism and cosmopolitanism,' in *For Love of Country?*, pp. 3–17, at p. 9 and *Cultivating Humanity: A Classical Defense of Reform in Liberal Education* (Cambridge, Mass., 1997), p. 60. The widespread use of the imagery (the first circle encompasses the self, the next one the immediate family, and so on, until we arrive at humanity) is reported in Heater, *Citizenship*, pp. 44–52. Veit Bader, 'For love of country', *Political Theory*, 27, 3 (1999), 379–97, at pp. 391ff. analyses its three assumptions.
36 Ulrich Beck, 'The cosmopolitan perspective: sociology in the second age of modernity', in Vertovec and Cohen, *Conceiving Cosmopolitanism*, pp. 61–85, p. 64. See also the criticism of Luke Martell, 'Global inequality, human rights and power: a critique of Ulrich Beck's cosmopolitanism', *Critical Sociology*, 35, 2 (2009), 253–72.
37 CBS, *60 Minutes: Punishing Saddam*, broadcast on 12 May 1996 and Madeline Albright, *Madam Secretary: A Memoir* (New York, 2003), both quoted in Thomas Pogge, 'Making war on terrorists – reflections on harming the innocent', *Journal of Political Philosophy*, 16, 1 (2008), 1–25, at p. 23.
38 For a full analysis, see Georg Cavallar, '"La société générale du genre humain": Rousseau on cosmopolitanism, international relations, and republican patriotism', in Paschalis M. Kitromilides (ed.), *From Republican Polity to National Community* (Oxford, 2003), pp. 89–109.
39 See, among others, several essays in Nussbaum et al., *For Love of Country* and the rather extreme example of Lee Harris, 'The cosmopolitan illusion', *Policy Review*, 118 (2003), 45–59.
40 Zolo, *Cosmopolis*, p. 153.
41 Timothy Brennan, *At Home in the World: Cosmopolitanism Now* (Cambridge, Mass. and London, 1997), the essays of David Chandler, Timothy Brennan and Peter Gowan in Daniele Archibugi (ed.), *Debating Cosmopolitics* (London, 2003), and Douzinas, *Human Rights and*

Empire, p. 176. See also the neo-Leninist cosmopolitanism of Michael Hardt and Antonio Negri in *Empire* (London and Cambridge, 2000) and *Multitude: War and Democracy in the Age of Empire* (New York, 2004).
42 Douzinas, *Human Rights and Empire*, pp. 291–8.
43 Toni Erskine, *Embedded Cosmopolitanism: Duties to Strangers and Enemies in a World of 'Dislocated Communities'* (Oxford, 2008), p. 72.
44 Ibid., p. 175.
45 Andrew Linklater, 'Cosmopolitanism', in Andrew Dobson and Robyn Eckersley (eds), *Political Theory and the Ecological Challenge* (Cambridge, 2006), pp. 109–27, at p. 124. See also Scrivener, *Ideal*, pp. 10ff., Dobson, 'Cosmopolitanism', pp. 175 and 179ff. Among many publications on globalization, see David Held and Anthony McGrew (eds), *Globalization Theory: Approaches and Controversies* (Oxford, 2007).
46 Julian Nida-Rümelin, 'Zur Philosophie des Kosmopolitismus', *Zeitschrift für Internationale Beziehungen*, 13, 2 (2006), 231–8, at p. 235. Thomas Kane claims in *Emerging Conflicts of Principle. International Relations and the Clash between Cosmopolitanism and Republicanism* (Aldershot, 2008) that international politics since the end of the Cold War have progressively become more ideological, with political actors siding either with republicanism, which favours self-rule and self-determination, or with cosmopolitanism, which tends to advocate international institutions, global governance, and collective decision-making. See my review in *Political Studies Review*, 7, 2 (2009), 256ff.
47 David A. Hollinger, 'Not universalists, not pluralists: the new cosmopolitans find their own way', in Vertovec and Cohen, *Conceiving Cosmopolitanism*, pp. 227–39, at pp. 230ff. Samuel Scheffler, 'Conceptions of cosmopolitanism', in idem, *Boundaries and Allegiances: Problems of Justice and Responsibility in Liberal Thought* (Oxford, 2001), pp. 111–30 suggests that weak moral cosmopolitanism is not only a very obvious and plausible choice, but also carries the day over strong moral cosmopolitanism.
48 Appiah, 'Cosmopolitan patriots', p. 639. Cosmopolitanism beyond Europe is, for instance, investigated by Camilla Fojas, *Cosmopolitanism in the Americas* (West Lafayette, Ind., 2005), Grace S. Fong, Nanxiu Qian and Harriet T. Zurndorfer (eds), *Beyond Tradition and Modernity: Gender, Genre, and Cosmopolitanism in Late Qing China* (Leiden, 2004), and Ifeoma Kiddoe Nwankwo, *Black Cosmopolitanism: Racial Consciousness and Transnational Identity in the Nineteenth-century Americas* (Philadelphia, 2005).

Select Bibliography

Aksu, Esref (ed.), *Early Notions of Global Governance: Selected Eighteenth-Century Proposals for 'Perpetual Peace'* (Cardiff, 2008).

Albrecht, Andrea, *Kosmopolitismus: Weltbürgerdiskurse in Literatur, Philosophie und Publizistik um 1800* (Berlin and New York, 2005).

Anderson, Amanda, *The Powers of Distance: Cosmopolitanism and the Cultivation of Detachment* (Princeton, 2001).

Anderson-Gold, Sharon, *Cosmopolitanism and Human Rights* (Cardiff, 2001).

Appiah, Kwame Anthony, 'Cosmopolitan patriots', *Critical Inquiry*, 23, 3 (1997), 617–39.

——, *Cosmopolitanism: Ethics in a World of Strangers* (New York, 2007).

Archibugi, Daniele, 'Cosmopolitical democracy', in eadem (ed.), *Debating Cosmopolitics* (London, 2003), pp. 1–15.

——, 'Cosmopolitan democracy and its critics: a review', *European Journal of International Relations*, 10, 3 (2004), 437–73.

—— and David Held (eds), *Cosmopolitan Democracy: An Agenda for a New World Order* (Cambridge, 1995).

Archibugi, Daniele, David Held and Martin Köhler (eds), *Re-imagining Political Community: Studies in Cosmopolitan Democracy* (Cambridge, 1998).

Bader, Veit, 'For love of country', *Political Theory*, 27, 3 (1999), 379–97.

Beck, Ulrich, *The Cosmopolitan Vision* (Cambridge, 2006).

——, 'The cosmopolitan perspective: sociology in the second age of modernity', in Vertovec and Cohen, *Conceiving Cosmopolitanism*, pp. 61–85.

—— and Edgar Grande, *Cosmopolitan Europe* (Cambridge, 2007).

Bellers, John, 'Some reasons for an European state' [1710], in George Clarke (ed.), *John Bellers: His Life, Times and Writings* (London, 1987), pp. 132–53.

Benhabib, Seyla, *The Rights of Others: Aliens, Residents, and Citizens* (Cambridge, 2004).

——, *Another Cosmopolitanism: With Commentaries by Jeremy Waldron, Bonnie Honig, and Will Kymlicka*, ed. Robert Post (Oxford, 2006).

Berman, Jessica, *Modernist Fiction, Cosmopolitanism, and the Politics of Community* (Cambridge, 2001).

Bluntschli, Johann Caspar, *Das moderne Völkerrecht der civilisirten Staten* [1868], 3rd edn. (Nördlingen, 1878).
Bolz, Norbert, Friedrich Kittler and Raimar Zons (eds), *Weltbürgertum und Globalisierung* (München, 2000).
Boucher, David, *Political Theories of International Relations* (Oxford, 1998).
——, *The Limits of Ethics in International Relations: Natural Law, Natural Rights, and Human Rights in Transition* (Oxford, 2009).
Bowden, Brett, 'Nationalism and cosmopolitanism: irreconcilable differences or possible bedfellows?', *National Identities*, 5, 3 (2003), 235–49.
Brassett, James, 'Cosmopolitanism vs. terrorism? Discourses of ethical possibility before and after 7/7', *Millennium: Journal of International Studies*, 36, 2 (2008), 121–47.
Breckenridge, Carol A., Homi K. Bhabha and Dipesh Chakrabarty (eds), *Cosmopolitanism* (Durham, NC and London, 2002).
Brennan, Timothy, *At Home in the World: Cosmopolitanism Now* (Cambridge, Mass. and London, 1997).
Brock, Gillian and Harry Brighouse (eds), *The Political Philosophy of Cosmopolitanism* (Cambridge, 2005).
Brown, Eric, 'Hellenistic cosmopolitanism', in Mary Louise Gill and Pierre Pellegrin (eds), *A Companion to Ancient Philosophy* (Oxford, 2006), pp. 549–58.
——, 'The emergence of natural law and the cosmopolis', in Stephen Salkever (ed.), *The Cambridge Companion to Greek Political Thought* (Cambridge, 2009), pp. 331–63.
Brown, Garrett Wallace, 'Kantian cosmopolitan law and the idea of a cosmopolitan constitution', *History of Political Thought*, 27, 4 (2006), 661–84.
Burgess, J. Peter, 'Dialektischer Kosmopolitismus', *Zeitschrift für Internationale Beziehungen*, 13, 2 (2006), 255–60.
Busch, H. J. and Horstmann, Axel, 'Kosmopolit, Kosmopolitismus', in Joachim Ritter (ed.), *Historisches Wörterbuch der Philosophie*, vol. 4 (1976), 1155–67.
Byrd, Sharon and Joachim Hruschka, 'From the state of nature to the juridical state of states', *Law and Philosophy*, 27, 6 (2008), 599–641.
Cameron, John, 'Reflections on cosmopolitanism and capabilities', *Development and Change*, 37, 6 (2006), 1273–76.
Caney, Simon, 'Global distributive justice and the state', *Political Studies*, 56, 3 (2008), 487–518.
Cavallar, Georg, *Pax Kantiana: Systematisch-historische Untersuchung des Entwurfs "Zum ewigen Frieden" (1795) von Immanuel Kant* (Wien, Köln, Weimar, 1992).

——, *Kant and the Theory and Practice of International Right* (Cardiff, 1999).

——, *The Rights of Strangers: Theories of International Hospitality, the Global Community, and Political Justice since Vitoria* (Aldershot, 2002).

——, '"La société générale du genre humain": Rousseau on cosmopolitanism, international relations, and republican patriotism', in Paschalis M. Kitromilides (ed.), *From Republican Polity to National Community* (Oxford, 2003), pp. 89–109.

——, *Die europäische Union – Von der Utopie zur Friedens- und Wertegemeinschaft* (Wien, 2006).

——, 'Zwischen Integration und Abgrenzung: das Fremdenrecht als Teil der Europa-Ideen', in Markus Kremer and Hans-Richard Reuter (eds), *Macht und Moral – Politisches Denken im 17. und 18. Jahrhundert* (Stuttgart, 2007), pp. 143–60.

Chernilo, Daniel, 'A quest for universalism: re-assessing the nature of classical social theory's cosmopolitanism', *European Journal of Social Theory*, 10, 1 (2007), 17–35.

Chhachhi, Amrita, 'Postscript: tensions and absences in the debate on global justice and cosmopolitanism', *Development and Change*, 37, 6 (2006), 1329–34.

Cheah, Pheng, 'What is a world? On world literature as world-making activity', *Daedalus*, 137, 3 (2008), 27–38.

—— and Bruce Robbins (eds), *Cosmopolitics: Thinking and Feeling beyond the Nation* (Minneapolis, 1998).

Cheneval, Francis, *Die Rezeption der „Monarchia" Dantes bis zur Editio Princeps im Jahre 1559: Metamorphosen eines philosophischen Werkes* (München, 1995).

——, *Philosophie in weltbürgerlicher Bedeutung: Über die Entstehung und die philosophischen Grundlagen des supranationalen und kosmopolitischen Denkens der Moderne* (Basel, 2002).

——, 'Auseinandersetzungen um die *civitas maxima* in der Nachfolge Christian Wolffs', *Studia Leibnitiana*, 33 (2001), 125–44.

——, 'Der kosmopolitische Republikanismus erläutert am Beispiel Anacharsis Cloots', *Zeitschrift für philosophische Forschung*, 58, 3 (2004), 373–96.

Cloots, Anacharsis, *Oeuvres* (München, 1980).

Cosgrove, Denis, 'Globalis and tolerance in early modern geography', *Annals of the Association of American Geographers*, 93, 4 (2003), 852–70.

Coulmas, Peter, *Weltbürger: Geschichte einer Menschheitssehnsucht* (Reinbek bei Hamburg, 1990).

Cowen, Tyler, *Creative Destruction: How Globalization is Changing the World's Cultures* (Princeton and Oxford, 2002).

Delanty, Gerard and Chris Rumford, *Rethinking Europe: Social Theory and the implications of Europeanization* (London and New York, 2005).
Dexter, Helen, 'The "new war" on terror, cosmopolitanism and the "just war" revival', *Government and Opposition*, 43, 1 (2008), 55–78.
Dingwerth, Klaus and Philipp Pattberg, 'Global governance as a perspective on world politics', *Global Governance*, 12 (2006), 185–203.
Dobson, Andrew, 'Thick cosmopolitanism', *Political Studies*, 54 (2006), 165–84.
Douzinas, Costas, *Human Rights and Empire: The Political Philosophy of Cosmopolitanism* (Abingdon and New York, 2007).
Easley, Eric S., *The War over 'Perpetual Peace': An Exploration into the History of a Foundational International Relations Text* (Houndmills, 2004).
Eisenstein, Elizabeth L., *Grub Street Abroad: Aspects of French Cosmopolitan Press from the Age of Louis XIV to the French Revolution* (Oxford, 1992).
Erskine, Toni, *Embedded Cosmopolitanism: Duties to Strangers and Enemies in a World of 'Dislocated Communities'* (Oxford, 2008).
Evans, Mark, 'World citizenship and the ethics of individual responsibility', in idem (ed.), *Ethical Theory in the Study of International Politics* (Hauppage, NY, 2004), pp. 35–54.
Fassbender, Bardo, 'Zwischen Staatsräson und Gemeinschaftsbindung: Zur Gemeinwohlorientierung des Völkerrechts der Gegenwart', in Herfried Münkler and Karsten Fischer (eds), *Gemeinwohl und Gemeinsinn im Recht: Konkretisierung und Realisierung öffentlicher Interessen* (Berlin, 2002), pp. 231–74.
——, 'Der Schutz der Menschenrechte als zentraler Inhalt des völkerrechtlichen Gemeinwohls', *Europäische Grundrechte-Zeitschrift*, 30, Heft 1–3 (2003), 1–16.
Ferry, Jean-Marc, *Europe, la voie kantienne: essai sur l'identité postnationale* (Paris, 2006).
Fine, Robert, *Cosmopolitanism* (London, 2007).
—— and Robin Cohen, 'Four cosmopolitanism moments', in Vertovec and Cohen (eds), *Conceiving Cosmopolitanism*, pp. 137–62.
Fink, Gonthier-Louis (ed.), *Cosmopolitisme, Patriotisme et Xénophobie en Europe au Siècle des Lumières* (Actes du Colloque, Strasbourg, 1987).
——, 'Kosmopolitismus – Patriotismus – Xenophobie: Eine französisch-deutsche Debatte im Revolutionsjahrzehnt 1789–1799', in Ortrud Gutjahr et al. (eds), *Gesellige Vernunft: Zur Kultur der literarischen Aufklärung* (Würzburg, 1993), pp. 23–42.
——, 'Das Wechselspiel zwischen patriotischen und kosmopolitisch-universalen Bestrebungen in Frankreich und Deutschland

(1750–1789)', in Ulrich Hermann (ed.), *Volk – Nation – Vaterland* (Hamburg, 1996), pp. 151–84.

Fisch, Jörg, 'Law as a means and as an end. Some remarks on the function of European and non-European law in the process of European expansion', in Wolfgang J. Mommsen and Jap de Moor (eds), *European Expansion and Law. The Encounter of European and Indigenous Law in 19th- and 20th-century Africa and Asia* (Oxford, 1991), pp. 15–38.

Fletcher of Saltoun, Andrew, 'An account of a conversation concerning a right regulation of governments for the common good of mankind' [1704], in *Selected Political Writings and Speeches*, ed. David Daiches (Edinburgh, 1979), pp. 106–37.

——, *Political Works*, ed. John Robertson (Cambridge, 1997).

Fojas, Camilla, *Cosmopolitanism in the Americas* (West Lafayette, Ind., 2005).

Fong, Grace S., Nanxiu Qian, and Harriet T. Zurndorfer (eds), *Beyond Tradition and Modernity: Gender, Genre, and Cosmopolitanism in Late Qing China* (Leiden, 2004).

Frith, Robert, 'Cosmopolitan democracy and the EU: the case of gender', *Political Studies*, 56 (2008), 215–36.

Fuchs, Susanne and Michael Zürn, 'Kosmopolitismus als Großtheorie?', *Zeitschrift für Internationale Beziehungen*, 13, 2 (2006), 247–54.

Gasper, Des, 'Cosmopolitan presumptions? On Martha Nussbaum and her commentators', *Development and Change*, 37, 6 (2006), 1227–1246.

Giri, Ananta Kumar, 'Cosmopolitanism and beyond: towards a multiverse of transformations', *Development and Change*, 37, 6 (2006), 1277–1292.

Grotius, Hugo, *The Law of War and Peace* [1625], trans. Francis W. Kelsey (Oxford, 1925).

——, *The Law of War and Peace*, ed. Richard Tuck, from the edition of Jean Barbeyrac (Indianapolis, 2005).

——, *Commentary on the Law of Prize and Booty* [1603], trans. Gwladys L. Williams (Oxford, 1950, reprint New York, 1964).

——, *Commentary on the Law of Prize and Booty* [1603], ed. Martine Julia van Ittersum (Indianapolis, 2006), accessed from http:/oll.libertyfund.org/title/1718/77251/1871412, on 15 February 2008.

Habermas, Jürgen, *The Inclusion of the Other: Studies in Political Theory*, ed. C. Cronin and P. de Greiff (Cambridge, Mass. and London, 1998).

——, *Postnational Constellation: Political Essays*, trans. M. Pensky (Cambridge, Mass. and London, 2001).

Harris, Lee, 'The cosmopolitan illusion', *Policy Review*, 118 (2003), 45–59.

Heater, Derek, *World Citizenship and Government: Cosmopolitan Ideas in the History of Western Political Thought* (Basingstoke, UK, 1996).

——, *World Citizenship: Cosmopolitan Thinking and its Opponents* (London and New York, 2002).
——, *A Brief History of Citizenship* (Edinburgh, 2004).
Hayden, Patrick, *Cosmopolitan Global Politics* (Aldershot, 2005).
Held, David, *Democracy and the Global Order: From the Modern State to Cosmopolitan Governance* (Oxford, 1995).
——, *Cosmopolitanism: A Defence* (Cambridge, 2003).
——, and Mathias Koenig-Archibugi (eds), *Global Governance and Public Accountability* (Malden, Mass., 2005).
Herrmann, Hans Peter, '"Ich bin fürs Vaterland zu sterben auch bereit": Patriotismus oder Nationalismus im 18. Jahrhundert?', in Ortrud Gutjahr et al. (eds), *Gesellige Vernunft: Zur Kultur der literarischen Aufklärung* (Würzburg, 1993), pp. 119–44.
Heuvel, Gerd van den, 'Cosmopolite, Cosmopoli(ti)sme', in Rolf Reichardt and Eberhard Schmidt (eds), *Handbuch politisch-sozialer Grundbegriffe in Frankreich 1680–1820* (München, 1986), pp. 41–55.
Hohendahl, Peter Uwe (ed.), *Patriotism, Cosmopolitanism, and National Culture: Public Culture in Hamburg 1700–1933* (Amsterdam and New York, 2003).
Hollinger, David A., *Cosmopolitanism and Solidarity: Studies in Ethnoracial, Religious, and Professional Affiliation in the United States* (Madison, Wisconsin, 2006).
——, 'Not universalists, not pluralists: the new cosmopolitans find their own way', in Vertovec and Cohen (eds), *Conceiving Cosmopolitanism*, pp. 227–39.
Hurrell, Andrew, *On Global Order: Power, Values, and the Constitution of International Society* (Oxford, 2007).
Jacob, Margaret C., *Strangers Nowhere in the World: The Rise of Cosmopolitanism in Early Modern Europe* (Philadelphia, 2006).
Jones, Charles, *Global Justice: Defending Cosmopolitanism* (Oxford, 1999).
——, 'Cosmopolitanism', in Donald M. Borchert (ed.), *Encyclopedia of Philosophy*, vol. 2 (Detroit et al., 2006), pp. 567–70.
Jones, Deiniol, 'The origins of the global city: ethics and morality in contemporary cosmopolitanism', *British Journal of Politics and International Relations*, 5, 1 (2003), 50–73.
Kant, Immanuel, 'Toward Perpetual Peace' [1795], in *Practical Philosophy*, trans. and ed. Mary J. Gregor (Cambridge, 1996), pp. 317–51.
——, 'The metaphysics of morals Part I: Metaphysical first principles of the doctrine of right' [1797], in *Practical Philosophy*, pp. 365–506.
Kirkbright, Suzanne (ed.), *Cosmopolitans in the Modern World: Studies on a Theme in German and Austrian Literary Culture* (München, 2000).

Kleingeld, Pauline, 'Six varieties of cosmopolitanism in late eighteenth-century Germany', *Journal of the History of Ideas*, 60 (1999), 505–24.

——, 'Kant's cosmopolitan patriotism', *Kant-Studien*, 94 (2003), 299–316, reprinted in Sharon Byrd and Joachim Hruschka (eds), *Kant and Law* (Aldershot, Burlington 2006), pp. 473–90.

——, 'Approaching perpetual peace: Kant's defence of a league of states and his ideal of a world federation', *European Journal of Philosophy*, 12 (2004), 304–25.

——, 'Kant's second thoughts on race', *Philosophical Quarterly*, 57 (2007), 573–92.

Kleingeld, Pauline and Eric Brown, 'Cosmopolitanism', in Edward N. Zalta (ed.), *The Stanford Encyclopedia of Philosophy* (2002 edn), at *http://plato.stanford.edu/archives/fall2002/entries/cosmopolitanism*, visited 23 November 2007.

Koskenniemi, Martti, *The Gentle Civilizer of Nations: The Rise and Fall of International Law 1870–1960* (Cambridge, 2002).

Küng, Hans, 'Global ethic: a response to my critics', *International Journal of Politics, Culture and Society*, 14, 2 (2000), 421–8.

Langlois, Anthony, 'Human rights and cosmopolitan liberalism', *Critical Review of International Social and Political Philosophy*, 10, 1 (2007), 29–45.

La Torre, Massimo, 'Global citizenship? Political rights under imperial conditions', *Ratio Juris*, 18, 2 (2005), 236–57.

Lederer, Markus and Philipp S. Müller (eds), *Criticizing Global Governance* (New York, 2005).

Lesaffer, Randall, 'War, peace, interstate friendship and the emergence of the *ius publicum Europaeum*', in Ronald G. Asch, Wulf Eckart Voß and Martin Wrede (eds), *Frieden und Krieg in der Frühen Neuzeit: Die europäische Staatenordnung und die außereuropäische Welt* (München, 2001), pp. 87–113.

Lettevall, Rebecka, and My Klockar Linder (eds), *The Idea of Kosmopolis: History, Philosophy and Politics of World Citizenship* (Huddinge, 2008).

Linklater, Andrew, *The Transformation of Political Community* (Cambridge, 1998).

——, 'Cosmopolitanism', in Andrew Dobson and Robyn Eckersley (eds), *Political Theory and the Ecological Challenge* (Cambridge, 2006), pp. 109–27.

Martens, Georg Friedrich von, *Einleitung in das positive europäische Völkerrecht auf Verträge und Herkommen gegründet* (Göttingen, 1796).

——, *A Compendium of the Law of Nations, Founded on the Treaties and Custom of the Modern Nations of Europe*, trans. William Cobbett (London, 1785).

Martini, Karl Anton Freiherr von, *Lehrbegriff des Natur-, Staats- und Völkerrechts* (1783; reprint Aalen, 1969).

——, *Erklärung der Lehrsätze über das allgemeine Staats- und Völkerrecht* (1791; reprint Aalen, 1969).

McGrew, Anthony, 'Liberal internationalism: between realism and cosmopolitanism', in Held David and Anthony McGrew (eds), *Governing Globalization: Power Authority and Global Governance* (Cambridge, 2002), pp. 267–89.

Meijer, Roel (ed.), *Cosmopolitanism, Identity and Authenticity in the Middle East* (Richmond, Surrey, 1999).

Meinecke, Friedrich, *Cosmopolitanism and the National State*, trans. Robert B. Kimber (Princeton, 1970).

Mignolo, Walter D., 'The many faces of cosmo-polis: border thinking and critical cosmopolitanism', in Breckenridge et al. (eds), *Cosmopolitanism* (Durham, NC and London, 2002), pp. 157–87.

Moellendorf, Darrel, *Cosmopolitan Justice* (Boulder, 2002).

Moser, Johann Jakob, *Versuch des neuesten europäischen Völkerrechts in Friedens- und Kriegszeiten*, 10 parts in 12 vols (Frankfurt am Main, 1777–80).

——, *Grundsätze des Völkerrechts, aus 'Versuch des neuesten Europäischen Völker-Rechts in Friedens- und Kriegszeiten'* [1777] (Frankfurt am Main, 1959).

Müller, Harald, 'Liberaler Kosmopolitismus: Eine partikularistische Emanation mit Unverträglichkeiten und Nebenwirkungen', *Zeitschrift für Internationale Beziehungen*, 13, 2 (2006), 239–45.

Muthu, Sankar, *Enlightenment against Empire* (Princeton and Oxford, 2003).

Neff, Stephen C., *War and the Law of Nations: A General History* (Cambridge, 2005).

Nida-Rümelin, Julian, 'Zur Philosophie des Kosmopolitismus', *Zeitschrift für Internationale Beziehungen*, 13, 2 (2006), 231–8.

Nussbaum, Martha C., et al., *For Love of Country?*, ed. Joshua Cohen (Boston, 2002).

——, *Cultivating Humanity: A Classical Defense of Reform in Liberal Education* (Cambridge, Mass., 1997).

——, 'Kant and Stoic cosmopolitanism', *Journal of Political Philosophy*, 5, 1 (1997), 1–25.

——, 'Standing against despairing detachment', 21 June 2003, at *http://evatt.labor.net.au/news/234.html*, visited 18 April 2008.

——, *Frontiers of Justice: Disability, Nationality, Species Membership* (Cambridge, Mass., 2006).

——, 'Reply: in defence of global political liberalism', *Development and Change*, 37, 6 (2006), 1313–28.

Nwankwo, Ifeoma Kiddoe, *Black Cosmopolitanism: Racial Consciousness and Transnational Identity in the Nineteenth-Century Americas* (Philadelphia, 2005).
Osterhammel, Jürgen, *Die Entzauberung Asiens: Europa und die asiatischen Reiche im 18: Jahrhundert* (München, 1998).
Pagden, Anthony, 'Stoicism, cosmopolitanism, and the legacy of European imperialism', *Constellations*, 7, 1 (2000), 3–22.
——, 'The genealogies of European cosmopolitanism and the legacy of European universalism', in Ronald G. Asch, Wulf Eckart Voß and Martin Wrede (eds), *Frieden und Krieg in der Frühen Neuzeit: Die europäische Staatenordnung und die außereuropäische Welt* (München, 2001), pp. 467–83.
——, *Peoples and Empires: A Short History of European Migration, Exploration, and Conquest, from Greece to the Present* (New York, 2003).
Penn, William, 'An Essay towards the present and future peace of Europe, by the establishment of an European dyet, parliament, or estates' [1693], in *The Peace of Europe, the Fruits of Solitude and other Writings*, ed. Edwin B. Bronner (London, 1993).
Perkins, Mary Anne, *Christendom and European Identity: The Legacy of a Grand Narrative since 1789* (Berlin, New York, 2004).
—— and Martin Liebscher (eds), *Nationalism versus Cosmopolitanism in German Thought and Culture, 1789–1914: Essays on the Emergence of Europe* (Lewiston, 2006).
Pieterse, Jan Nederveen, 'Emancipatory cosmopolitanism: towards an agenda', *Development and Change*, 37, 6 (2006), 1247–57.
Pitts, Jennifer, *A Turn to Empire: The Rise of Imperial Liberalism in Britain and France* (Princeton and Oxford, 2005).
Pogge, Thomas, 'Cosmopolitanism and sovereignty', in Chris Brown (ed.), *Political Restructuring in Europe: Ethical Perspectives* (London and New York, 1994), pp. 89–122.
——, 'Making war on terrorists – reflections on harming the innocent', *Journal of Political Philosophy*, 16, 1 (2008), 1–25.
Price, Richard, *Political Writings*, ed. D. O. Thomas (Cambridge, 1991).
Pufendorf, Samuel, *Elements of Universal Jurisprudence* [1660], trans. William Abbott Oldfather, vol. 15 of the *Classics of International Law* (reprint New York, 1964).
——, *The Law of Nature and Nations* [1672], trans. C. H. Oldfather and W. A. Oldfather (Oxford, 1934, reprint New York, 1964).
——, *The Political Writings of Samuel Pufendorf*, ed. Craig L. Carr, trans. Michael J. Seidler (New York and Oxford, 1994).
Purdy, Daniel L., *The Tyranny of Elegance: Consumer Cosmopolitanism in the Era of Goethe* (Baltimore and London, 1998).

Rawls, John, *The Law of Peoples with 'The Idea of Public Reason Revisited'* (Cambridge, 1999).
Richter, Ingo K., Sabne Berking and Ralf Müller-Schmid (eds), *Building a Transnational Civil Society* (Houndmills, 2006).
Roosevelt, Grace, 'Rousseau versus Rawls on international relations', *European Journal of Political Theory*, 5, 3 (2006), 301–20.
Rorty, Amélie Oksenberg and James Schmidt (eds), *Kant's Idea for a Universal History with a Cosmopolitan Aim: A Critical Guide* (Cambridge, 2009).
Rumford, Chris (ed.), *Cosmopolitanism and Europe* (Liverpool, 2007).
Scheffler, Samuel, 'Conceptions of Cosmopolitanism', in *Boundaries and Allegiances: Problems of Justice and Responsibility in Liberal Thought* (Oxford, 2001), pp. 111–30.
Schlereth, Thomas J., *The Cosmopolitan Ideal in Enlightenment Thought: Its Form and Fuction in the Ideas of Franklin, Hume, and Voltaire, 1694–1790* (Notre Dame, 1977).
Scrivener, Michael, *The Cosmopolitan Ideal in the Age of Revolution and Reaction, 1776–1832* (London, 2007).
Sellars, John, 'Stoic cosmopolitanism and Zeno's Republic', *History of Political Thought*, 28, 1 (2007), 1–29.
Shabani, Omid A. Payrow, 'Cosmopolitan justice and immigration: a critical theory perspective', *European Journal of Social Theory*, 10, 1 (2007), 87–98.
Singer, Peter, *One World: The Ethics of Globalization* (New Haven, 2002).
Smith, Adam, *An Inquiry into the Nature and Causes of the Wealth of Nations* [1776], eds R. H. Campbell, A. S. Skinner and W. B. Todd (Oxford, 1976).
——, *Lectures on Jurisprudence*, eds R. L. Meek, D. D. Raphael and P. G. Stein (Oxford, 1978).
Steiger, Heinhard, 'From the international law of Christianity to the international law of the world citizen – reflections on the formation of the epochs of the history of international law', *Journal of the History of International Law*, 3 (2001), 180–93.
Tan, Kok-Chor, *Justice without Borders: Cosmopolitanism, Nationalism and Patriotism* (Cambridge, 2004).
Tesón, Fernando R., *A Philosophy of International Law* (Boulder, Colorado, 1998).
Thielking, Sigrid, *Weltbürgertum: Kosmopolitische Ideen in Literatur und politischer Publizistik seit dem 18: Jahrhundert* (München, 2000).
Tönnies, Sibylle, *Cosmopolis Now: Auf dem Weg zum Weltstaat* (Hamburg, 2002).
Tuck, Richard, *The Rights of War and Peace: Political Thought and the International Order From Grotius to Kant* (Oxford, 1999).

Van der Dungen, Peter, 'The Abbé de Saint-Pierre and the English "Irenists" of the eighteenth century (Penn, Bellers and Bentham)', *International Journal of World Peace*, 17, 2 (2000), 5–31.
Vattel, Emer de, *The Law of Nations or the Principles of Natural Law* [1758], trans. Charles G. Fenwick, in James Brown Scott (ed.), *The Classics of International Law* (Washington, 1916).
Verdross, Alfred, 'Les règles internationales concernant le traitement des étrangers', *Recueil des Cours*, 37, 3 (1931), 327–412.
——, *Völkerrecht* [1937], 5th edn (Wien, 1964).
—— and Bruno Simma, *Universelles Völkerrecht: Theorie und Praxis*, 3rd edn (Berlin, 1984).
Vertovec, Steven and Cohen, Robin (eds), *Conceiving Cosmopolitanism: Theory, Context, and Practice* (Oxford, 2002).
Vitoria, Francisco de, *Vorlesungen I und II (Relectiones): Völkerrecht, Politik, Kirche*, eds Ulrich Horst, Heinz-Gerhard Justenhoven and Joachim Stüben (Stuttgart, Berlin, Köln, 1995 and 1997).
——, 'On the American Indians', in *Political Writings*, eds Anthony Padgen and Jeremy Lawrance (Cambridge, 1991), pp. 231–92.
——, 'On the law of war', in *Political Writings*, pp. 293–327.
Voltaire, *Political Writings*, ed. and trans. David Williams (Cambridge, 1994).
Wagar, W. Warren, *The City of Man: Prophecies of a World Civilization in Twentieth-Century Thought* (Boston, 1963).
Waldron, Jeremy, 'Who is my Neighbor? Proximity and humanity', *The Monist*, 86 (2003), 333–54.
——, 'Cosmopolitan norms', in Seyla Benhabib, *Another Cosmopolitanism*, pp. 83–101.
Ward, Robert, *An Enquiry into the Foundation and History of the Law of Nations in Europe from the Time of the Greeks and the Romans to the Age of Grotius*, 2 vols (London, 1795).
Weichlein, Siegfried, 'Cosmopolitanism, patriotism, nationalism', in Tim Blanning and Hagen Schulze (eds), *Unity and Diversity in European Culture c.1800* (Oxford, 2006), pp. 77–99.
Williams, Howard, *Kant's Critique of Hobbes: Sovereignty and Cosmopolitanism* (Cardiff, 2003).
Wolff, Christian, *Ius gentium methodo scientifica pertractatum, in quo ius gentium naturale ab eo, quod voluntarii, pactitii et consuetudinarii est, accurate distinguitur* [1749], trans. Joseph H. Drake (reprint New York, 1964).
——, *Institutiones juris naturae et genitum*, ed. Marcel Thomann, in *Gesammelte Werke*, vol. 26 (reprint Hildesheim: Georg Olms Verlag, 1969).

Wyduckel, Dieter, 'Recht, Staat und Frieden im Jus Publicum Europaeum', in Heinz Duchhardt (ed.), *Zwischenstaatliche Friedenswahrung in Mittelalter und Früher Neuzeit* (Köln, Wien, 1991), p. 185–204.

Ypi, Lea L., 'Statist Cosmopolitanism', *Journal of Political Philosophy*, 16, 1 (2008), 48–71.

Zanetti, Véronique, 'Nach dem 11. September: Paradigmenwechsel im Völkerrecht?', *Deutsche Zeitschrift für Philosophie*, 50, 3 (2002), 455–69.

Zolo, Danilo, *Cosmopolis: Prospects for World Government* (Cambridge, 1997).

Zurbuchen, Simone, *Patriotismus und Kosmopolitismus: Die Schweizer Aufklärung zwischen Tradition und Moderne* (Zürich, 2003).

Index

Africa, African 40, 100, 119
Albrecht, Andrea 12
Albright, Madeline 137
alliance(s) 25, 55, 57, 58, 60, 65, 75, 82, 92, 103, 138
ambiguity 19, 37
Amerindians, Native Americans 5, 13, 18, 20, 22–4, 29, 34, 53, 55–6
analogy
  domestic analogy 26, 29, 32, 44, 54, 75–7, 83, 91, 113
anarchy 65
  international anarchy 43, 58–9, 72–5, 79, 92, 107
  see also state of nature
Anderson, Amanda 12, 129
Anghie, Antony 18, 35, 36
Appiah, Anthony 3, 11, 129, 138, 140
argument
  agricultural argument 13, 27, 29, 32, **33–5**, 37, 65, 68
Arneil, Barbara 33
Austin, John **98–9**, 118
Austria, Austrian 91, 122

balance of power 4, 13, 15, 44–5, 51, 62, 75, 80, 85, 90, 92, 95, 97, 99, 107, 135
barbarian(s), barbarianism 20–1, 22, 25, 31, 46, 50, 118
Beck, Ulrich 3, 10, 137
Bellers, John 10, 13, 53, **55–6**, 59, 62, 95
Benhabib, Seyla 2, 3, 11, 110, 131–2, 136
Bentham, Jeremy 13, 42, **49–51**, 52, 54, 98, 128, 131
Bernstein, Eduard 55
Bluntschli, Johann Caspar 15, 97, **117–21**, 124
Bowden, Brett 13, 18, 19, 30, 36, 136
Bull, Hedley 14, 103–4
Burke, Edmund vii, 41, 42, 50, **51–2**, 62, 100, 106, 128
Bush, George W. 1, 18, 135

Carens, Joseph 110, 127, 136

Catholicism, Catholics, Catholic Church 20–4, 55, 91, 114, 122
Charles V 23, 44, 80
Cheneval, Francis 12, 32, 61, 78
China 28, 30, 37, 70
Christianity 4, 15, 20, 22, 24, 25, 27, 31, 54–6, 59, 97, 100–1, 105, 108
Christians 18, 21, 24, 25–7, 55, 56, 100
'citizen(s) of the world' 5, 7, 40, 60
civilization 25, 31–2, 34, 48–9
civitas maxima 33, 78, 89, 92, 96, 116
  see also commonwealth, global commonwealth; Wolff, Christian
Cloots, Anacharsis 9, 10, 14, 15, 62, 85, **102–4**, 105, 108, 130, 138
colonialism, colonies 6, 13, **17–38**, 47, 50–1, 62, 64, 66, 80, 128, 136
  see also imperialism
commerce, commercial 5, 8, 11, 26, 30, 46, 48, 50, 53, 58, 61, 69, 120, 131, 137
commercial society 32, 46, 59, 69–70, 130–1, 138
  see also cosmopolitanism, economic or commercial
commonwealth 43, 45, 60, 67, 76, 99
  global commonwealth 8, 33, 48, 64, 78, 87, 89, 109, 124
  juridical commonwealth (Kant) 68
community 43, 44, 45, 61, 139, 140
  international community 2, 6, 7, 8, 9, 10, 20, 24, 28, 45, 51, 67, 69, 92, 93, 97, 103, 105, 107, **109–**27, 134, 135,
  original community, idea of 33–4, 42, 64, 68, 81
  see also commonwealth, global commonwealth; Europe; society, international society; union
confederation 5, 57–9, 61, 79, 105
contract 2, 14, 28, 43, 73, 78, 93, 103, 107, 112, 116, 129, 132
contractual or duelling school 88, 97, 98
corruption 51, 57–8, 61, 116

cosmopolitanism
concept of 1, **8–11**
contractual 14–15, 64, 52, 53, 64, 68, 103, 130
cultural **9**, 33, 42, 69–70, 89
Cynic and Stoic 7–8, 24
economic or commercial **10, 44–8**, 50–1, 69–70, 130, 137
and Enlightenment 39–42, 62
epistemological or intellectual **10**, 33, 46
legal 13, 14, 15, 20, 23, 37, 65, 100, 104, 108, 126, 132, 133; *see also* contractual
moral 8–9, 23, 33, 40, 48, 51, 56, 66, 67, 76, 90, 111, 128, 129, 130, 131, 132, 135, 137, 138
natural law 9; *see also* cosmopolitanism, moral
political 5, **9**, 10, 13, 14, 32–3, 62, 102, 103, 131, 132, 133, 135, 137, 138; *see also* legal cosmopolitanism
thin and thick versions **10–11**
Covell, Charles 83
Cromarty, earl of 57
culture
cultural relativism 99–100

Davenant, Charles 62
democracy 2, 49, 55
cosmopolitan democracy 1, 9
democratic peace proposition 47, 48, 59
Diogenes 7
dominion 26, 27, 29, 113
Douzinas, Costas 130, 138
droit public européen 86, 107
Dutch 13, 26, 29, 35, 85, 86, 111, 114

England 33, 40, 47, 49, 53, 56, 61, 133
Enlightenment **4–6**, 10, 12, 13, 39–42, 62
British 13–14, **39–62**
'cosmopolitan Enlightenment' 39–42
'Enlightenment project' 4–5, 36
equality 4, 9, 20, 29, 37, 42, 46, 57, 67, 91, 96, 102, 107, 125, 126, 127, 136
Erskine, Toni 139
Europe, European, Europeans 6, 12, 13, 15, **17–63**, 64, 65, 66, 69, 74, 75, 79, 80, 82, **85–108**, 110, 115, 117, 118, 119, 120, 122, 128, 129, 130

see also union, European Union
Eurocentrism 9, 17, 19–20, 35, 39–40, 54, 65, 73, 106, 117, 129, 133–4
Europeanism 8, 15, 40, 51, 56, 62, 100–1, 105–6, 107, 137, 140
pacifist and imperialist 56
see also colonialism
Europeanization 1, 15, 51

Fassbender, Bardo 134
federation 3, 15, 27, 49, 53–6, 65, 69, 70, 79, 81–4, 105
see also world republic
First World War 15, 86, 110, 120, 121, 123, 134
Fisch, Jörg 36
Fletcher of Saltoun, Andrew 13, 14, **56–61**, 62, 79, 130
foreigner(s) 27, 28, 59, 112, 114, 116, 119, 123, 127
Forster, Georg 9, 66
freedom 5, 26, 32, 41, 42, 45, 46, 54, 57, 64, 67, 70, 84, 88, 89, 90, 91, 95, 96, 102, 103, 104, 109, 115, 125, 126, 127
freedom of travel 64
see also hospitality rights
French Revolution 39, 40, 51, 62–3, 85, 99, **102–7**, 121

Geismann, Georg 72
Gentili, Alberico 19, 25, 27, 28, 30, 36, 101, 111
German, Germany 3, 10, 12, 24, 34, 39, 41, 52, 66, 83, 85, 93, 96, 100, 104–6, 122, 128, 136, 137
Gibbon, Edward 62, 99
globalization 1, 131, 138, 139
Goethe, Johann Wolfgang von 40, 104, 106, 136
Grewe, Wilhelm 86
Grotius, Hugo 7, 8, 12, 13, 14, 19, 24–8, 29, 32, 33, 36 37, 42, 68, 70, 74, **78–9**, 80, 84, 87, 92, 110–11, 112, 113, 115, 128, 133, 137, 138

Habermas, Jürgen 3, 9, 11, 131
Hamann, Johann Georg 71
Hardenberg, Friedrich von, known as 'Novalis' 105
Hastings, Warren 51, 52
Heater, Derek 12
hegemony 13, 57, 62, 80, 138
Held, David 2, 7, 9, 138

INDEX

Hegewisch, Dietrich Hermann 10, 41, 130
Henry IV 49, 56, 95
Herder, Johann Gottfried 40, 66, 69, 136
historicism 117, 118, 120
historiography 90, 120
history, historical **4–8**, 12, 17, 18, 19, 24, 36, 47, 66, 69, 83, **99–100**, 108, 111, **119–20**, 123, 128, 129
Hobbes, Thomas 42, 43, 45, 65, 72, 73, 76, 77, 78, 79, 85, 87, 88, 91, 93, 97, 111
   Hobbesian school of thought 87–8, 98, 121
hospitality 2, 21, 111–12
   right of hospitality 21, 22, 23, 28, 64, 65, 111–13, 114, 123–4
human rights 3, 8–9, 21, 23, 25, 37, 41, 47, 48, 103, 110, 120, 123, 124, 130, 133, 137, 138
   international human rights 123, 125, 134, 135
   see also cosmopolitanism, moral humanism
   civic humanism 58–9, 130
Hume, David 13, 30, 39, 41, **43–5**, 46, 48, 51, 54, 65, 80
Hurrell, Andrew 133

immigration, 2, 28, **109–27**, 135
   right of 15–16, **109–27**, 136
impartiality 10, 21, 23, 31, 40, **125–7**
imperialism 8, 13, 18, 37, 38, 120, 122, 128
   cultural imperialism 19, 138
   see also colonialism
individualism
   normative individualism 9, 14, 43, 78, 85, 138
inequality 131, 132
Innocent IV 27
Institut de droit international 117
intervention 10, 36, 37, 47, 102, 119, 131, 135
   humanitarian intervention 7, 21, 29, 135
Ittersum, Martine Julia van 24, 26, 128

Jacob, Margret J. 11
Japan, Japanese 29, 70, 119
jurisprudence 84, 87, 111, 131
Justi, Johann Heinrich Gottlob von 66
justice 2, 20–3, 26, 34, 35, 44, 50, 54, 67, 74, 75, 77, 86, 88, 93, 95, 107, 112, 115, 119, 129, 131, 138
   idea of natural justice 94, 125–7
   International Court of Justice 134
   see also impartiality
just-war theory 23, 73, 74, 85, 86, 87, 88, 98, 121, 135

Kant, Immanuel 2, 6, 7, 8, 9, 10, 12, **14–15**, 33, 41, 42, 46, 60, 61, 63, **64–84**, 85, 96, 101, 103, 104, 105, 106, 107, 121, 126, 132, 133, 134, 136, 138, 139
   Kant and forms of cosmopolitanism 66–70
   Kant and racism 65–6
   Kant and the 'miserable comforters' 70–81
   see also republic, world republic; right, cosmopolitan right (Kant)
Keal, Paul 18–19
Kelsen, Hans 15, 110, 122
Kleingeld, Pauline 82, 105
Koskenniemi, Martti 37–8, 87, 122, 125, 134

La Torre, Massimo 6
Lauterpacht, Hersch 7, 95, 111, 123, 125
law
   international law 4, 7, 12, 16, 17, 18–20, 36, 50, 53, 55, 87, 89, 90, 93, 97, 98, 109, 110, 115, 117, 118, 121, 122, 123, 124, 132, 133, 134, 135
   law of nations *see* law, international law; nation, right of nations
   natural law 3, 26, 27, 28, 31, 32, 34, 35, 36, 44, 47, 52, 59, 76, 77, 79, 80, 81, 83, 87, 88–98, 99, 102, 109, 110–17, 118, 119, 121–7, 129, 134, 135
   natural lawyers 15, 16, 33, 37, 55, 64, 65, 68, 70–5, 78, 81, 84, 85, 88–98, 107, 110–17, 119, 127, 129, 133, 134
   necessary law 77–8, 89, 115
   permissive law 78
   positive law 15, 32, 33, 43, 85, 92, 96, 97, 123, 124, 135
   rational law 90; *see also* law, natural law
   voluntary law 33, 87–9, 90, 92, 96, 109, 115
liberalism 2, 8, 50, 131
   imperial liberalism 50, 133

neo-liberalism 131, 138
Locke, John 10, 13, 27, 32, 33–4, 42–3, 52, 65, 68, 78, 128, 133
London 6, 58–9, 61, 71, 101
Louis XIV 44, 80, 93

Machiavelli 59, 60
Martens, Georg Friedrich von 15, 85, 86, 96–8, 102, 107, 135
Martini, Karl Anton Freiherr von 15, 85, 90–3, 94, 95, 96, 100, 107, 124, 135
Mignolo, Walter 14, 64
Mill, John Stuart 50
Mission, Christian 22–3, 30–1
monarchy, universal 44, 53, 57, 80, 95, 97
Monbron, Fougeret de 5–6
monism 122, 124
Montesquieu, Baron de 40–1, 48, 52
morality 52, 60, 67, 71, 79, 87, 114, 115, 134
    international morality 17, 89, 96, 135
Moser, Johann Jacob 15, 85, 86, 91, 93–6, 97, 98, 99, 101, 107, 122, 135
Musgrave, Sir Christopher 57, 58, 60
Muthu, Sankar 24

Nafziger, James 109–10
nationalism 1, 8, 9, 39, 40, 62, 104, 106, 121, 136
nation
    cultural nation (*Kulturnation*) 106
    right of nations 44, 70, 72, 73, 75, 76, 77, 78, 80, 81–3, 84, 85
    see also law, international law
nature
    state of nature 42–3, 48, 54, 68, 72–3, 75, 78, 79, 81, 83, 88, 91, 93, 132
Neff, Stephen 87–8, 101, 121
Nussbaum, Arthur 85, 86, 97, 101
Nussbaum, Martha 2, 3, 7–8, 9, 11, 79, 132, 137

pacifism 13, 54, 55, 101
Pagden, Anthony 62
Paine, Thomas 47–9
patriotism 8, 11–13, 40, 42, 45, 47, 60–2, 102, 104, 106, 107, 132, 136, 137
    cosmopolitan patriotism 137
    see also nationalism
peace 21, 27, 45, 46, 47, 53, 54, 55, 56, 71, 80, 81, 82, 83, 85, 88, 91, 105, 107, 124
    global peace 40
    peace projects 15, 53–6, 90, 92, 95, 96, 102
    perpetual peace 39, 97
    see also democracy, democratic peace proposition; justice; law, international law; law, natural law; right, right of nations
Penn, William 53–5, 58, 62, 95
philosophy 3, 13, 44, 64, 66, 67, 81, 90, 122, 131, 139
    philosophy of history 66, 83, 119
    political philosophy 2, 12, 78
Pieterse, Jan Nederveen 12
Pitts, Jennifer 52, 128, 133
Pogge, Thomas 9
positivism 86, 87, 94, 111,
    legal positivism 13, 15, 35, 36, 84, 93, 96–8, 99, 110, 111, 118, 121, 122, 123–5, 133, 134, 135
Price, Richard 5, 8, 42,
Priestley, Joseph 61, 62
property 25, 26, 32, 33, 42, 43, 58, 68, 111, 112, 113, 126,
    theory of property in Grotius 27–8
    in Vattel 33–5
Pufendorf, Samuel (von) 13, 14, 15, 17, 19, 28–9, 30, 37, 44, 47, 57, 70, 74, 78, 79, 80, 84, 110–14, 115, 116, 119, 120, 125, 126, 127, 128, 135, 137
punishment 88, 121
    theory of punishment in Grotius 26–7

Quakers 53, 55

racism, racist 6, 9, 39, 41, 65–6
Rawls, John 2, 125, 127
relativism 3, 9, 31, 47, 99–100, 101, 129, 132
    see also universalism
Remec, Peter 90
republic 97, 138
    European republic 49, 74, 75, 89–90, 99, 101; *see also* Europe; union, European Union; peace, peace projects
    'republic of letters' 41
    world republic 14, 15, 69, 81–4, 103–4, 132–3
republicanism, republican 6, 47, 59, 61, 68

INDEX

civic republicanism 8, 58; *see also* civic humanism
cosmopolitan republicanism (Cloots) 102–4; *see also* legal cosmopolitanism
right, rights 9, 13, 14, 15, 17, 19, 20–37, 41, 42, 45, 46, 48, 58, 65, 68, 69, 71, 73, 74, 76, 77, 86, 88, 89, 90, 91, 93–8, 100, 103, 109–27, 129, 132, 135
  cosmopolitan right (Kant) 64, 68, 104
  imperfect right 28, 112–14
  international human rights 134
  international right 15, 78–84
  perfect right 28, 30, 112, 113, 114
  see also human rights; immigration, right of; law; law, natural law; nation, right of nations
Rousseau, Jean-Jacques 39, 42, 59, 61, 65, 66, 69, 72–3, 78, 95, 102, 103, 105, 115, 137, 138, 139

Saint-Pierre, Abbé de 8, 39–40, 54, 56, 61, 65, 72, 73, 78, 92, 94–6, 101, 102, 105, 107
Schiller, Friedrich 41, 106
Schmitt, Carl 72, 86
Scotland 56, 57, 58, 61
Scott, James Brown 20
Scrivener, Michael 11
Seymour, Sir Edward 57
Sidney, Algernon 61
Simma, Bruno 122, 124, 134
Smith, Adam 30, **45–7**, 58–9, 62, 64, 67, 69, 74, 99, 114, 130, 131, 137
societas humanis generic 15, 107
society
  anarchical society 91
  international society 7, 18, 23, 43, 44; *see also* international community
  of states 15, 107, 111, 120
  see also commercial society
sovereignty 3, 4, 9, 15, 18, 19, 20, 24, 29, 31, 32, 34, 36, 44, 54, 70, 81, 83, 89, 95, 98, 102, 103, 104, 107, 110, 111,113, 115–16, 119–25, 127, 133, 134, 136
Spain, Spaniards, Spanish 5, 20, 21–4, 39, 100
state
  state of nature 42–3, 48, 54, 68, 72, 73, 75, 78, 79, 81, 83, 88, 91, 93, 132; *see also* anarchy

world state *see* republic, world republic
Steiger, Heiner 4, 101
Suárez, Francisco 30, 36, 85, 111, 123, 134
system
  Westphalian system *see* Westphalian order

theory
  international legal theory 36, 85–9, 134–5
Turks 5, 40, 54, 55, 56, 65, 100

union 49, 56, 57, 58
  European Union 1, 39, 59, 61, 79, 130
United Dutch East India Company 26
United States 6, 120, 137
  US Supreme Court 109
universalism 1, 2–3, 6, 9, 11, 18, 47, 52, 65, 100, 101, 106, 117
utilitarianism, utilitarian 34, 44, 47, 50, 51, 54, 98, 114, 131
  see also Jeremy Bentham

Vattel, Emer de 12, 13, 14, 15, 17, 19, 27, **33–7**, 51, 65, 70, 72, **74–8**, **79–81**, 84, 85, 86, 87, 88, **89–90**, 91, 92, 97, 100, 101, 107, **115–17**, 119, 120, 123, 124, 126, 129, 135
Verdross, Alfred 15, 86, **121–4**, 126, 134, 135
Vitoria, Francisco de 10, 12, 13, **17–24**, 25, 26, 27, 28, 30, 31, 36, 37, 52, 55, 64, 109, 110, 111, 112, 114, 116, 119, 120, 123, 124, 129
Voltaire 40, 42

Waldron, Jeremy 131–2
Walzer, Michael 14, 110, 124
war
  state of war 53, 56, 72, 107
  see also state of nature, anarchy
Ward, Robert 15, 85, **98–101**, 121
Westphalian order 4, 15
Wheaton, Henry 17
Wieland, Christoph Martin 9, 42, 136
Williams, Robert 17–18, 20, 35
Wolff, Christian 12, 13, 14, 17, **30–3**, 36, 37, 47, 64, 68, 69, 73, 74, 78, 80, 86, 89, 91, 92, 94, 96, 101, 115, 116, 124, 128, 134, 139

Zurbuchen, Simone 12